Women poe
the English Civil War

MANCHEStER
1824

Manchester University Press

Women poets of the English Civil War

Edited by
Sarah C. E. Ross and
Elizabeth Scott-Baumann

Manchester University Press

Published by Manchester University Press
Altrincham Street, Manchester M1 7JA
www.manchesteruniversitypress.co.uk

British Library Cataloguing-in-Publication Data
A catalogue record for this book is available from the British Library

ISBN   978 0 7190 8624 3 hardback
ISBN   978 1 5261 2870 6 paperback

First published 2018

The publisher has no responsibility for the persistence or accuracy of URLs for any
external or third-party internet websites referred to in this book, and does not guarantee
that any content on such websites is, or will remain, accurate or appropriate.

Typeset
by Toppan Best-set Premedia Limited
Printed in Great Britain
by CPI Group (UK) Ltd, Croydon, CR0 4YY

Contents

Contents

Contents

Contents

Contents

Illustrations

Acknowledgements

Women poets of the English Civil War has been several years in the making, and has involved numerous delightful collaborations, not least that between the two editors. We would like to thank Elizabeth Clarke for her early discussions, and all of our colleagues who have encouraged us to edit this anthology. Those who have supported it along the way are too numerous to list, but we could particularly like to thank Marie-Louise Coolahan, Alice Eardley, Elizabeth Hageman, Pamela Hammons, Peter C. Herman, Laura Knoppers, Paul Salzman, Nigel Smith, Mihoko Suzuki, Margaret Thickstun, and Gillian Wright. The Society for the Study of Early Modern Women and its members have done so much to foster research in this area, and we are grateful to our colleagues there for their encouragement and support.

Sarah Ross would like to thank Elizabeth Gray, Nikki Hessell, and Ingrid Horrocks, and her colleagues in the Early Modern Women's Research Network at the University of Newcastle, particularly Patricia Pender for discussion and contention over the politics of modernisation. Paul Salzman has provided wise counsel on editorial practice, and the contributors to our volume *Editing Early Modern Women* have taught me much about the politics of editing women's texts. I have also learned much from discussion of the anthology with colleagues at 'Editing Early Texts: Practice and Protocol' (Wellington, 2012), 'Katherine Philips 350' (Dublin, 2014), and the ANZAMEMS biennial conference in Brisbane (2015).

Elizabeth Scott-Baumann would like to thank Alice Eardley, Jonathan Healey, Sarah Lewis, Mary Ann Lund, and David Norbrook. Massey University provided a Visiting Research Fellowship in 2012, and the Leverhulme Trust's generous Early Career Fellowship 2012–15 allowed time for this alongside other projects. King's College London has provided financial and collegial support of many kinds, and gratitude is due to successive heads of department Jo McDonagh and Richard Kirkland and all members of the London Shakespeare Centre.

It is only fitting for a student-focused anthology that a number of postgraduate students have provided invaluable assistance. The anthology would not have been completed without the editorial assistance of Jake Arthur, Hannah Crummé, Bonnie Etherington, and Leigh McLennon. Clare Whitehead was an exemplary postdoctoral research assistant. We would particularly like to thank Bonnie for her work in the initial preparation of the texts, and Clare and Jake for their efforts in the anthology's final stages. We are also more broadly indebted to discussion of the poems in this anthology with our undergraduate and graduate students at King's College London, Massey University, and Victoria University of Wellington: many a line we think of in fresh and fascinating ways thanks to their questions and insights.

We have received invaluable financial assistance from King's College London, Massey University, and the Faculty of Humanities and Social Sciences at Victoria University of Wellington. Permission for images from Hester Pulter's manuscript has been graciously provided by the University of Leeds Library. Nottinghamshire Archives DD/Hu2 is the copyright of the Hutchinson family, and we are grateful to them and to the Team Manager: Archives and Local Studies of Nottinghamshire Archives for permission to reproduce extracts.

We would like to thank Matthew Frost at Manchester University Press for taking on this project, and for his patience and support. Fiona Little was an astute, rigorous, and efficient copy editor and Danielle Shepherd an equally meticulous and thoughtful production editor. We are very grateful for their work on the book.

Finally, thanks to the Scott-Baumann family, Benjie, Edward, and William Way, and to Andru, Milly, and Henry Isac, all of whom have lived with and supported this project and all the others.

Timeline

Year	Historical events	Literary events
1483		Geoffrey Chaucer's *Troilus and Criseyde* published
1533	Elizabeth I born	
1557		Richard Tottel's *Songs and Sonnets* published, containing ninety-six poems ascribed to Thomas Wyatt
1566	James VI born	
1575		George Gascoigne's *The Noble Art of Venery or Hunting* published
1580s		Philip Sidney completes his first version of *The Countess of Pembroke's Arcadia*
1588	Spanish Armada defeated by English forces	
1589	James VI marries a Danish princess, Anna	

1590		The first revised edition of Philip Sidney's *The Countess of Pembroke's Arcadia* published
		The first three cantos of Edmund Spenser's *The Faerie Queene* published
1591		Ludovico Ariosto's *Orlando Furioso* published, translated by John Harington
		Philip Sidney's *Astrophel and Stella* published
		Edmund Spenser's *Complaints* published
1593		William Shakespeare's *Venus and Adonis* published
		The second revised edition of Philip Sidney's *The Countess of Pembroke's Arcadia* published
1594	Nine Years War begins	
1595		Philip Sidney's *An Apology for Poetry* published
		Edmund Spenser's *Amoretti* published
1596	Elizabeth Stuart (eldest daughter of James VI and the future Queen of Bohemia) born	Edmund Spenser's *The Faerie Queene* republished with Cantos IV–VI
		Edmund Spenser's *Prothalamion* published

1599		Christopher Marlowe's *The Passionate Shepherd to his Love* published
		Mary and Philip Sidney's translation of the Psalms presented to Queen Elizabeth
1600	Charles Stuart (the future Charles I) born	
1601		Pliny the Elder's *The History of the World: Commonly Called the Natural History of C. Plinius Secundus* published, translated by Philemon Holland
1603	Elizabeth I dies	
	James VI and I crowned	
1605	Hester Pulter likely to have been born	Guillaume de Saluste Du Bartas's *Bartas: His Divine Weeks and Works* published, translated by Josuah Sylvester
1610		Galileo Galilei's *Sidereus Nuncius* published
1611		Aemilia Lanyer's *Salve Deus Rex Judaeorum* published
		John Speed's *History of Great Britain* published
1612	Anne Bradstreet born	Michael Drayton's *Poly-Olbion* published
1613	Elizabeth Stuart marries Frederick, Elector Palatine	

1614		Walter Ralegh's *History of the World* published
1615		William Camden's *Annales*, volume 1, published
1616		Ben Jonson's 'To Penshurst' published
1618	Thirty Years War begins Hester Pulter likely to have married Arthur Pulter	
1619	Elizabeth Stuart and Frederick, Elector Palatine, are crowned in Bohemia for a reign that lasts only a year	
1620	Lucy Hutchinson born Elizabeth Stuart and Frederick, Elector Palatine, flee Bohemia for the Netherlands	
1623	?Margaret Cavendish born	William Shakespeare's *Mr William Shakespeare's Comedies, Histories and Tragedies* published
1625	James VI and I dies Charles I is crowned, and, shortly after, marries a Catholic French princess, Henrietta Maria	William Camden's *Annales*, volume 2, published

1628	William Laud becomes Bishop of London	
	George Villiers, first Duke of Buckingham and favourite of Charles I, is assassinated	
	Charles I begins eleven years of 'personal rule' without calling parliament	
	Anne Bradstreet marries Simon Bradstreet	
1630	Anne and Simon Bradstreet leave England and sail to the New World	
1632	Katherine Philips born	
1633	William Laud becomes Archbishop of Canterbury	John Donne's *Poems* published
		George Herbert's *The Temple* published
1634		John Milton's *Comus* performed at Ludlow Castle
		Francis Quarles's *Emblems* published
1637		John Milton's *Comus* published anonymously
1638	Lucy Hutchinson marries Colonel John Hutchinson	
1639	Bishops' Wars begin in Scotland	

1640   First meeting of the Short Parliament, which is dissolved by Charles I less than a month later

First meeting of the Long Parliament, which cannot be dissolved without its own consent

The Root and Branch Petition is presented to parliament, demanding the abolition of episcopacy

1641   Bishops of the Church of England are excluded from the House of Lords

William Laud, Archbishop of Canterbury, is imprisoned

Thomas Wentworth, Earl of Strafford, a chief minister of Charles I and supporter of Archbishop William Laud, is tried and executed

Henrietta Maria flees to the Netherlands with her eldest daughter and the crown jewels

English Protestant settlers in Ireland are massacred during the Irish Uprising

1642   Civil War begins

Charles I travels through England, making clandestine preparations for war

1643	Henrietta Maria returns to England	
	Parliament passes the Licensing Order to impose pre-publication censorship on the printing trade	
1644	Henrietta Maria flees to Paris, followed by various courtiers, including Margaret Cavendish	
1645	Margaret Cavendish marries William Cavendish, the Marquess of Newcastle-upon-Tyne and a recent self-exile from England	John Milton's *Poems* published
		Hester Pulter is likely to have begun work on her poetry
	William Laud, Archbishop of Canterbury, is executed	
1647		Nathaniel Ward's *The Simple Cobbler of Agawam* published
1648	Long Parliament is purged of those members opposed to the trial of Charles I for high treason, and is subsequently known as the Rump Parliament	Robert Herrick's *Hesperides* and *His Noble Numbers* published
	The High Court of Justice is established to try Charles I for high treason	
	Margaret and William Cavendish leave France for the Netherlands	

	Charles Cavendish, Margaret's brother, is executed after the siege of Colchester	
	Katherine Philips marries James Philips	
1649	The trial of Charles I begins, and culminates in his execution	*Eikon Basilike* published and attributed to Charles I
	Rump Parliament votes to abolish the English monarchy and declares England a commonwealth	
	Charles I's eldest son, Charles Prince of Wales, proclaimed King of Britain, France, and Ireland by the Scottish Parliament	
1650		Anne Bradstreet's *The Tenth Muse Lately Sprung up in America* published
1650s		Lucy Hutchinson is likely to have begun work on *De rerum natura*
1651	Charles II and his army defeated by Oliver Cromwell's forces at the Battle of Worcester	Thomas Hobbes's *Leviathan* published
1652	Charles II flees England for France	

1653	Protectorate begins, under the rule of Oliver Cromwell Rump Parliament disbanded	Margaret Cavendish's *Poems and Fancies* and *Philosophical Fancies* published William Davenant's *Certain Verses Written by Several of the Author's Friends* published
1654	The High Court of Justice sentences a leading royalist, Colonel John Gerard, to death	
1655		Lucy Hutchinson is likely to have begun work on 'To Mr Waller upon his Panegyric to the Lord Protector'
1656		Margaret Cavendish's *Philosophical and Physical Opinions* published Abraham Cowley's *Poems* published
1657	Oliver Cromwell declines the crown of England	
1658	Oliver Cromwell dies Richard Cromwell succeeds his father as Lord Protector	
1659	Richard Cromwell resigns the position of Lord Protector	

1660	Charles II returns to England, and offers most of his enemies a general pardon through the Declaration of Breda in April and the Act of Indemnity and Oblivion on August	John Dryden's *Astraea redux* published Lucy Hutchinson begins work on *Order and Disorder*
	Margaret and William Cavendish return to England	
	The trials and executions of the regicides of Charles I begin	
1661	Charles II is crowned at Westminster Abbey	Alexander Brome's *Songs and Other Poems* published
1662	Elizabeth Stuart, Queen of Bohemia and sister to Charles I, dies	
	James Philips is cleared by the House of Commons of signing the death warrant of Colonel John Gerard	
1663		Katherine Philips's translation of Corneille's *Pompey* published
1664	Katherine Philips dies	Margaret Cavendish's revised edition of *Poems and Fancies* published
		Lucy Hutchinson begins work on *Elegies* and *Memoirs of the Life of Colonel Hutchinson*
		Katherine Philips's *Poems* published

1665		Robert Hooke's *Micrographia* published
1666	Great Fire of London	Margaret Cavendish's *Observations upon Experimental Philosophy* published
1667		John Milton's *Paradise Lost* published
1671		John Milton's *Paradise Regained* published, containing *Samson Agonistes*
1672	Anne Bradstreet dies	
1673	Margaret Cavendish dies	
1674		Revised edition of John Milton's *Paradise Lost* published
1678	Hester Pulter dies	Anne Bradstreet's *Several Poems* published
1681	Lucy Hutchinson dies	Andrew Marvell's *Miscellaneous Poems* published

Introduction

Women poets of the English Civil War

This anthology brings together extensive selections of poetry by the five most prolific and prominent women poets of the English Civil War: Anne Bradstreet, Hester Pulter, Margaret Cavendish, Katherine Philips, and Lucy Hutchinson. Some of these women are more familiar to students and teachers than others. Katherine Philips and Margaret Cavendish have enjoyed fame (or endured notoriety) as women poets since the first publication of their work in the 1650s and 1660s, and brief selections of their poems have appeared for a number of years in *The Norton Anthology of English Literature*. Anne Bradstreet is relatively well known as America's first woman poet, after her emigration to New England with her deeply religious family in the 1630s. Hester Pulter's and Lucy Hutchinson's poetry has come to light only very recently, as manuscripts have been discovered. Before that, Hutchinson was familiar to students and scholars of the English Civil War as the author of one of the period's most important historical documents, the *Memoirs* of her parliamentarian husband, Colonel John Hutchinson. Hester Pulter was not known at all. Whether their work has been known for centuries or only a couple of decades, however, all five women whose poetry is collected in this anthology are attracting new and concerted attention as poets at the centre of a rich and diverse culture of poetry by seventeenth-century women.

For women writers, the decades of the English Civil War were of special importance. Women's literacy increased exponentially over the seventeenth century as a whole, and it is that century (rather than the conventional literary-critical period of 'The Renaissance', from 1500 to 1640 or 1660) that sees a great burgeoning in the volume of literary writing by women. A relaxation of the licensing of published writing during the years of the Civil War itself meant that a larger number of women than ever before entered into print, from the radical prophetess Anna Trapnel to the Quaker Margaret Fell and to the poets Elizabeth Major, An Collins, and the anonymous (but presumably female) author of *Eliza's Babes*. Women's writing also thrived in networks and communities of manuscript writing and exchange, but these manuscript-based texts have been far less visible to literary history than the printed tradition. Hester Pulter's and Lucy Hutchinson's poems exemplify the extent and depth of women's poetry in manuscript culture, as do the extensive manuscript-based activities of Katherine Philips. This anthology presents these manuscript poems alongside those that were printed in the volumes of Anne Bradstreet (*The Tenth Muse*, 1650; *Several Poems*, 1678), Margaret Cavendish (*Poems and Fancies*, 1653 and 1664), and Philips (*Poems*, 1664 and 1667). Together, these texts reveal the diversity and complexity of women's poetry in the mid-century, and enable a more comprehensive understanding of a seventeenth-century women's poetic culture that traversed political affiliations and material forms.

Prominent male poets and their complex works loom large in seventeenth-century literary history. Robert Herrick, Thomas Carew, Richard Lovelace, and John Suckling are known for the delights of poems that invite us to 'Gather ye rosebuds while ye may', rallying a Cavalier poetics of friendship and pleasure against political defeat. Andrew Marvell's poetry is famously oblique, his 'Horatian Ode' on Cromwell's return from Ireland epitomising his nuanced celebration – or critique – of the revolutionary general. John Milton, author of *Paradise Lost*, is perhaps the greatest poetic heavyweight of all, his poems tackling politics and theology, boldly attempting 'to justify the ways of God to men'. *Paradise Lost* was not published until 1667, but it is a poem of the English Civil War in that its ideas and intensity bear a strong relationship to the turmoil of the English mid-century, and its multiple revolutions in political and religious thought. Some historians have called the English Civil War 'the last of the European wars of religion', indicating the extent to which religious ideas and religious disagreement created the conflict of the 1640s.[1] Others emphasise the radical experiment of political republicanism, almost 150 years before the French Revolution. Of equal importance are the associated epistemological and philosophical revolutions out of which, arguably, emerge the early modern self as an individual and a public entity. For all of these reasons, the poetry of the canonical, male Civil War writers is well known for the intensity of its political and philosophical thought, as well as for its poetic and stylistic qualities. In some aspects, these poets are not just male but masculinist, in the Cavaliers' reputations for libertinism and their lyrics about homosocial drinking and heterosexual erotic love, while Milton's sexual politics remain a topic of fervent critical debate.

Like the poetry of their male contemporaries, that of Bradstreet, Pulter, Cavendish, Philips, and Hutchinson is closely tied to the ideas and conflicts of the English Civil War. Philips, Cavendish, and Pulter were royalists of varying stances, and express their support for the king and his allies. Anne Bradstreet wrote as a puritan in the New World who had fled religious persecution, and she recalls in ideal terms the good old days of Queen Elizabeth's reign. Lucy Hutchinson was a fervent republican and, like *Paradise Lost*, her Restoration poems evoke the bitter disillusionment of personal and political loss. Each poet also deploys poetic forms and modes that were fashionable at the time, writing elegies, dialogues, panegyrics, and epic. Each of these five women also felt, geographically, the impact of Civil War, writing from locations as diverse as Hertfordshire in England, Cardiganshire in Wales, Antwerp on the European continent, and Massachusetts Bay in the New World. Abraham Cowley famously wrote of the English Civil War and republic that 'A warlike, various, and tragical age is best to write *of*, but worst to write *in*.' The women whose verse is collected in this anthology felt the privations of war in diverse and multiple ways, but their poetry attests to a rich literary response to the political events of the century.

This anthology presents a complex and rewarding poetic culture that is both uniquely women-centred and integrally connected to the male canonical poetry for which the era is justifiably famous. In subsequent sections, the Introduction will delineate the historical contexts in which – and about which – these poets write: the English Civil War; the relationship between religious conflict and poetry; the networks and communities within which these women situated themselves; the transformative scientific and philosophical culture of the seventeenth century; the genres in which these poets wrote; and the physical forms taken by their poetry, in print and manuscript.

The English Civil War

The earliest poem in this anthology, Anne Bradstreet's elegy on Sir Philip Sidney, dates from 1638, and by that year the events that would lead to the outbreak of Civil War in England were already in motion. In 1625 James I of England (James VI of Scotland) died and was succeeded by his son Charles. During the first few years of his rule Charles became frustrated with the checks on his power by parliament, particularly its objection to some of his religious and economic policies, and in 1629 he suspended parliament altogether. During the subsequent period of 'personal rule', over a decade, he continued to raise taxes and implement controversial religious policy.

The Scots were increasingly troubled by Charles's attempts to impose religious conformity and, faced with a major uprising in the late 1630s, Charles decided to send in troops. Requiring further levels of taxation to fund this military action, and hoping for support, he called parliament (the 'Short Parliament') but dismissed it again when it refused his demands. Another parliament that was called in 1640 (the 'Long Parliament'), when Charles was faced with a successful Scottish army occupying the north of England, became a mouthpiece of opposition to the king, which was now strongly motivated by both religious and political principles.

In 1641 a rebellion of Irish Catholics in which many Protestant settlers were killed was both provoked by fear at the increasing power of puritan parliamentarians in England and inspired by the Scots' uprising. After an unsuccessful attempt to have leading parliamentarians arrested, Charles raised his standard in Nottingham in August 1642, effectively initiating the Civil War. After a series of indecisive military clashes, in 1645 parliament established the very effective 'New Model Army' led by Thomas Fairfax with Oliver Cromwell as his cavalry commander, and at the Battle of Naseby Charles's forces were defeated. The king fled and surrendered himself to the Scots. 1648 saw a renewal of military action often known as the Second Civil War, culminating in the powerful New Model Army enforcing a purge ('Pride's Purge') of parliament, which resulted in a 'Rump' of MPs sympathetic to its demands. On 30 January 1649, after a trial for treason, Charles I was executed (the 'regicide'), sending shockwaves around Europe. As this discussion makes clear, this was a conflict involving Scotland, Wales, and Ireland as well as England. Indeed, England, Scotland, and Ireland had only been united under the same monarch since 1603. As neither 'Britain' nor 'United Kingdom' were terms used in this period, though, 'English' is a useful, if problematic, shorthand for the Civil War.

In 1650 parliament passed an act obliging all men to take the Oath of Engagement: 'I do declare and promise, that I will be true and faithful to the Commonwealth of England, as it is now established, without a King or House of Lords'. In a further consolidation of power, parliamentary commander Oliver Cromwell led an offensive in Ireland which brutally suppressed rebellion by killing thousands of Catholics. Meanwhile Charles I's son had himself crowned King of Scotland. In 1651 Cromwell's forces defeated him at the Battle of Worcester and Charles fled to Europe, thus ending the Civil War.

Oliver Cromwell was made Lord Protector in 1653 and dismissed the Rump Parliament. From July to December 1653 Cromwell and the army nominated a ruling assembly (variously called the 'Barebones Parliament', or the 'Parliament of Saints') before the calling of the First Protectorate Parliament. This period saw further polarisation of views about Cromwell's rule. He was strongly supported by the army, and he was offered the crown by those who hoped he would be a more unifying force if he became the monarch. Even though he refused the crown, his title and increasing state powers led many of the opposite political persuasion to fear that he was becoming increasingly monarchical in his rule (and a protector was actually less limited by common law than a king).

In 1658 Cromwell died and was succeeded by his son Richard. A combination of dynastic succession in a non-monarchical state, Richard's relative lack of charisma, increasing economic disarray, and faction-fighting resulted in a state of chaos, and in April 1660, after fresh elections had been held, parliament invited Charles II to return and assume power. In May 1660 Charles officially became King Charles II at the 'Restoration'. His return was greeted with widespread celebration, though dissenting voices were appalled by the apparent failure of the country's republican experiment.

While Charles I's last word is reputed to have been 'Remember', one of Charles II's early acts was of enforced forgetting. The Act of Indemnity and Oblivion made it illegal to mention 'any name or names, or other words of reproach tending to revive the memory of the late differences or the occasions thereof'. The poems in this anthology represent many of the various means by which writers attempted to preserve memories of the conflict, to rewrite these into narratives coloured by their own principles, or to erase these through recourse to seemingly non-political modes or subjects. Writers also represented political events through contemporary discourses of international expansion, science, philosophy, and gender politics, as well as the profoundly personal losses of family, friends, land, and religious autonomy.

Critics have debated whether royalist or republican, Catholic or puritan, or other positions in between these, were more sympathetic ideologies to women's autonomy. Certainly women of all persuasions became more publicly articulate in this period, with publications attributed to women rising steeply. For many women, any cultural prohibitions against women writing were outweighed by the impulse to speak out in their other identities as royalists, parliamentarians, Levellers, nobles or Catholics.

Religion, war, and poetry

Religious debate was central to the English Civil War. The absolutism of Charles I's personal rule may have aggravated parliament over a number of years, but it was conflict over forms of worship and church governance in Scotland and in England that led to outright conflict. After Henry VIII's initial break in the 1530s, Elizabeth I had cut ties between England and the Roman (Catholic) church once and for all, and confirmed Protestant worship as the form of the Church of England, but tension between milder and 'hotter' Protestants simmered through the later decades of the sixteenth century and into the seventeenth. Puritans, broadly speaking, were the more purist Protestants who desired plainer and more individualised modes of worship than the Church of England offered, disdaining elaborate ceremonies and ornaments, and, especially in Scotland, arguing against church governance by a hierarchy of bishops. English puritans met their *bête noir* in the 1630s in Archbishop William Laud, whose views on ceremonial worship and on theology were antithetical to those of puritans; many were also uneasy about the openly Catholic affiliations of Charles I's Spanish wife, Henrietta Maria, and her circle. When the Scottish Bishops' War erupted in 1638, then, the tone was set for a prolonged conflict, in which Anglican royalists – those who were loyal to the king and to the Church of England – were pitched against parliamentarians and more radical puritans, whose religious views ranged widely from Scots-style Presbyterians to Quakers, Baptists, and sects such as the Ranters, Diggers, and Levellers.

If religious debate was central to the Civil War, so was religious expression central to the writing of the period. The Reformation of the western Christian church from the early sixteenth century was in part precipitated by a desire for closer individual interaction with the words of the Bible; Reformation Christianity was inherently a religion of words. The English Reformation was accompanied by a proliferation of religious translations, prayers, and treatises in vernacular languages, including striking female-authored examples such as *The Mirror or Glass of the Sinful Soul* (1544) by Princess Elizabeth (later Elizabeth I) and Queen Katherine Parr's *The Lamentation of a Sinner* (1547). Much of the writing by men and women that proliferated in the Civil War years was religious in nature, and included multiple poetic modes: Psalm paraphrases and translations, devotional lyrics, and occasional meditations – meditational poems focusing on a particular moment or occasion in everyday life, or of public prominence – biblical epics (such as Cowley's *Davideis*), and meditational retreats from the world. Even the latter can be seen as highly politicised. The meditational poems of Henry Vaughan and Thomas Traherne have

6

been described as 'poetry of Anglican survivalism', retreating from the political world that threatened them;[2] at the other end of the religious and political spectrum, Anne Bradstreet's 'David's Lamentation for Saul and Jonathan', a delicate poetic paraphrase of 2 Samuel 1:19, carries political connotations as oblique as any poem of Andrew Marvell's. Its ambiguity is illustrated by readings which see it, alternatively, as a lament for the death of King Charles I or as 'a reminder of Charles's role in bringing about his own destruction'.[3]

The women poets in this anthology came from and allied themselves to a full range of positions on the religious and political spectrum. Anne Bradstreet's birth and marital families were among a group of devout puritans who emigrated from Lincolnshire to Massachusetts Bay in 1630 in order to escape persecution for their dissenting religious views, and to found an ideal religious community. Bradstreet spent her adult life in Massachusetts Bay, where her father, Thomas Dudley, and her husband, Simon Bradstreet, both served as early governors. Hester Pulter, in contrast, was an ardent Anglican and royalist, associating religion strongly with her deposed monarch and his queen, and it is possible that her royalist and Church of England allegiances saw her isolated from her husband and her immediate community during the Civil War years. Her husband, Arthur, was the patron of a Presbyterian minister in their local parish church, and some of Pulter's religious lyrics suggest that she felt herself to be excluded from communal worship. Katherine Philips's allegiances were also royalist and Anglican, and she wrote a number of religious poems that have been read as important expressions of loyalty to Anglicanism in Wales, where, in the 1650s, it had a tenuous hold.[4]

Margaret Cavendish is arguably the most secular of the poets featured in this anthology: religion does not appear for her to have been a motivating force, ideologically or poetically, and she was disparaging about the extensive religious writings of her stepdaughters, Jane Cavendish and Elizabeth Brackley. For Lucy Hutchinson, however, independent puritan religion is at the forefront of her politics and her poetic expression. Hutchinson and her parliamentarian husband, like Anne Bradstreet's, dissented from the high Anglicanism of the Church of England, and were in favour of the right of Protestant congregations to form voluntarily and freely. After the restoration of the monarchy in 1660, Hutchinson continued to be closely allied to Nonconformist preachers in London (those who did not conform to the Act of Uniformity in religion of 1662).

Given the centrality of religion to identity and affiliation in the seventeenth century, it might be expected that religious outlook would determine the networks and communities in which women wrote. To a large extent it did: Bradstreet was particularly deeply entwined in the small New English puritan community in which she lived, and Hutchinson's dissenting alliances had a close bearing on her writing in the 1660s and 1670s. However, the fault lines of religious and political conflict in the period often ran directly through families, marriages, and communities, in complex and unpredictable ways. Katherine Philips, for example, was a royalist while her husband James was a parliamentarian; the royalist Hester Pulter's sister was a close associate of the republican Milton; and Lucy Hutchinson's brother, Sir Allen Apsley, was a prominent royalist. The communities (or lack thereof) in which women poets wrote are often complex and diverse.

Networks and communities

One of the most intriguing questions about the Civil War poetic culture in which the women in this anthology engaged is the extent to which it developed in isolation or in conversation with other poets. Some of the social environments in which male poets wrote were closed to women poets, such as professional institutions (the Inns of Court) or academic institutions (the universities or the Royal Society), though women poets also often gained more oblique access to such circles. Lucy Hutchinson's literary commonplace book shows her collecting poetry which circulated among Inns of Court poets, probably through her brother, the royalist Sir Allen Apsley. Margaret Cavendish visited the Royal Society and corresponded with some of its members, while Philips associated with the circle of the royalist musician Henry Lawes in the 1650s, and had one of her plays performed during a very successful trip to Dublin. Anne Bradstreet's poetry seems to have circulated reasonably widely in the settler community in Massachusetts Bay, and even Hester Pulter, supposedly shut up in her country grange, had connections to London networks and even possibly to Milton.

Anne Bradstreet's education was, like that of most women in this anthology, received at home – in her case, in the home of the Earl of Lincoln, to whom her father, Thomas Dudley, served as a gentleman steward. Her stay in the home of the earl, however, was short: after time in the market town of Boston, Lincolnshire, Dudley and his family sailed for Massachusetts Bay in April 1630, part of a group of Lincolnshire puritans helping to establish a colony in the New World. Anne was eighteen years old, newly married to Simon Bradstreet, a Cambridge graduate and a fellow puritan emigrant, and in the fledgling Massachusetts Bay community, she seems to have found a readership for her poems among a small but highly-educated coterie of puritan men and women.

She addressed her poems explicitly to her father, describing him as the author of a quarternion poem (a poem on a theme in four parts) like her own, and asking this poet-patriarch to bestow his 'mild aspect' on her 'ragged lines' ('To her Most Honoured Father Thomas Dudley Esquire, these Humbly Presented'). Other readers included Nathaniel Ward, who returned to England in 1646, and her brother-in-law John Woodbridge, who returned to England in 1647.

Bradstreet's poems appeared in London, printed in *The Tenth Muse* (1650), after Woodbridge took her manuscripts with him, probably without her permission, when he travelled there in 1647. The volume's title celebrates Bradstreet as *The Tenth Muse Lately Sprung up in America*, but it is to an English Civil War audience that the publication is directed. Bradstreet's declared poetic and political heroes are Sir Philip Sidney and Elizabeth I, and her greatest poetic influences are her father and Guillaume de Saluste Du Bartas, the French writer whose extended religious poetry was enormously popular (in Josuah Sylvester's translation) in England in the first part of the seventeenth century. Several of her poems speak directly to the circumstances of the English Civil War, not least *A Dialogue between Old England and New, Concerning their Present Troubles, Anno 1642*, in which Old England laments her social and political woes, and her daughter (New England) offers sympathy and relief. Bradstreet lived her entire adult life in New England, and later poems that are included in the posthumous *Several Poems* (Boston, 1678) speak to a more domestic context; but via *The Tenth Muse* and its publication in London in the first year of the English republic, she is emphatically a woman poet of the English Civil War.

Hester Pulter's birth family also appears to have been one in which girls received a high level of education. Her father, Sir James Ley, was Chief Justice of the King's Bench in Ireland, and went on to become Lord Chief Justice and Lord High Treasurer of England; he was himself a writer, and is described by Milton as 'that old man eloquent' in a sonnet written to Pulter's sister Lady Margaret Ley in the 1640s. Pulter repeatedly describes her writing context, at the country estate of Broadfield, Hertfordshire, in the 1640s and 1650s, as one of isolation, insisting that she is 'shut up in a country grange' and 'tied to one habitation'. It is clear that Broadfield was a site of melancholy for her, not least because of the absence of her adult daughters, whom she repeatedly exhorts in her poems to leave London and to visit her there, but there are records of her visiting London during these years. Her poems attest to an acute awareness of contemporary literary culture, echoing the court and country poetry of Carew and Herrick; the prolific culture of royalist elegies on Charles I's death; and the emblem traditions of George Wither and

Francis Quarles. Resonances between several of her poems and those of Marvell have led to speculation that she may have known Marvell's poems in manuscript.

Of all the works in this anthology, however, Pulter's poems appear to have had the least impact on contemporary readers. Pulter addresses numerous poems to her adult daughters, inviting them to join her in the country; and her series of emblem poems is didactic, addressed to her children and to royalist women more broadly. She evokes the trope of royalist friendship that is central also to Katherine Philips's verse, but there is no evidence of her poetry circulating beyond the sole existing manuscript of her work. This manuscript has been annotated by an early eighteenth-century antiquarian, whose notes suggest an interest in her family connections as much as her poetry; and some later additions to the volume indicate that it was passed down the family line. Beyond these familial readers, there appears to have been no audience for her verse, its reception history reinforcing the poetic trope of isolation that runs through much of it.

Katherine Philips describes her literary life in Wales in similar terms of isolation, and Cardiganshire was, indeed, remote from London, but much of her life was spent in, or influenced by, city culture and specifically that of London and Dublin. Philips was educated at a London girls' school (rather than at home, as were all the other poets in this anthology), and mingled in some court circles, probably partly through her school friend Mary Aubrey. She married James Philips of Cardiganshire, Wales, at the age of sixteen in 1648; in contrast to life in London, married life in Cardigan may have seemed quiet, but Philips corresponded widely and actively, cultivating her 'Society of Friendship' and circulating her poetry among friends and wider circle of acquaintance. She wrote often to Sir Charles Cotterell, master of ceremonies for Charles II, and he provided a key link to court circles, presenting copies of her poems in mauscript and in print to the Duchess of York and Charles II. Such correspondence was a lively and critical form of literary engagement for many women, as well as men, in the seventeenth century, and provided for Philips a way of selecting an appropriate coterie of readers for her poems. At the same time, she also explored and exploited her rural location in developing a distinctive poetry of retreat in poems such as 'A Country Life', 'Invitation to the Country', and 'A Retired Friendship, to Ardelia, 23 August 1651'.

Philips travelled to Dublin in the early 1660s, and this trip was to prove remarkably fruitful. Philips's contact with an Anglo-Irish elite including Robert Boyle, Earl of Orrery, and Wentworth Dillon, Earl of Roscommon, saw her translating a play by the French dramatist Corneille.

Under her title of *Pompey*, Philips's play was performed and printed in Dublin in 1663. Her correspondence tells of her rivalry with an English court circle including Edmund Waller, who was also translating Corneille's play at this time. The prominence given to *Pompey* in both Dublin and London no doubt contributed to the publication of her *Poems* (1664), a volume about which she loudly protested. Whether or not that publication was in fact approved by her, there was a market for the poetry of 'Orinda', her sobriquet.

Margaret Cavendish had access to some of the most prominent social circles and experienced some of the most wide-ranging European travel of any writer, let alone woman writer, in the mid-seventeenth century. Her works both bear the marks of these people and places and also reject these as Cavendish claims to prioritise unlearnedness and natural wit over social interaction and cultural engagement. This is as much a carefully constructed identity as Philips's 'Orinda', though, as we will see from the evidence of her actual participation in intellectual culture.

Margaret Cavendish was born to the Lucas family in Essex. She moved to Oxford with her sister and there became a maid of honour to Charles I's wife, Queen Henrietta Maria, following the court into exile in Paris. It was here that she met her husband, William Cavendish, a royalist commander and widower whose daughters were also poets and who was himself a minor Cavalier poet and a very significant patron of other poets and writers. As royalists in exile the couple lived first in Paris and then Antwerp, moving into the house of the painter Rubens (who had died some years previously). In both cities they mingled with some of the most prominent thinkers of their day, both English émigrés and continental Europeans, including the royalist political theorist Thomas Hobbes, the philosopher René Descartes, and William's brother the prominent mathematician Charles Cavendish. Though Margaret writes with some ambivalence about her interactions with many of these men, the discussion in the Cavendish household must have fostered her interests particularly in natural philosophy, and after they had returned to England she would visit the Royal Society in 1667. Though they lived abroad, the political events of the later 1640s and 1650s touched the Cavendishes sharply. In 1648 Margaret's brother Charles Lucas was executed after the siege of Colchester, and in 1651 she suffered some humiliation when she returned to England with her brother-in-law to try to regain Cavendish land sequestered by the new regime. Nor were Margaret and her husband rewarded at the Restoration for their loyalty to the new king's father in the ways she had evidently expected. Poems such as 'A Dialogue between a Bountiful Knight and a Castle Ruined in War' show that Cavendish felt the degradations of Civil War had indelibly marked the places she inhabited. She and William lived both at Bolsover Castle, Derbyshire (where dramas by Ben Jonson were put on for Charles I before the war), and Welbeck Abbey, Nottinghamshire (making them almost neighbours of the Hutchinsons, and the husbands seem to have shared mutual respect despite their opposing political views).

Lucy Hutchinson was born into the royalist Apsley family, though her mother's puritan inclinations may have instigated her own later puritanism and shift away from royalism. Her father was lieutenant of the Tower of London, so she was brought up in an unusual setting, and one which may have provided surprising access to intellectual circles rather than seclusion from them; she recounts how her mother assisted Sir Walter Ralegh with some of his scientific experiments when he was imprisoned in the tower. Her brother Sir Allen Apsley was a royalist officer and MP (notorious for a drunken episode in the House of Commons) and perhaps had a formative influence on his sister through his access to London literary circles. Her religious and political views were one of the features that attracted her husband, John Hutchinson, to her, and her to him, and Lucy Hutchinson's marriage only further developed her opposition to aspects of state religion and the court. She and her husband were activist republicans and Independents in religion. Their circles were of high social standing but diverse in political persuasion, from the Apsley family and their Wilmot relatives (Anne Wilmot, Lucy Hutchinson's cousin, was the mother of the notorious libertine poet John Wilmot, Earl of Rochester) to the Earl of Anglesey (to whom she dedicated her Lucretius translation) and the Nonconformist preacher John Owen, whose sermons both Hutchinson and Lady Anglesey attended and whose Latin theological treatise Hutchinson translated. After the Restoration, Hutchinson felt her intellectual and social circles disintegrating around her, though this period seems also to have seen renewed productivity in her poetic career. Hutchinson's most personal (and also arguably, most political) poems are the elegies on her husband, which instead of bolstering the kind of community represented by Katherine Philips in defeat, represent a poetry of isolation. These are poems profoundly connected to place, as they meditate on the bereaved wife's experience of the estate where she had lived with her husband. These poems turn inside out many of the tropes of country house poetry (most prominently used by Ben Jonson in 'To Penshurst'), which often presents the richness, plenitude, and order of the estate ruled by the perfect master. With her husband gone and her hopes for a godly republic shattered, Hutchinson represents Owthorpe as an elegiac and dystopian landscape.

Philosophy and science

While the Civil War wrought damage across the landscapes in which these poets lived, their perspective on the world around them was also transformed by the period's rapid developments in natural philosophy. John Donne wrote that 'new philosophy calls all in doubt',

And freely men confess that this world's spent,
When in the planets, and the firmament
They seek so many new; they see that this
Is crumbled out again to his atomies.[5]

As this famous quotation suggests, philosophy in the period was both profoundly revolutionary and profoundly poetic. Donne gives a vivid sense of the loss as well as gain that came with scientific discoveries, and his words would also come to reflect the country's mixed feelings about the triumphs and devastations of Civil War and political revolution some three decades later.

The terms 'philosophy' and particularly 'new philosophy' would come in the seventeenth century to represent something closer to what we now call science. The word 'science' derives from the Latin for 'knowledge', and 'philosophy' from the Greek for 'love of knowledge'. The term 'natural philosophy' was used to describe investigation of the natural world – what we now think of as biology, chemistry, and physics – but while these modern disciplines probably would not identify themselves with philosophy, the early modern discipline incorporated more imaginative and conjectural approaches. The mid-seventeenth century saw a shift to 'experimental philosophy'. Again, the terms 'experiment' and 'philosophy' may seem divergent today, but convey the nature of scientific enquiry in this period. The work of scholars including Francis Bacon earlier in the century had led to a focus on empirical methods, on evidence and observation rather than book learning or enquiry through imagination. The Royal Society was founded in 1660 on Baconian principles, becoming England's first scientific institution. It was granted a royal charter by Charles II in 1663 and the full title 'The Royal Society of London for Improving Natural Knowledge'. As its name and charter make clear, the society was connected to the Restoration court, with Charles as its patron, and he may have seen it as an important step in building national pride after the Civil War period. The Curator of Experiments was Robert Hooke, and he put on a dazzling display of experiments for Margaret Cavendish's famous visit to the society in 1667. Her poems on telescopic and microscopic vision ('Of Stars' and 'A World in an Earring') are inspired by contemporary use of optical instruments as well as critical of their presumption to truth; rejecting Royal Society principles, she often concludes that the imagination can be as precise and productive a tool as vision or reason.

The terms that are now often used for this period's philosophy, 'the scientific revolution' and 'the new science', are as value-laden as those used for its political phases, such as 'Interregnum' and 'Restoration'. Both 'revolution' and 'new' suggest what their proponents (and later scholars) have wanted to see occurring, but the period saw continuity as well as transformation in thinking about the natural world. Writers like Hester Pulter, Margaret Cavendish, and Lucy Hutchinson bridge these aspects of seventeenth-century philosophy, both prescient and nostalgic. Pulter's poetic depictions of her garden and surrounding landscape owe much to the moralistic and religious view of the natural world propounded in Pliny's *Natural History*, translated by Philemon Holland in 1601; at the same time, 'A Solitary Complaint' reveals a strikingly modern understanding of Copernican astronomical theory, as confirmed by Galileo. When Lucy Hutchinson translated the Roman poet Lucretius' *De rerum natura* ('Of the nature of things'), she was reworking an ancient poem which still shocked her contemporaries. Cavendish was somewhat retrograde in her rejection of experimentation and instruments, but also very modern in her critique of the objectivity claimed by contemporary scientists and also in her environmental consciousness. She ventriloquises the hare, stag, and oak in order to assert their equal claim to subjecthood and sensibility.

Early modern philosophy and science also raised questions about poetic language. Thomas Sprat, in his 1667 history of the Royal Society (which was also a kind of manifesto), saw the society's members as having resolved 'to reject all the amplifications, digressions, and swellings of style' and to promote 'a close, naked, natural way of speaking; positive expressions; clear senses; a native easiness: bringing all things as near the mathematical plainness'. Hutchinson's Lucretius translation, her *Order and Disorder*, and Cavendish's atomist poems in *Poems and Fancies* all defend the poet's choice to write in verse for subjects that might seem better suited to prose. Pulter's occasional and religious poems, such as 'A Solitary Complaint' and 'The Circle ["Those that the hidden chemic art profess"]', are often surprising in the extent to which contemporary scientific theory becomes the basis of extended poetic tropes, with Donne's metaphysical poems likely to be one influence on her.

The gendering of early modern natural philosophy has been much debated, and its formal institutions were indeed exclusively male in membership; the Royal Society allowed Cavendish to visit but did not admit female members to its fellowship until 1945. But the philosophical poems by these women poets suggest another story, one dominated by powerful female figures, such as Venus in the *De rerum natura* and Nature in Cavendish's poems. Pulter is, again, a striking case, as her protestations of isolation belie a familiarity with contemporary alchemical thought and Galilean astronomical theory that she puts to detailed and sophisticated use. It is difficult to know exactly what her sources were (for example, if she read Galileo she would have had to do so in Latin or Italian), but her poetry illustrates both the diffusion of new scientific ideas in the period and women poets' interest in them.[6]

Genre

The range of poetic genres in which these women wrote testifies to the diversity of their education, environment, and influence, as well as religious and political leanings. Some choices of poetic genre – for example, religious lyrics and elegies – are particularly prevalent, and reflect the particularities of women's education and cultural capital. At the same time, however, and just as intriguingly, the women represented in this anthology participate in a full spectrum of seventeenth-century genres, including philosophical poems, dialogues, political complaints, and epics; and they do so as innovatively as their male counterparts. Poetic fashions also changed across the decades covered, and we will see each poem representing a particular and distinctive manifestation of any one genre, with continuities as well as changes revealing much about seventeenth-century women's engagements with poetic forms and about the most popular Civil War genres.

Women's close relationship to the Bible, through education and reading practices, is evident in the wide and various range of religious genres that they use. Katherine Philips's '2 Corinthians 5:19', written on Good Friday 1653, is a kind of verse that was based on devotional practice, advocated by many influential churchmen such as Bishop Joseph Hall and widely popular among male and female poets. Such meditations, along with the devotional lyrics represented in Hester Pulter's work, often bear a close relationship to the meditational lyrics of Donne and Herbert, favourites of women readers in the seventeenth century. (Donne's secular love lyrics also influenced both Philips and Hutchinson; see, for example, Philips's 'Friendship in Emblem or the Seal, to my Dearest Lucasia' and Hutchinson's 'Another on the Sunshine'). Women's religious lyrics may once have been regarded as a lesser sort of writing, 'private' and personal, but the religious nature of the conflict during the Civil War also means that these poems' languages of devotion are often highly politicised. Pulter's 'Must I thus ever interdicted be?', for example, expresses a personal experience of God's love, but also seems to make a statement about being excluded from communal worship at her local parish church.

Women also wrote longer-form biblical poems, in part under the influence of Guillaume de Saluste Du Bartas, whose long poems on sacred and secular history, the *Divine Weeks and Works*, were enormously popular. Anne Bradstreet is explicit about her poetic debt to 'great Bartas', whose name recurs throughout her verse. Her longest poem, *The Four Monarchies*, is a lengthy verse explication of the Assyrian, Persian, Greek, and Roman monarchies using them to interpret the history of the world and to reflect obliquely on the central political events of the English mid-century. Lucy Hutchinson's *Order and Disorder* is a lengthy poetic retelling of Genesis that can be most easily compared to Milton's *Paradise Lost*, but its deliberately plainer language and closer adherence to Scripture also reflect its relationship to Du Bartas's work and to a wider culture of poetic biblical paraphrases.

Elegy is another favourite genre for women writers, and the poets in this anthology put it to an intriguingly wide range of uses. It has been said of elegy and its popularity with women writers that 'grief provided a position from which women could speak',[7] and its basis in child-loss poetry is illustrated in this anthology in poems by Bradstreet (on the death of her granddaughter Elizabeth), Pulter (on the death of her daughter Jane), and Philips (on the death of her infant son Hector). Elegy is, however, put to many and various uses. Bradstreet's 'elegies' for Sir Philip Sidney, Elizabeth I, and Du Bartas are really retrospective encomiums, harking back to the 'halcyon days' of English Protestantism; they are different in kind from Pulter's elegies for King Charles I, which were contemporaneous to his death, and deeply influenced by an outpouring of royalist elegies on his death in 1649. Margaret Cavendish's 'Upon the Funeral of my Dear Brother, Killed in these Unhappy Wars' is personal as well as political, as are Lucy Hutchinson's elegies on the death of her husband. These poems radically revise the genre again, appropriating what had become a royalist form (through its identification with mourning of the king) and using it to republican ends.

Poems of friendship, of retirement, and of invitation to rural retreat are also common across the royalist lyrics of Pulter and Philips. Philips circulated poetry in a 'Society of Friendship', her articulations of friendship to Lucasia, Rosania, and Ardelia often delineating a space outside the tumult of state politics; see, for example, 'Invitation to the Country' and 'A Retired Friendship, to Ardelia, 23 August 1651'. Friendship in these poems coincides with a call to rural retreat that echoes the classical retirement poetry of Horace, in a Horatian stoicism that became associated with royalists in the Civil War period. Pulter, too, addresses her poems to royalist 'friends', and advocates a retreat from the city to the country (see, for example, her 'Invitation into the Country, to my Dear Daughters'). These poems can be read in relation to each other as well as to poems of a similar nature by Cowley and Marvell; each speaks to the poetic 'mainstream', and also illustrates ways in which these tropes are, in some cases, feminised, enabling an expanded exploration of that central, evolving trope in seventeenth-century personal and political poetry.

The women in this anthology write in a wide range of other genres, many of which have very particular political resonances in the period. The female-voiced complaint poem has classical and biblical precedents, as well as medieval and early modern histories of use for political commentary. Hester Pulter's 'The Complaint of Thames, 1647' is in this mode, as is Bradstreet's female-voiced dialogue poem *A Dialogue between Old England and New*. But Bradstreet's 'The Flesh and the Spirit', like Margaret Cavendish's 'A Dialogue between the Body and the Mind', is in the medieval tradition of dialogues between body and soul rather than in the vein of the contentious dialogue poem that was a popular Civil War genre. Cavendish's dialogues between mankind and hare or oak tree are different again, drawing on literary traditions of a moralised landscape and its animal inhabitants and placing her as a leading voice of environmental consciousness.

Hester Pulter's emblem poems are also indebted to a moralised reading of the natural world, drawing heavily in her case on Pliny's *Natural History*, in its English translation by Philemon Holland (1601), and similar sources. Emblems were popular in England from the 1580s, drawing on European models and consisting of three parts – a motto, an image, and a poem – in order to draw a moral from the natural world or from religious belief. Pulter's emblems are purely poetic (without image or motto) but they draw on previous models and encapsulate divine and moral 'truths' for her children and for royalist readers.[8] These are unapologetically didactic poems, drawing on images from the natural word in order to correct the ills of English republican society. Lucy Hutchinson's translation of Lucretius' *De rerum natura*, excerpted in this anthology, takes a radically different approach to the world. It is the first translation into English of a linguistically difficult, ideologically radical Latin poem that is instructive yet also allusive and epic; it can be read alongside Cavendish's different, but equally materialist, 'A World Made by Atoms' and 'Nature Calls a Council', and alongside Pulter's philosophically speculative lyrics.

What emerges in our selection of poems – approximately twenty lyrics or extracts of longer poems for each author – is a corpus of poetry by mid-seventeenth-century women that is extensive, complex, and formally diverse, showing that women poets used all the genres adopted by their male peers, and indeed led the way in the formation of some key Civil War genres.

Forms of publication

The decades of the English Civil War and the Cromwellian republic saw an unprecedented number of women writers enter into print. The publication of Anne Bradstreet's *The Tenth Muse* in 1650 exemplifies the printing of poetry for political ends: her historical verse spoke directly to religious puritans and political republicans in the year after the regicide, and *A Dialogue between Old England and New* could be seen as a metaphor for exactly the way in which Bradstreet's political voice spoke back to the country from which she had emigrated. The publication of *The Tenth Muse* also illustrates the questions concerning authorisation to publish which surround a number of prominent women's printed texts in this period. Bradstreet's brother-in-law John Woodbridge is believed to have taken her manuscript poems to London without her knowledge: certainly, she later wrote that the poems of *The Tenth Muse* were 'snatched' from her side 'by friends less wise than true, / Who thee abroad exposed to public view' ('The Author to her Book'). Katherine Philips also publicly decried the printing of her *Poems* in 1664, claiming that the volume was not authorised. It is, however, unclear whether Bradstreet and Philips were entirely ingenuous in their public expressions of violation.

These reactions indicate the extent to which print publication was often still regarded in the mid-seventeenth century as inappropriate for women, although these are important transitional decades when even prominent male writers such as Andrew Marvell demurred from publishing their poems in print. Women of the sixteenth and seventeenth centuries had written prevalently in manuscript, circulating and 'publishing' their works in coteries and networks that ranged from the very small to the more extensive. Anne Bradstreet's poems circulated in a relatively small family and community coterie in New England, and Hester Pulter's poems seem to have circulated within her family first and foremost. Katherine Philips, however, was an enormously successful and prolific manuscript poet, cultivating an audience for verses that ranged from friends she knew well to readers of whom she knew little. When Philips's *Poems* (1664) was printed, her work was already widely known, and indeed the printed volume may have been a pirate edition, provided to the printers by an admiring reader.

The examples of Bradstreet and Philips illustrate the ways in which manuscript circulation and print publishing existed in a continuum with each other in this period (and, indeed, well into the eighteenth century). The first five cantos of Lucy Hutchinson's *Order and Disorder* were printed anonymously in 1679, and several copies of the other fifteen cantos seem to have circulated in manuscript. Her elegies, however, seem to have remained private, perhaps on account of their great political sensitivity. It is important to remember that politically sensitive male authors' poetry often remained unprinted in this period, too. The poetry of Andrew Marvell, for example, was unprinted until 1681, and even then, 'An Horatian Ode upon Cromwell's Return from Ireland' was cancelled from most copies, probably because its apparent praise of Cromwell was out of step with prevailing political sentiment.

Margaret Cavendish is alone among the poets in this anthology in boldly prioritising the print publication of her work. Her folios represent a thoroughgoing monumentalisation of herself as they foreground her name and title and her authorial voice, through the many prefaces addressing various components of her readership. Her work was also promoted by her husband, William Cavendish, both during her life and after her death, when he published a collection of letters and poems about his wife. Nor did she regard the printing of her work as bestowing an inviolable fixity upon it. Cavendish probably keenly oversaw, if not conducted, the editing of her own work. *Poems and Fancies* was first printed in 1653, and she made large numbers of amendments to it before its second printing in 1664.

The final seventeenth-century publications of Katherine Philips's and Anne Bradstreet's poems were posthumous: *Poems by the Most Deservedly Admired Mrs Katherine Philips* (1667) was published three years after Philips's death of smallpox, and *Several Poems, Compiled with Great Variety of Wit and Learning* (1678) was published six years after Bradstreet's death. All of these volumes claim, less and more explicitly, that the revisions to the poems that they contain were made by the author, but it is hard to be sure of the extent to which this is the case. *Poems* (1667) is a handsome folio volume, prefaced with a bust of the poet and a plethora of celebratory poems: the volume begins the celebration of Katherine Philips as 'The Matchless Orinda', and her poems were read, circulated, and copied to a greater extent than any other early modern woman writer. Bradstreet's *Several Poems*, printed in Boston, established her as America's first poet, a context in which she has primarily been read ever since. With these posthumous editions begins another story, one of the reception and reading of Civil War women's poetry from their deaths until the present day – and one in which this anthology seeks to intervene.

Women's poetic engagement in the political, social, and literary cultures of seventeenth-century England has long been elided, rendering only partial our sense of Civil War poetics. Much women's poetry of the period, underrepresented in the print culture, became invisible to future centuries, and its participation in the social, poetic, and political cultures of its time was lost from view. 'Women's poetry' of the English Civil War is, in the formulation of this anthology, simply that authored by women: this point of genesis aside, the poems are as diverse in genre, poetics, and political sentiment as those by men, and they provide as rich and as varied an experience of seventeenth-century poetic culture as those hitherto better-known texts. Drawing on the multiple material contexts in which women's poetry occurred, and on the immediate, revised, and posthumous versions of these poems, this anthology presents the works of women poets whose works emerge out of, reflect upon, and contribute to Civil War poetic culture. Here, Bradstreet, Pulter, Philips, Cavendish, and Hutchinson can be read in depth alongside each other, and can take their places in the poetic canon of Civil War and seventeenth-century England.

Notes

1 David Loewenstein and John Morrill, 'Literature and Religion', in David Loewenstein and Janel Mueller (eds), *The Cambridge History of Early Modern English Literature* (Cambridge: Cambridge University Press, 2002), pp. 664–713 (p. 664).
2 See Claude J. Summers and Michael Schoenfeldt, 'Herrick, Vaughan, and the Poetry of Anglican Survivalism', in John R. Roberts (ed.), *New Perspectives on the Seventeenth-Century Religious Lyric* (Columbia and London: University of Missouri Press, 1994), pp. 46–74.
3 See Elizabeth Wade White, *Anne Bradstreet: The Tenth Muse* (New York: Oxford University Press, 1971), p. 250; and Mihoko Suzuki, 'What's Political in Seventeenth-Century Women's Political Writing?', *Literature Compass*, 6 (2009): 927–41 (p. 935).
4 John Kerrigan, *Archipelagic English: Literature, History, and Politics, 1603–1707* (Oxford: Oxford University Press, 2008).
5 John Donne, *An Anatomy of the World* (1611), lines 205, 209–12.
6 See Sarah Hutton, 'Hester Pulter (c. 1596–1678). A Woman Poet and the New Astronomy', *Etudes Epistémè*, 14 (2008): 77–87.
7 See Danielle Clarke, *The Politics of Early Modern Women's Writing* (London: Pearson Education, 2001), pp. 166–67.
8 See Alice Eardley, *Lady Hester Pulter: Poems, Emblems, and* The Unfortunate Florinda (Toronto: Iter Inc. and the Centre for Reformation and Renaissance Studies, 2014), pp. 27–29.

Further reading

Anne Bradstreet

Gray, Catharine, *Women Writers and Public Debate in Seventeenth-Century Britain* (Basingstoke: Palgrave Macmillan, 2007)

Hensley, Jeannine (ed.), *The Works of Anne Bradstreet*, with a foreword by Adrienne Rich (Cambridge, MA: Belknap Press of Harvard University Press, 1967)

Jed, Stephanie, '*The Tenth Muse*: Gender, Rationality and the Marketing of Knowledge', in Margo Hendricks and Patricia Parker (eds), *Women, 'Race', and Writing in the Early Modern Period* (London and New York: Routledge, 1994), pp. 195–208

Pender, Patricia, 'Disciplining the Imperial Mother: Anne Bradstreet's *A Dialogue between Old England and New*', *Meridian*, 18, *Women's Writing 1550–1750*, ed. Jo Wallwork and Paul Salzman (Melbourne, 2001): 115–31

Pender, Patricia, *Early Modern Women's Writing and the Rhetoric of Modesty* (Basingstoke: Palgrave Macmillan, 2012)

Prescott, Anne Lake, 'A Year in the Life of King Saul: 1643', in Kevin Killeen, Helen Smith, and Rachel Willie (eds), *The Oxford Handbook of The Bible in Early Modern England, c. 1530–1700* (Oxford: Oxford University Press, 2015), pp. 412–26

Round, Philip H., *By Nature and by Custom Cursed: Transatlantic Civil Discourse and New England Cultural Production, 1620–1660* (Hanover and London: University Press of New England, 1999)

Suzuki, Mihoko, 'What's Political in Seventeenth-Century Women's Political Writing?', *Literature Compass*, 6 (2009): 927–41

Wade White, Elizabeth, *Anne Bradstreet: The Tenth Muse* (New York: Oxford University Press, 1971)

Wiseman, Susan, *Conspiracy and Virtue: Women, Writing, and Politics in Seventeenth-Century England* (Oxford: Oxford University Press, 2006)

Wright, Gillian, *Producing Women's Poetry, 1660–1730: Text and Paratext, Manuscript and Print* (Cambridge: Cambridge University Press, 2013)

Hester Pulter

Archer, Jayne, 'A "Perfect Circle"? Alchemy in the Poetry of Hester Pulter', *Literature Compass*, 2 (2005), DOI: 10.1111/j.1741-4113.2005.00160.x (accessed 27 April 2017)

Brady, Andrea, 'Dying with Honour: Literary Propaganda and the Second English Civil War', *Journal of Military History*, 70 (2006): 9–30

Chedgzoy, Kate, *Women's Writing in the British Atlantic World: Memory, Place and History, 1550–1700* (Cambridge: Cambridge University Press, 2007)

Clarke, Elizabeth, 'Introducing Hester Pulter and the Perdita Project", *Literature Compass*, 2 (2005), DOI:10.1111/j.1741-4113.2005.00159.x (accessed 27 April 2017)

Clarke, Elizabeth, 'Women in Church and in Devotional Spaces', in Laura Lunger Knoppers (ed.), *The Cambridge Companion to Early Modern Women's Writing* (Cambridge: Cambridge University Press, 2009), pp. 110–23

Eardley, Alice, 'Lady Hester Pulter's Date of Birth', *Notes and Queries*, 57 (2010): 498–501

Eardley, Alice (ed.), *Lady Hester Pulter: Poems, Emblems, and* The Unfortunate Florinda (Toronto: Iter Inc. and the Centre for Reformation and Renaissance Studies, 2014)

Ezell, Margaret J. M., 'The Laughing Tortoise: Speculations on Manuscript Sources and Women's Book History', *English Literary Renaissance*, 38 (2008): 331–55

Hutton, Sarah, 'Hester Pulter (c. 1596–1678): A Woman Poet and the New Astronomy', *Etudes Epistémè*, 14 (2008): 77–87

Marcus, Leah, 'Herrick's "Hesperides" and the "Proclamation Made for May"', *Studies in Philology*, 76.1 (1979): 49–74

Marcus, Leah, *The Politics of Mirth: Jonson, Herrick, Milton, Marvell, and the Defense of Old Holiday Pastimes* (Chicago: University of Chicago Press, 1986)

Nevitt, Marcus, 'The Insults of Defeat: Royalist Responses to Sir William Davenant's *Gondibert* (1651)', *The Seventeenth Century*, 24 (2009): 287–304

Nixon, Scott, '"Aske me no more" and the Manuscript Verse Miscellany', *English Literary Renaissance*, 29 (1999): 97–130

Robson, Mark, 'Reading Hester Pulter Reading', *Literature Compass*, 2 (2005), DOI:10.1111/j.1741-4113.2005.00162.x (accessed 27 April 2017)

Robson, Mark, 'Swansongs: Reading Voice in the Poetry of Lady Hester Pulter', *English Manuscript Studies 1100–1700*, 9 (2000): 238–56

Ross, Sarah C. E., 'Tears, Bezoars, and Blazing Comets: Gender and Politics in Hester Pulter's Civil War Lyrics', *Literature Compass*, 2 (2005), DOI:10.1111/j.174 1-4113.2005.00161.x (accessed 27 April 2017)

Ross, Sarah C. E., *Women, Poetry, and Politics in Seventeenth-Century Britain* (Oxford: Oxford University Press, 2015)

Katherine Philips

Anderson, Penelope, *Friendship's Shadows: Women's Friendship and the Politics of Betrayal in England, 1640–1705* (Edinburgh: Edinburgh University Press, 2012)

Andreadis, Harriette, 'Reconfiguring Early Modern Friendship: Katherine Philips and Homoerotic Desire', *Studies in English Literature, 1500–1900*, 46 (2006): 523–42

Andreadis, Harriette, 'The Sapphic-Platonics of Katherine Philips, 1632–1664', *Signs: Journal of Women in Culture and Society*, 15 (1989): 34–60

Applegate, Joan, 'Katherine Philips's "Orinda upon Little Hector": An Unrecorded Musical Setting by Henry Lawes', *English Manuscript Studies 1100–1700*, 4 (1993): 272–80

Barash, Carol, *English Women's Poetry, 1649–1714: Politics, Community and Linguistic Authority* (Oxford: Oxford University Press, 1996)

Brady, Andrea, 'The Platonic Poems of Katherine Philips', *The Seventeenth Century*, 25 (2010): 300–22

Chalmers, Hero, *Royalist Women Writers, 1650–1689* (Oxford: Clarendon Press, 2004)

Coolahan, Marie-Louise, '"We live by chance, and slip into Events": Occasionality and the Manuscript Verse of Katherine Philips', *Eighteenth-Century Ireland*, 18 (2003): 9–23

Gray, Catherine, 'Katherine Philips and the Post-Courtly Coterie', *English Literary Renaissance*, 32 (2002): 426–51

Hageman, Elizabeth H., 'Treacherous Accidents and the Abominable Printing of Katherine Philips's 1664 *Poems*', in W. Speed Hill (ed.), *New Ways of Looking at Old Texts, III: Papers of the Renaissance English Text Society, 1997–2001* (Tempe, AZ: ACMRS, 2004), pp. 85–95

Hageman, Elizabeth H. and Sununu, Andrea, '"More Copies of It Abroad than I Could Have Imagin'd": Further Manuscript Texts of Katherine Philips, "The Matchless Orinda"', *English Manuscript Studies 1100–1700*, 5 (1995): 127–69

Hageman, Elizabeth H. and Sununu, Andrea, 'New Manuscript Texts of Katherine Philips, "the Matchless Orinda"', *English Manuscript Studies 1100–1700*, 4 (1993): 174–216

Katherine Philips and Other Writers, a special issue of *Women's Writing*, 23 (2016)

Kerrigan, John, *Archipelagic English: Literature, History, and Politics, 1603–1707* (Oxford: Oxford University Press, 2008)

Loscocco, Paula, '"Manly Sweetness": Katherine Philips among the Neoclassicals', *Huntington Library Quarterly*, 56 (1993): 259–79

Loxley, James, 'Unfettered Organs: The Polemical Voices of Katherine Philips', in Danielle Clarke and Elizabeth Clarke (eds), *'This Double Voice': Gendered Writing in Early Modern England* (New York: St Martin's Press, 2000), pp. 230–48

Orvis, David L. and Ryan Singh Paul, *The Noble Flame of Katherine Philips: A Poetics of Culture, Politics, and Friendship* (Pittsburgh, PA: Duquesne University Press, 2015)

Salzman, Paul, *Reading Early Modern Women's Writing* (Oxford: Oxford University Press, 2006)

Scott-Baumann, Elizabeth, *Forms of Engagement: Women, Poetry, and Culture, 1640–1680* (Oxford: Oxford University Press, 2013)

Shifflett, Andrew, '"How Many Virtues Must I Hate": Katherine Philips and the Politics of Clemency', *Studies in Philology*, 94 (1997): 103–35

Thomas, Patrick (ed.), *The Collected Works of Katherine Philips, The Matchless Orinda*, vol. 1: *The Poems*; vol. 2: *The Letters* (Stump Cross, Essex: Stump Cross Books, 1990)

Wright, Gillian, 'Textuality, Privacy and Politics: Katherine Philips's Poems in Manuscript and Print', in James Daybell and Peter Hinds (eds), *Material Readings of Early Modern Culture* (Basingstoke: Macmillan, 2010), pp. 163–82

Margaret Cavendish

Battigelli, Anna, *Margaret Cavendish and the Exiles of the Mind* (Lexington: University Press of Kentucky, 1998)

Brady, Andrea, 'Dying with Honour: Literary Propaganda and the Second English Civil War', *Journal of Military History*, 70 (2006): 9–30

Chalmers, Hero, *Royalist Women Writers, 1650–1689* (Oxford: Clarendon Press, 2004)

Clucas, Stephen (ed.), *A Princely Brave Woman: Essays on Margaret Cavendish, Duchess of Newcastle* (Aldershot: Ashgate, 2003)

Dodds, Lara, *The Literary Invention of Margaret Cavendish* (Pittsburgh: Duquesne University Press, 2013)

Hutton, Sarah, 'In Dialogue with Thomas Hobbes: Margaret Cavendish's Natural Philosophy', *Women's Writing*, 4 (1997): 421–32

Hutton, Sarah, 'Margaret Cavendish and Henry More', in Stephen Clucas (ed.), *A Princely Brave Woman: Essays on Margaret Cavendish, Duchess of Newcastle* (Aldershot: Ashgate, 2003), pp. 185–98

Johns, Adrian, *The Nature of The Book: Print and Knowledge in the Making* (Chicago and London: University of Chicago Press, 1998)

Mendelson, Sarah H., (ed.), *Ashgate Critical Essays on Women Writers in England, 1550–1700* (series editor Mary Ellen Lamb), vol. 7: *Margaret Cavendish* (Aldershot: Ashgate, 2009)

Nate, Richard '"Plain and Vulgarly Express'd": Margaret Cavendish and the Discourse of the New Science', *Rhetorica*, 19 (2001): 403–17

Norbrook, David, 'Margaret Cavendish and Lucy Hutchinson: Identity, Ideology and Politics', *In-Between: Essays and Studies in Literary Criticism*, 9 (2000): 179–203

Osmond, Rosalie, *Mutual Accusations: Seventeenth-Century Body and Soul Dialogues in their Literary and Theological Context* (Toronto: Toronto University Press, 1990)

Rees, Emma L. E., *Margaret Cavendish: Gender, Genre, Exile* (Manchester: Manchester University Press, 2003)

Salzman, Paul, *Reading Early Modern Women's Writing* (Oxford: Oxford University Press, 2006)

Sarasohn, Lisa T., *The Natural Philosophy of Margaret Cavendish: Reason and Fancy during the Scientific Revolution* (Baltimore: Johns Hopkins University Press, 2010)

Scott-Baumann, Elizabeth, '"Bake'd in the Oven of Applause": The Blazon and the Body in Margaret Cavendish's Fancies', *Women's Writing*, 15 (2008): 86–106

Spiller, Elizabeth, *Science, Reading, and Renaissance Literature: The Art of Making Knowledge, 1580–1670* (Cambridge: Cambridge University Press, 2004)

Stark, Ryan John, 'Margaret Cavendish and Composition Style', *Rhetoric Review*, 17 (1999): 264–81

Whitaker, Katie, *Mad Madge: Margaret Cavendish, Duchess of Newcastle, Royalist, Writer and Romantic* (London: Chatto & Windus, 2003)

Wright, Joanne H., 'Reading the Private in Margaret Cavendish: Conversations in Political Thought', in David Armitage (ed.), *British Political Thought in History, Literature and Theory, 1500–1800* (Cambridge: Cambridge University Press, 2006), pp. 212–34

Lucy Hutchinson

Anderson, Penelope, *Friendship's Shadows: Women's Friendship and the Politics of Betrayal in England, 1640–1705* (Edinburgh: Edinburgh University Press, 2012)

Gillespie, Katharine, 'Shades of Representation: Lucy Hutchinson's Ghost and the Politics of the Representative', in Catharine Gray and Erin Murphy (eds), *Milton Now: Alternative Approaches and Contexts* (Basingstoke: Palgrave Macmillan, 2014), pp. 195–214

Further reading

Goldberg, Jonathan, 'Lucy Hutchinson Writing Matter', *English Literary History*, 73 (2006): 275–301

Hammons, Pamela, 'Polluted Palaces: Gender, Sexuality and Property in Lucy Hutchinson's "Elegies"', *Women's Writing*, 13 (2006): 392–415

Hirst, Derek, 'Remembering a Hero: Lucy Huchinson's *Memoirs* of her Husband', *English Historical Review*, 119 (2004): 682–91

Hutchinson, Lucy, *The Works of Lucy Hutchinson*, vol. 1: *The Translation of Lucretius*, ed. Reid Barbour and David Norbrook, with Latin text by Maria Cristina Zerbino (Oxford: Oxford University Press, 2012)

Keeble, N. H., '"But the Colonel's Shadow": Lucy Hutchinson, Women's Writing, and the Civil War', in Thomas Healy and Jonathan Sawday (eds), *Literature and the English Civil War* (Cambridge: Cambridge University Press, 1990), pp. 227–47

Lobo, Giuseppina Iacono, 'Lucy Hutchinson's Revisions of Conscience', *English Literary Renaissance*, 42 (2012): 317–41

Longfellow, Erica, *Women and Religious Writing in Early Modern England* (Cambridge: Cambridge University Press, 2004)

Lucy Hutchinson, a special issue of *The Seventeenth Century*, 30 (2015)

Mayer, Robert, 'Lucy Hutchinson: A Life of Writing', *The Seventeenth Century*, 22 (2007): 305–35

Norbrook, David, 'John Milton, Lucy Hutchinson, and the Republican Biblical Epic', in Mark R. Kelley, Michael Lieb, and John T. Shawcross (eds), *Milton and the Grounds of Contention* (Pittsburgh: Duquesne University Press, 2003), pp. 37–63

Norbrook, David, 'Lucy Hutchinson and *Order and Disorder*: The Manuscript Evidence', *English Manuscript Studies 1100–1700*, 9 (2000): 257–91

Norbrook, David, 'Lucy Hutchinson's "Elegies" and the Situation of the Republican Woman Writer', *English Literary Renaissance*, 27 (1997): 468–521

Norbrook, David, 'Lucy Hutchinson: Theology, Gender and Translation', *The Seventeenth Century*, 30 (2015): 139–62

Norbrook, David, 'Lucy Hutchinson versus Edmund Waller: An Unpublished Reply to Waller's "A Panegyrick to my Lord Protector"', *The Seventeenth Century*, 11 (1996): 61–86

Norbrook, David, 'Margaret Cavendish and Lucy Hutchinson: Identity, Ideology and Politics', *In-Between: Essays and Studies in Literary Criticism*, 9 (2000): 179–203

Norbrook, David, 'Memoirs and Oblivion: Lucy Hutchinson and the Restoration', *Huntington Library Quarterly*, 75 (2012): 233–82

Norbrook, David, 'Milton, Lucy Hutchinson and the Lucretian Sublime', *Tate Papers*, 13 (2010), http://www.tate.org.uk/research/publications/tate-papers/13/milton-lucy-hutchinson-and-the-lucretian-sublime (accessed 21 April 2017)

Norbrook, David, '"Words more than civil": Republican Civility in Lucy Hutchinson's "The Life of John Hutchinson"', in Jennifer Richards (ed.), *Early Modern Civil Discourses* (Basingstoke: Palgrave Macmillan, 2003), pp. 68–84

Norbrook, David, Philip Hardie, and Stephen Harrison (eds), *Lucretius and the Early Modern* (Oxford: Oxford University Press, 2015)

Ross, Sarah C. E., *Women, Poetry, and Politics in Seventeenth-Century Britain* (Oxford: Oxford University Press, 2015)

Salzman, Paul, *Reading Early Modern Women's Writing* (Oxford: Oxford University Press, 2006)

Scott-Baumann, Elizabeth, 'Lucy Hutchinson's *Elegies* and the Seventeenth-Century Country House Poem', *Literature Compass*, 4 (2007): 664–76

Scott-Baumann, Elizabeth, 'Lucy Hutchinson, the Bible and *Order and Disorder*', in *The Intellectual Culture of Puritan Women* (Basingstoke: Palgrave, 2010), pp. 176–89

Suzuki, Mihoko (ed.), *Ashgate Critical Essays on Women Writers in England, 1550–1700* (series editor Mary Ellen Lamb), vol. 5: *Anne Clifford and Lucy Hutchinson* (Aldershot: Ashgate, 2009)

Wilcher, Robert, '"Adventurous Song" or "presumptuous folly": The Problem of "utterance" in John Milton's *Paradise Lost* and Lucy Hutchinson's *Order and Disorder*', *The Seventeenth Century*, 21 (2006): 304–14

Wiseman, Susan, *Conspiracy and Virtue: Women, Writing, and Politics in Seventeenth-Century England* (Oxford: Oxford University Press, 2006)

The English Civil War

Holmes, Clive, *Why was Charles I Executed?* (London: Hambledon Continuum, 2006)

Morrill, John (ed.), *The Impact of the English Civil War* (London: Collins and Brown, 1991)

Summers, Claude J., and Ted-Larry Pebworth (eds), *The English Civil Wars in the Literary Imagination* (Columbia and London: University of Missouri Press, 1999)

Worden, Blair, *The English Civil Wars 1640–1660* (London: Phoenix, 2009)

Religion, war, and poetry

Hill, Christopher, *Puritanism and Revolution* (London: Secker & Warburg, 1958)

Longfellow, Erica, *Women and Religious Writing in Early Modern England* (Cambridge: Cambridge University Press, 2004)

Loxley, James, *Royalism and Poetry in the English Civil Wars: The Drawn Sword* (Basingstoke: Macmillan, 1997)

McDowell, Nicholas, *The English Radical Imagination: Culture, Religion, and Revolution, 1630–1660* (Oxford: Oxford University Press, 2003)

Norbrook, David, *Writing the English Republic: Poetry, Rhetoric and Politics, 1627–1660* (Cambridge: Cambridge University Press, 1999)

Smith, Nigel, *Literature and Revolution in England, 1640–1660* (New Haven: Yale University Press, 1994)

Summers, Claude J., and Ted-Larry Pebworth (eds), The *English Civil Wars in the Literary Imagination* (Columbia and London: University of Missouri Press, 1999)

Networks and communities

Anderson, Penelope, *Friendship's Shadows: Women's Friendship and the Politics of Betrayal in England, 1640–1705* (Edinburgh: Edinburgh University Press, 2012)

Barash, Carol, *English Women's Poetry, 1649–1714: Politics, Community and Linguistic Authority* (Oxford: Oxford University Press, 1996)

Ross, Sarah C. E., *Women, Poetry, and Politics in Seventeenth-Century Britain* (Oxford: Oxford University Press, 2015)

Wright, Gillian, *Producing Women's Poetry, 1660–1730: Text and Paratext, Manuscript and Print* (Cambridge: Cambridge University Press, 2013)

Philosophy and science

Clucas, Stephen, *Magic, Memory and Natural Philosophy in the Sixteenth and Seventeenth Centuries* (Farnham: Ashgate Variorum, 2011)

Hutton, Sarah, and Lynette Hunter (eds), *Women, Science and Medicine 1500–1700* (Stroud, Gloucestershire: Sutton Publishing, 1997)

Merchant, Carolyn, *The Death of Nature: Women, Ecology and the Scientific Revolution*, rev. edn (San Francisco: Harper San Francisco, 1990)

Merchant, Carolyn, 'Getting Back to the Death of Nature: The Scientific Revolution and the Death of Nature', *Isis*, 97 (2006): 513–33

Nussbaum, Martha, *The Therapy of Desire: Theory and Practice in Hellenistic Ethics* (Princeton: Princeton University Press, 1994)

Rogers, John, *The Matter of Revolution: Science, Poetry and Politics in the Age of Milton* (Ithaca: Cornell University Press, 1996)

Spiller, Elizabeth, *Science, Reading, and Renaissance Literature: The Art of Making Knowledge, 1580–1670* (Cambridge: Cambridge University Press, 2004)

Sutton, John, 'Soul and Body', in Peter Anstey (ed.), *The Oxford Handbook of British Philosophy in the Seventeenth Century* (Oxford: Oxford University Press, 2013), pp. 285–307

Genre

Clarke, Danielle, *The Politics of Early Modern Women's Writing* (London: Pearson Education, 2001)

Clarke, Elizabeth, 'The Garrisoned Muse: Women's Use of the Religious Lyric in the Civil War Period', in Claude J. Summers and Ted-Larry Pebworth (eds), *The English Civil Wars in the Literary Imagination* (Columbia and London: University of Missouri Press, 1999), pp. 130–43

Kerrigan, John, *Motives of Woe: Shakespeare and 'Female Complaint', a Critical Anthology* (Oxford: Clarendon Press, 1991)

Lewalski, Barbara K., 'The Lady of the Country House Poem', in Gervase Jackson-Stops, Gordon J. Schochet, Lena Cowen Orlin, and Elisabeth Blair MacDougall (eds), *The Fashioning and Functioning of the British Country House* (Hanover and London: National Gallery of Art, Washington, and University Press of New England, 1989), pp. 261–76

Lilley, Kate, 'True State Within: Women's Elegy 1640–1700', in Isobel Grundy and Susan Wiseman (eds), *Women, Writing, History, 1640–1740* (London: Batsford, 1992), pp. 72–92

Osmond, Rosalie, *Mutual Accusations: Seventeenth-Century Body and Soul Dialogues in their Literary and Theological Context* (Toronto and London: University of Toronto Press, 1990)

Ross, Sarah C. E., *Women, Poetry, and Politics in Seventeenth-Century Britain* (Oxford: Oxford University Press, 2015)

Scott-Baumann, Elizabeth, *Forms of Engagement: Women, Poetry, and Culture, 1640–1680* (Oxford: Oxford University Press, 2013)

Forms of publication

Ezell, Margaret J. M., 'The Laughing Tortoise: Speculations on Manuscript Sources and Women's Book History', *English Literary Renaissance*, 38 (2008): 331–55

Ezell, Margaret J. M., *The Patriarch's Wife: Literary Evidence and the History of the Family* (Chapel Hill and London: University of North Carolina Press, 1987)

Johns, Adrian, *The Nature of The Book: Print and Knowledge in the Making* (Chicago and London: University of Chicago Press, 1998)

Millman, Jill Seal, and Gillian Wright (eds), *Early Modern Women's Manuscript Poetry* (Manchester: Manchester University Press, 2005)

Ross, Sarah C. E., *Women, Poetry, and Politics in Seventeenth-Century Britain* (Oxford: Oxford University Press, 2015)

Scott-Baumann, Elizabeth, *Forms of Engagement: Women, Poetry, and Culture, 1640–1680* (Oxford: Oxford University Press, 2013)

Other topics

Achinstein, Sharon, *Literature and Dissent in Milton's England* (Cambridge: Cambridge University Press, 2003)

Corns, Thomas, *Uncloistered Virtue: English Political Literature, 1640–1660* (Oxford: Clarendon Press, 1992)

Harris, Johanna, and Elizabeth Scott-Baumann (eds), *The Intellectual Culture of Puritan Women, 1558–1680* (Basingstoke: Palgrave Macmillan, 2010)

King, Kathryn, 'Political Verse and Satire: Monarchy, Party and Female Political Agency', in Sarah Prescott and David E. Shuttleton (eds), *Women and Poetry 1660–1750* (Basingstoke: Palgrave Macmillan, 2003), pp. 203–22

Le Doeuff, Michèle, *The Sex of Knowing*, trans. Kathryn Hamer and Lorraine Code (London: Routledge, 2003; first pub. in French, 1998)

McColley, Diane Kelsey, *Poetry and Ecology in the Age of Milton and Marvell* (Aldershot: Ashgate, 2007)

Ng, Su Fang, *Literature and the Politics of Family in Seventeenth-Century England* (Cambridge: Cambridge University Press, 2007)

Patterson, Annabel, *Censorship and Interpretation: The Conditions of Writing and Reading in Early Modern England* (Madison: University of Wisconsin Press, 1984)

Pritchard, Allan, 'Marvell's "The Garden": A Restoration Poem?', *Studies in English Literature, 1500–1900*, 23 (1983): 371–88

Suzuki, Mihoko, 'What's Political in Seventeenth-Century Women's Political Writing?', *Literature Compass*, 6 (2009): 927–41

Watson, Robert N., *Back to Nature: The Green and the Real in the Late Renaissance* (Philadelphia: University of Pennsylvania Press, 2006)

Anne Bradstreet (1612–1672)

Anne Bradstreet was born in Northampton, England, in 1612, the daughter of Thomas Dudley and his wife Dorothy Yorke. Thomas Dudley, a military man and a law clerk, took up a position in 1619 as steward to Theophilus Clinton, fourth Earl of Lincoln, at Sempringham, Lincolnshire, and he remained there in service for almost five years. Dudley was himself a man of great 'Natural and Acquired Abilities', according to a later memoir by Cotton Mather, 'known to have a very good pen … [and] succinct and apt expression', and the years in the earl's household are likely to have been formative for the young Anne. It is possible that she received some of her education alongside the earl's children, whose tutor was the Elizabethan poet Thomas Lodge. Certainly, the household would have provided a rich wider environment for reading encounters and cultural exchange, including activity by women: the countess, Elizabeth Clinton, was the author of *The Countess of Lincoln's Nursurie* (1622).

In 1624, Thomas Dudley moved his family from the Earl of Lincoln's estate to the market town of Boston, Lincolnshire, in order to enter the congregation of the prominent puritan John Cotton, at that point the resident preacher at St Botolph's church. In 1628 Anne married Simon Bradstreet, who had also served the Earl of Lincoln under Dudley's stewardship; he was a Cambridge graduate and the son of another Lincolnshire Nonconformist preacher, and at the time of their marriage, he was serving as steward to Frances Rich, the dowager Countess of Warwick. In March 1630, the Dudley family, with Anne and Simon Bradstreet, set sail with a core group of Boston puritans for the New World, settling first in Newtowne (now Cambridge), and later in Ipswich and then North Andover, Massachusetts. Thomas Dudley, whose house at Newtowne reputedly contained a library of eight hundred books, rapidly became the colony's deputy governor. He served for several years in prominent public positions, including posts as deputy governor and governor of the colony. So, too, did Simon Bradstreet, and both men were influential in the establishment of Harvard College.

The first of Bradstreet's eight children was born in Newtowne in 1632, and her years of child-rearing clearly coincided with poetic writing, which seems to have been shared within a small coterie of educated readers in the Massachusetts Bay colony. She wrote a poem presenting her quarternions (poems on a theme divided into four parts) to her father, referring to a 'four' of his own authorship. She describes her 'ragged lines' as 'meanly clad' emulations of his mode, instigating the rhetoric of authorial modesty that permeates her verse at the same time as intimating the importance of her father as a poetic model. Thomas Dudley could also trace ancestry, through the Dudley line, to the family of Philip and Mary Sidney, and Bradstreet's earliest printed poem, her nostalgic elegy in memory of Sir Philip Sidney, describes the 'self-same blood' that flows 'yet in my veins' (line 28). A sense of connection to the Sidneys was cultivated within the Dudley family, and other of Bradstreet's poems, including the elegies on Elizabeth I and on the French Huguenot poet Guillaume de Saluste Du Bartas, also articulate her emulation of Elizabethan England's preeminent Protestant and poetic role models.

Her poems appear to have been taken without her consent to London by her brother-in-law John Woodbridge, who travelled there in 1647; they were published as *The Tenth Muse Lately Sprung up in America* in 1650. Bradstreet's poems are prefaced in the volume by numerous short prefatory endorsements: the authors of these are a combination of New English and 'old' English puritans, attesting to a New England reading community but also inserting her writing into the context of Civil War conflict. *A Dialogue between Old England and New, Concerning their Present Troubles, Anno 1642* speaks very directly to the English Civil War context, and *The Four Monarchies* provides examples of monarchical failure in the Assyrian, Persian, Greek, and Roman histories. Some commentators have seen Bradstreet's praise of Elizabeth I as an endorsement of monarchy, but this nostalgic evocation of a Protestant female ruler does not undercut the strong support of parliament that is evident in her poetry of the 1650s.

Bradstreet continued to write until her death in 1672. A fire in 1666 destroyed her North Andover house and most of her papers, including lines she had written towards an ending of *The Four Monarchies* (see lines 3452–53 of that poem). Her poems after this date seem to have been predominantly personal: a second, posthumous edition of her poetry was published as *Several Poems* in 1678 (see Figure 1), and includes several additional poems that attest to her life as a wife, mother, and grandmother. Until recently it has been on these more personal poems, and on her publication as America's first female poet, that her poetic reputation has rested. Only more recently have the aesthetics and political contributions of her 1650s poems to their English Civil War context begun to be more fully explored.

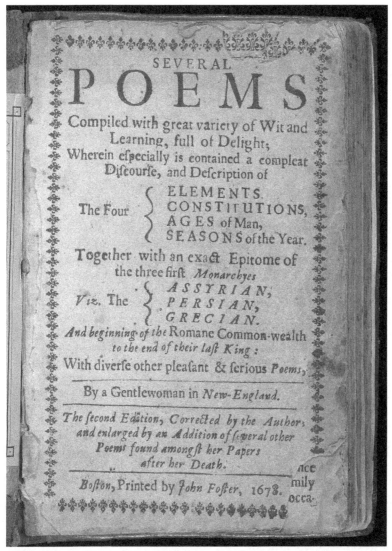

Figure 1 Title page to Anne Bradstreet, *Several Poems, Compiled with Great Variety of Wit and Learning* (Boston, 1678).

From *The Tenth Muse Lately Sprung up in America* (1650)

The Prologue

To sing of wars, of captains, and of kings,
Of cities founded, commonwealths begun,
For my mean pen are too superior things,
And how they all, or each, their dates have run:
Let poets and historians set these forth,   5
My obscure verse shall not so dim their worth.

But when my wond'ring eyes and envious heart
Great Bartas' sugared lines do but read o'er,
Fool, I do grudge, the Muses did not part
'Twixt him and me that over-fluent store;   10
A Bartas can do what a Bartas will,
But simple I, according to my skill.

From schoolboy's tongue, no rhetoric we expect,
Nor yet a sweet consort from broken strings,
Nor perfect beauty, where's a main defect: 15
My foolish, broken, blemished Muse so sings,
And this to mend, alas, no art is able,
'Cause nature made it so irreparable.

Nor can I, like that fluent sweet-tongued Greek
Who lisped at first, speak afterwards more plain.   20
By art, he gladly found what he did seek,
A full requital of his striving pain.
Art can do much, but this maxim's most sure:
A weak or wounded brain admits no cure.

8] *Bartas*: Guillaume de Saluste Du Bartas (1544–90), a French Huguenot poet. His
lengthy biblical creation epics were translated into English by Josuah Sylvester as
Bartas: His Divine Weeks and Works (1605), and were enormously influential on
biblical poetry in seventeenth-century Britain. See Bradstreet, 'In Honour of Du
Bartas, 1641'.
14] *consort*: accord, or harmony.
19–20] *Greek*: Demosthenes (384–322 BC), a great Athenian orator who, according
to legend, trained himself to overcome a speech impediment.

I am obnoxious to each carping tongue   25
Who says my hand a needle better fits;
A poet's pen all scorn I should thus wrong,
For such despite they cast on female wits.
If what I do prove well, it won't advance,
They'll say it's stol'n, or else, it was by chance.   30

But sure the antique Greeks were far more mild,
Else of our sex, why feignèd they those nine,
And poesy made Calliope's own child?
So, 'mongst the rest, they placed the arts divine.
But this weak knot they will full soon untie;   35
The Greeks did nought but play the fool and lie.

Let Greeks be Greeks, and women what they are,
Men have precedency, and still excel,
It is but vain, unjustly to wage war;
Men can do best, and women know it well.   40
Preeminence in each and all is yours,
Yet grant some small acknowledgement of ours.

And o, you high-flown quills that soar the skies,
And ever with your prey still catch your praise,
If e're you deign these lowly lines your eyes,   45
Give wholesome parsley wreath, I ask no bays:
This mean and unrefinèd ore of mine
Will make your glist'ring gold but more to shine.

Note

'The Prologue' is the second poem in *The Tenth Muse* (1650), directly
following a prefatory poem to Bradstreet's father. It adopts a posture of
female authorial modesty, and includes a number of strikingly pointed
comments about the perceived position of women in relation to poetic
traditions (see Pender, *Early Modern Women's Writing and the Rhetoric of
Modesty*). See also Bradstreet's 'The Author to her Book'.

28] *despite*: contempt.
32] *nine*: the nine muses, in Greek mythology the deities who preside over music,
    poetry, the arts, and sciences.
33] *Calliope*: the muse of heroic poetry.
46] *bays*: the bay laurel wreath, a classical emblem of distinction in poetry.

From The Four Monarchies

The Assyrian being the first, beginning under Nimrod, 131 years after the flood

When time was young, and world in infancy,
Man did not strive for sovereignty,
But each one thought his petty rule was high,
If of his house he held the monarchy.
This was the golden age, but after came   5
The boisterous son of Cush, grandchild to Ham,
That mighty hunter who, in his strong toils,
Both beasts and men subjected to his spoils;
The strong foundation of proud Babel laid,
Erech, Akkad, and Calneh also made.   10
These were his first, all stood in Shinar land;
From thence he went Assyria to command,
And mighty Nineveh he there begun,
Not finished till he his race had run.
Resen, Caleh, and Rehoboth likewise   15
By him to cities eminent did rise.
Of Saturn, he was the original,
Whom the succeeding times a god did call.
When thus with rule he had been dignified,
One hundred fourteen years he after died.   20

6–16] These lines are inspired by Genesis 10:6–12, on the conquests and spreading of the descendants of Noah.

7] *That mighty hunter*: Nimrod, the first great king of the Old Testament and a mighty huntsman (Genesis 10:8–9).

9] *Babel*: Babylon or the Tower of Babel. Babylon was one of the cities founded by Nimrod (Genesis 10:10). The construction of the Tower of Babel (Genesis 11:1–9) is often linked to Nimrod; the tower ambitiously reached for heaven, but God confused the languages of the builders so that they could no longer work together.

10] *Erech, Akkad, and Calneh*: ancient cities in Iraq and Iran.

11] *Shinar*: Mesopotamia

13] *Nineveh*: an ancient Assyrian city founded by Nimrod (Genesis 10:11), described in the book of Jonah as a doomed city of great 'wickedness' (Jonah 1:2).

15] *Resen, Caleh, and Rehoboth*: other ancient cities founded by Nimrod (Genesis 10:12).

17] *Saturn*: Nimrod and Saturn are sometimes equated.

Bellus

Great Nimrod dead, Bellus, the next his son,
Confirms the rule his father had begun,
Whose acts and power is not for certainty
Left to the world by any history.
But yet this blot for ever on him lies: 25
He taught the people first to idolise.
Titles divine he to himself did take,
Alive and dead, a god they did him make.
This is that Bell the Chaldees worshippèd,
Whose priests in stories oft are mentionèd;   30
This is that Bell to whom the Israelites
So oft profanely offered sacred rites;
This is Beelzebub, god of Ekronites,
Likewise Baalpeor of the Moabites.
His reign was short, for as I calculate,   35
At twenty-five ended his regal date.

Ninus

His father dead, Ninus begins his reign,
Transfers his seat to the Assyrian plain,
And mighty Nineveh more mighty made,
Whose foundation was by his grandsire laid: 40
Four hundred forty furlongs walled about,
On which stood fifteen hundred towers stout.
The walls one hundred sixty foot upright,
So broad three chariots run abreast there might.
Upon the pleasant banks of Tigris' flood   45
This stately seat of warlike Ninus stood.
This Ninus for a god his father canonised,
To whom the sottish people sacrificed.

21] *Bellus*: equated here with the Levantine god Ba'al, who was later pejoratively referred
    to as Beelzebub.
29] *Bell*: a form of the general honorific 'Bel' or 'Ba'al' for 'lord'.
29] *Chaldees*: of Chaldea, an ancient Semitic nation, and another name for Aramaic,
    a language used in the Old Testament.
33] *Beelzebub*: a demon; a false god (2 Kings 1:2–3; Matthew 12:24; Mark 3:22).
34] *Baalpeor of the Moabites*: a local branch of Ba'al worship at the mountain Moab,
    associated with licentiousness (Numbers 25:3; Joshua 22:17).
48] *sottish*: foolish.

This tyrant did his neighbours all oppress:
Where'er he warred he had too good success.   50
Barzanes, the great Armenian king,
By force his tributary he did bring.
The Median country he did also gain,
Pharmus their king he caused to be slain.
An army of three millions he led out   55
Against the Bactrians (but that I doubt);
Zoroaster, their king, he likewise slew,
And all the greater Asia did subdue;
Semiramis from Menon did he take,
Then drown himself, did Menon, for her sake.   60
Fifty-two years he reigned (as we are told);
The world then was two thousand nineteen old.

Semiramis

This great oppressing Ninus dead and gone,
His wife Semiramis usurped the throne;
She like a brave virago played the rex   65
And was both shame and glory of her sex:
Her birthplace was Philistines' Ashkelon,
Her mother, Docreta, a courtesan;
Others report she was a vestal nun,
Adjudged to be drowned for what she'd done,   70
Transformed into a fish by Venus' will,
Her beauteous face (they feign) retaining still;

56] *Bactrians*: ancient people located in Central Asia. Bactria was a powerful Indo-Greek
   kingdom in the third and second centuries BC.
59] *Semiramis*: legendary Assyrian queen and protagonist of ancient, medieval, and
   modern legends. In Assyrian mythology, she was the daughter of a fish goddess and
   the god of wisdom, and was raised by doves. Semiramis is sometimes credited with
   founding the city of Babylon and its famous gardens, watered by 'Euphratian flood'
   (line 121). See Bradstreet, 'In Honour of that High and Mighty Princess', lines
   67–70.
65] *virago*: a warrior woman. See 'In Honour of that High and Mighty Princess', line
   52.
67] *Ashkelon*: one of five cities said to be owned by the Philistines. See 'David's Lamenta-
   tion for Saul and Jonathan'.
69] *she*: Docreta.
71] According to Ovid's *Metamorphoses*, Venus turns herself into a fish.

Sure from this fiction Dagon first began,
Changing the woman's face into a man.
But all agree that from no lawful bed   75
This great renowned empress issued,
For which she was obscurely nourished,
Whence rose that fable, she by birds was fed.
This gallant dame unto the Bactrian war,
Accompanying her husband Menon far,   80
Taking a town, such valour she did show,
That Ninus of her amorous soon did grow
And thought her fit to make a monarch's wife,
Which was the cause poor Menon lost his life.
She flourishing with Ninus long did reign,   85
Till her ambition caused him to be slain,
That having no compeer, she might rule all,
Or else she sought revenge for Menon's fall.
Some think the Greeks this slander on her cast,
As on her life licentious, and unchaste,   90
And that her worth deserved no such blame,
As their aspersions cast upon the same.
But were her virtues more, or less, or none,
She for her potency must go alone.
Her wealth she showed in building Babylon,   95
Admired of all, but equalised of none;
The walls so strong and curiously were wrought,
That after ages, skill by them was taught.
With towers and bulwarks made of costly stone,
Quadrangle was the form it stood upon;   100
Each square was fifteen thousand paces long,
An hundred gates it had of metal strong;
Three hundred sixty foot the walls in height,
Almost incredible they were in breadth.
Most writers say six chariots might affront   105
With great facility, march safe upon't.
About the wall a ditch so deep and wide
That, like a river long, it did abide.

73] *Dagon*: a deity of the Philistines, represented as a fish-tailed man (Judges 16:23; 1
　　Chronicles 10:10; and 1 Samuel). See also Milton, *Samson Agonistes*.
87] *compeer*: someone of equal rank, a co-ruler.

Three hundred thousand men here day by day
Bestowed their labour, and received their pay.   110
But that which did all cost and art excel,
The wondrous temple was, she reared to Bell,
Which in the midst of this brave town was placed
(Continuing till Xerxes it defaced),
Whose stately top beyond the clouds did rise,   115
From whence astrologers oft viewed the skies.
This to describe in each particular,
A structure rare I should but rudely mar:
Her gardens, bridges, arches, mounts and spires
All eyes that saw, or ears that hear, admires;   120
On Shinar plain, by the Euphratian flood,
This wonder of the world, this Babel stood.
An expedition to the East she made,
Staurobates, his country to invade.
Her army of four millions did consist   125
(Each man believe it, as his fancy list).
Her camels, chariots, galleys in such number,
As puzzles best historians to remember;
But this is marvellous, of all those men
(They say) but twenty e'er came back again.   130
The river Indus swept them half away,
The rest Staurobates in fight did slay;
This was last progress of this mighty queen,
Who in her country never more was seen.
The poets feigned her turned into a dove,   135
Leaving the world to Venus soared above,
Which made the Assyrians many a day
A dove within their ensigns to display.
Forty-two years she reigned, and then she died
But by what means we are not certified.   140

[...]

114] *Xerxes*: Xerxes I, son of Darius I (486–465 BC), regained Egypt and crushed a
   rebellion in Babylon before launching his invasion of Greece (480 BC).
122] *Babel*: Babylon.
124–38] Elizabeth Wade White suggests that Bradstreet drew on Sir Walter Ralegh's
   History of the World (1614); see book I, chapter 12.

The third monarchy, being the Grecian, beginning under
Alexander the Great in the 112 *Olympiad*

[...]

Fair Cleopatra next, last of that race,	3265

Fair Cleopatra next, last of that race,   3265
Whom Julius Caesar set in royal place;
Her brother by him lost his traitorous head
For Pompey's life, then placed her in his stead.
She with her paramour, Mark Anthony
Held for a time, the Egyptian monarchy,   3270
Till great Augustus had with him a fight;
At Actium slain, his navy put to flight.
Then poisonous asps she sets unto her arms
To take her life, and quit her from all harms,
For 'twas not death nor danger she did dread,   3275
But some disgrace in triumph to be led.
Here ends at last the Grecian monarchy,
Which by the Romans had its destiny.
Thus king and kingdoms have their times and dates,
Their standings, overturnings, bounds and fates: 3280
Now up, now down, now chief, and then brought under,
The heavens thus rule, to fill the world with wonder.
The Assyrian monarchy long time did stand,
But yet the Persian got the upper hand.
The Grecian them did utterly subdue,   3285
And millions were subjected unto few.
The Grecian longer than the Persian stood,
Then came the Roman like a raging flood,
And with the torrent of his rapid course,
Their crowns, their titles, riches bears by force.   3290
The first was likened to a head of gold,
Next arms and breast of silver to behold,

3265] *Cleopatra*: Cleopatra VII, the last Ptolemaic queen (c. 69–30 BC). Cleopatra initially ruled alongside her brother Ptolemy XIII. To earn his favour, Ptolemy had Caesar's political rival Pompey (Pompeius Magnus) beheaded. However, this reportedly enraged Caesar, and after the Romans defeated Ptolemy in 47 BC, he installed Cleopatra as sole ruler.

3272] *At Actium slain*: the Battle of Actium, 31 BC, in which the fleet of Octavian (later Emperor Augustus) defeated the fleets of Mark Antony and Cleopatra.

3273] *poisonous asps*: small venomous snakes with which Cleopatra is said to have committed suicide.

The third, belly and thighs of brass in sight,
And last was iron, which breaketh all with might.
The stone out of the mountains then did rise, 3295
And smote those feet, those legs, those arms and thighs;
Then gold, silver, brass, iron and all that store,
Became like chaff upon the threshing floor.
The first a lion, second was a bear,
The third a leopard, which four wings did rear, 3300
The last more strong and dreadful than the rest,
Whose iron teeth devoured every beast,
And when he had no appetite to eat,
The residue he stamped under feet;
But yet this lion, bear, this leopard, ram, 3305
All trembling stand before that powerful lamb.
With these three monarchies now have I done,
But how the fourth, their kingdoms from them won,
And how from small beginnings it did grow,
To fill the world with terror and with woe, 3310
My tired brain leaves to a better pen;
This task befits not women like to men.
For what is past, I blush, excuse to make,
But humbly stand, some grave reproof to take;
Pardon to crave for errors is but vain, 3315
The subject was too high beyond my strain.
To frame apology for some offence
Converts our boldness into impudence.
This my presumption (some now) to requite,
Ne sutor ultra crepidam may write. 3320

After some days of rest, my restless heart,
To finish what's begun new thoughts impart,
And maugre all resolves, my fancy wrought
This fourth to the other three, now might be brought.
Shortness of time and inability 3325
Will force me to a confused brevity,

3298] *chaff upon the threshing floor*. See Daniel 2:31–35, which Bradstreet adapts.
3304] *residue he stamped under feet*: See Daniel 7:3–7.
3306] *that powerful lamb*: Bradstreet closes Daniel's Vision of the Four Beasts with the image of Jesus as the Lamb of God. See John 1:29.
3320] *Ne sutor ultra crepidam*: This Latin phrase, 'Cobbler, stick to the last' (that is, 'stick to what you know') is, with the addition of *quidem* (indeed), also found on the title page of Nathaniel Ward's *Simple Cobbler of Agawam*.
3323] *maugre*: in spite of.

Yet in this chaos, one shall easily spy
The vast limbs of a mighty monarchy.
What e'er is found amiss take in best part,
As faults proceeding from my head, not heart.   3330

The Roman Monarchy, being the fourth and last, beginning
Anno Mundi, 3213

Stout Romulus, Rome's founder, and first king,
Whom vestal Rhea into th'world did bring,
His father was not Mars as some devised,
But Aemulus in armour all disguised;
Thus he deceived his niece, she might not know   3335
The double injury he then did do.
Where shepherds once had cotes, and sheep their folds,
Where swains and rustic peasants made their holds,
A city fair did Romulus erect,
The mistress of the world, in each respect;   3340
His brother Remus there by him was slain,
For leaping o'er the walls with some disdain.
The stones at first were cemented with blood,
And bloody hath it proved, since first it stood.
This city built and sacrifices done,   3345
A form of government he next begun;
A hundred senators he likewise chose,
And with the style of patres, honoured those.
His city to replenish, men he wants,
Great privileges then to all he grants   3350
That will within these strong built walls reside,
And this new gentle government abide.
Of wives there was so great a scarcity,
They to their neighbours sue for a supply;
But all disdain alliance then to make,   3355
So Romulus was forced this course to take:
Great shows he makes at tilt and tournament,

3331–36] To protect his claim, the usurper Amulius made his niece Rhea a nun to the
    Roman goddess Vesta. According to legend, the god Mars raped her and she gave
    birth to Romulus and Remus. Plutarch gives an alternative account in which Amulius
    himself raped her and then ordered the killing of the twins she bore.
3337] *cotes*: shelters for animals.
3341] In legend, Romulus kills his brother Remus and names the city Rome.
3348] *patres*: literally, 'fathers', a formal collective term for patrician senators.

41

To see these sports, the Sabines all are bent;
Their daughters by the Romans then were caught,
For to recover them a field was fought; 3360
But in the end, to final peace they come,
And Sabines, as one people, dwelt in Rome.
The Romans now more potent 'gin to grow,
And Fidenates they wholly overthrow.
But Romulus then comes unto his end. 3365
Some feigning say to heav'n he did ascend;
Others, the seven and thirtieth of his reign,
Affirm, that by the senate he was slain.

Numa Pompilius

Numa Pompilius is next chosen king,
Held for his piety some sacred thing; 3370
To Janus he that famous temple built,
Kept shut in peace, but ope when blood was spilt;
Religious rites and customs instituted,
And priests and flamines likewise he deputed,
Their augurs strange, their habit and attire, 3375
And vestal maids to keep the holy fire.
Goddess Egeria this to him told,
So to delude the people he was bold;
Forty-three years he ruled with general praise,
Accounted for some god in after days. 3380

Tullus Hostilius

Tullus Hostilius was third Roman king,
Who martial discipline in use did bring.

3358] *Sabines*: ancient people of central Italy. According to legend, Romulus invited
the Sabines to a festival and abducted their women; this resulted initially in a war
but ultimately in a treaty and co-rulership between Romulus and the Sabine King
Titus Tatius.
3364] *Fidenates*: inhabitants of Fidenae, upstream from Rome.
3369] Numa Pompilius, legendary second King of Rome, reigned from 715 to 673
BC.
3371] *Janus*: god of door and gate.
3374] *flamines*: priests serving a particular deity.
3377] *Egeria*: a water nymph, said to be the wife and advisor of Numa Pompilius.
Perhaps an invention by which Numa legitimised his religious reforms.
3381] *Tullus Hostilius*: the third King of Rome, who reigned from 673 to 642 BC.

War with the ancient Albans he did wage,
The strife to end six brothers did engage:
Three called Horatii on the Romans' side,   3385
And Curiatii three, Albans provide;
The Romans conquer, others yield the day,
Yet for their compact, after false they play.
The Romans, sore incensed, their general slay,
And from old Alba fetch the wealth away;   3390
Of Latin kings this was long since the seat,
But now demolished, to make Rome great.
Thirty-two years did Tullus reign, then die,
Leaves Rome in wealth and power still growing high.

Ancus Marcius

Next Ancus Marcius sits upon the throne,   3395
Nephew unto Pompilius dead and gone;
Rome he enlarged, new built again the wall
Much stronger, and more beautiful withal.
A stately bridge he over Tiber made,
Of boats and oars no more they need the aid.   3400
Fair Ostia he built this town, it stood
Close by the mouth of famous Tiber flood.
Twenty-four year th'time of his royal race,
Then unto death unwillingly gives place.

Tarquinius Priscus

Tarquin, a Greek at Corinth born and bred,   3405
Who for sedition from his country fled,
Is entertained at Rome, and in short time,
By wealth and favour doth to honour climb.
He after Marcius' death the kingdom had,
A hundred senators he more did add;   3410

3383–86] According to Roman legend, the struggle between Rome and Alba Longa
(in Latium) in the reign of King Tullus Hostilius (seventh century BC) was decided
by the single combats of three Roman brothers, the Horatii, against three Latin
brothers, the Curiatii. Two of the former were killed and all three of the latter.
3395] *Ancus Marcius*: the fourth King of Rome, who reigned from 642 to 617 BC.
3405] *Tarquin*: Lucius Tarquinius Priscus, the fifth King of Rome, who reigned from
616 to 578 BC.

Wars with the Latins he again renews,
And nations twelve of Tuscany subdues.
To such rude triumphs as young Rome then had,
Much state and glory did this Priscus add.
Thirty-eight years this stranger born did reign,   3415
And after all, by Ancus' sons was slain.

Servius Tullius

Next Servius Tullius sits upon the throne,
Ascends not up by merits of his own,
But by the favour and the special grace
Of Tanaquil, late queen, obtains the place.   3420
He ranks the people into each degree,
As wealth had made them of ability;
A general muster takes, which by account,
To eighty thousand souls then did amount.
Forty-four years did Servius Tullius reign,   3425
And then by Tarquin Priscus' son was slain.

Tarquinius Superbus, the last Roman King

Tarquin the proud, from manners called so,
Sat on the throne when he had slain his foe.
Sextus, his son, did (most unworthily)
Lucretia force, mirror of chastity.   3430
She loathed so the fact, she loathed her life,
And shed her guiltless blood with guilty knife.
Her husband sore incensed to quit this wrong,
With Junius Brutus rose, and being strong,
The Tarquins they from Rome with speed expel,   3435
In banishment perpetual to dwell;

3417] *Servius Tullius*: the sixth King of Rome, reigning from 578 and 534 BC.
3417–20] After the death of the fifth king, Tarquinius Priscus, his widow, Tanaquil, procured the crown for her favourite Servius Tullius.
3427] *Tarquin*: Lucius Tarquinius Suberbus, the seventh and last King of Rome, who reigned from 534 to 509 BC.
3430] *Lucretia*: According to legend she was raped by Sextus, son of Tarquinius Superbus, and having revealed this to her husband took her own life. After her death her husband conspired with Junius Brutus to overthrow Superbus, and the Romans expelled the Tarquins from Rome. Ovid tells Lucretia's story in *Fasti*, book II.

The government they change, a new one bring,
And people swear ne'er to accept of king.

The end of the Roman monarchy, being the fourth and last

An Apology

To finish what's begun was my intent,   3440
My thoughts and my endeavours thereto bent;
Essays I many made but still gave out,
The more I mused, the more I was in doubt.
The subject large, my mind and body weak,
With many more discouragements did speak.   3445
All thoughts of further progress laid aside,
Though oft persuaded, I as oft denied;
At length resolved, when many years had passed,
To prosecute my story to the last;
And for the same, I hours not few did spend,   3450
And weary lines (though lank) I many penned,
But 'fore I could accomplish my desire,
My papers fell a prey to the raging fire.
And thus my pains (with better things) I lost,
Which none had cause to wail, nor I to boast.   3455
No more I'll do since I have suffered wrack,
Although my monarchies their legs do lack,
Nor matter is it this last, the world now sees,
Hath many ages been upon his knees.

Note

The Four Monarchies has in recent times been dismissed as tedious in narrative and in meter, but it is likely to have held more appeal for contemporary readers accustomed to providential and typological readings of history. Bradstreet's ambitious work draws on Sir Walter Ralegh's *History of the World* and Du Bartas's *Divine Weeks and Works*; and her father also penned an extended quarternion poem (a poem on a theme divided into four parts, like this one). Her poetic style implies didactic aims, but she refrains from sustained comments on the events she recounts,

---

3440] 'An Apology' occurs only in the 1678 text. We have included it here for the explanation it offers of the poem's truncated ending.

suggesting that part of the poem's instruction is the practice of reading history as a map to the present. Focusing on individual leaders and the ebb and flow of their power, Bradstreet seems to suggest the transience of monarchical power and to comment on the violence those upheavals entails. Such insight might be applied to the perceived corruption of Charles I's reign, or indeed of the English monarchy generally. Notably, though, Bradstreet compresses the last fourth monarchy in a 'weary' and 'confused brevity'. Wiseman suggests that the fourth monarchy, nearest to the present, 'demands that she bring political problems within the frame of contemporary history', and so finally engage in the kind of explicit political comment she avoids throughout (*Conspiracy and Virtue*, p. 93). The poem ends somewhat abruptly. 'An Apology' is added to the end of the 1678 text, claiming that she is incapable of imparting the political lesson that her long history implies in its structure and style.

Anne Bradstreet

A Dialogue between Old England and New, Concerning their Present Troubles, Anno 1642

New England

Alas, dear Mother, fairest queen and best,
With honour, wealth, and peace, happy and blessed;
What ails thee hang thy head, and cross thine arms?
And sit i'th'dust, to sigh these sad alarms?
What deluge of new woes thus overwhelm   5
The glories of thy ever-famous realm?
What means this wailing tone, this mourning guise?
Ah, tell thy daughter, she may sympathise.

Old England

Art ignorant, indeed, of these my woes?
Or must my forcèd tongue these griefs disclose?   10
And must myself dissect my tattered state,
Which 'mazèd Christendom stands wond'ring at?
And thou a child, a limb, and dost not feel
My weakened fainting body now to reel?
This physic purging potion I have taken   15
Will bring consumption, or an ague quaking,
Unless some cordial thou fetch from high,
Which present help may ease my malady.
If I decease, dost think thou shalt survive?
Or by my wasting state dost think to thrive?   20
Then weigh our case; if't be not justly sad,
Let me lament alone, while thou art glad.

New England

And thus, alas, your state you much deplore
In general terms, but will not say wherefore.
What medicine shall I seek to cure this woe,   25
If th'wound's so dangerous I may not know?
But you, perhaps, would have me guess it out:

24] *wherefore*: why.

47

What, hath some Hengist, like that Saxon stout,
By fraud and force usurped thy flow'ring crown,
And by tempestuous wars thy fields trod down?   30
Or hath Canutus, that brave valiant Dane,
The regal, peaceful sceptre from thee ta'en?
Or is't a Norman, whose victorious hand
With English blood bedews thy conquered land?
Or is't intestine wars that thus offend?   35
Do Maud and Stephen for the crown contend?
Do barons rise and side against their king,
And call in foreign aid to help the thing?
Must Edward be deposed? Or is't the hour
That second Richard must be clapped i'th'Tower?   40
Or is the fatal jar again begun
That from the red, white pricking roses sprung?
Must Richmond's aid the nobles now implore,
To come and break the tushes of the boar?

28–30] *Hengist*: an Anglo-Saxon leader, the traditional founder of the Kentish royal house (perhaps mythical). The Anglo-Saxon Chronicle describes him deposing Vortigern and becoming the Kentish king in 455 AD, and defeating the British in successive battles.

31] *Canutus*: Cnut, King of England, Norway, and Denmark (c. 995–1035). Cnut's invasions of England from 1015 resulted in the division of the realm, Cnut receiving Mercia and probably Northumbria, and Edmund Ironside retaining Wessex. But in 1016 Edmund died and Cnut succeeded to the entire kingdom.

33–34] William of Normandy invaded and conquered England at the Battle of Hastings in 1066.

35] *intestine wars*: civil wars.

36] *Maud and Stephen*: Henry I's daughter Matilda and nephew Stephen. In 1125, Stephen swore fealty to Matilda as Henry's successor; but after Henry's death in 1135 he proclaimed himself king. His reign was troubled by internal wars, with Matilda reigning briefly as queen in 1141. Stephen declared Matilda's son Henry of Anjou his heir and successor in 1153.

37] *barons rise*: The English baronage united against the tyrannical reign of King John, forcing him to sign the Magna Carta in 1215.

39] Edward II was deposed by his queen, Isabella, and her lover, Roger Mortimer, in 1327.

40] *second Richard*: Richard II succeeded to the English throne as a minor in 1377. Henry of Bolingbroke was supported by parliament in a bid for the throne in 1399. Bolingbroke became Henry IV of England; Richard was imprisoned and apparently murdered in the following year.

41] *jar*: conflict, dissension; here, the War of the Roses, a series of dynastic wars between the rival houses of Lancaster and York for the English throne, beginning in 1455 and ending with Henry Tudor's victory over Richard III at the Battle of Bosworth in 1485.

43–44] *Richmond*: Henry Tudor, Earl of Richmond, defeated the unpopular Richard III, whose personal device (emblem) was the white boar. *tushes*: tusks.

If none of these, dear Mother, what's your woe? 45
Pray, do not fear Spain's bragging armado.
Doth your ally, fair France, conspire your wrack?
Or do the Scots play false behind your back?
Doth Holland quit you ill, for all your love?
Whence is this storm? From earth, or heaven above? 50
Is it drought, is it famine, or is it pestilence?
Dost feel the smart, or fear the consequence?
Your humble child entreats you, show your grief,
Though arms nor purse she hath for your relief;
Such is her poverty, yet shall be found 55
A suppliant for your help, as she is bound.

Old England

I must confess, some of those sores you name,
My beauteous body at this present maim;
But foreign foe, nor feignèd friend I fear,
For they have work enough (thou knowst) elsewhere; 60
Nor is it Alcie's son, and Henry's daughter,
Whose proud contention cause this slaughter;
Nor nobles siding, to make John no king,
French Lewis unjustly to the crown to bring;
No Edward, Richard, to lose rule and life, 65
Nor no Lancastrians to renew old strife;
No crook-backed tyrant now usurps the seat,
Whose tearing tusks did wound, and kill, and threat;

46] *armado*: armada, a fleet of ships. Philip II of Spain's famous Spanish Armada was
defeated by the naval forces of Elizabeth I in 1588.

47–49] More general references to England's relations with France, Scotland, and the
Netherlands. England's support of the Netherlands in its revolt against Spanish rule
contributed to the conflict between England and Spain.

57–82] Old England responds point by point to New England's account of English
historical events in lines 23–56. See notes above.

61] *Alcie's son, and Henry's daughter*: Alcie is Adela, Countess of Blois (c. 1067–1137),
the mother of Stephen, who contended with Matilda, daughter of Henry I, for the
English throne.

64] *French Lewis*: King Louis VIII of France (1187–1226), whom English barons
approached in a request for support against King John's tyranny. King Louis invaded
England in 1216, but John's death later that year, and the succession of his infant
son Henry III, removed his already slight claim to the English throne.

67] *crook-backed tyrant*: Richard III was famously hunchbacked.

No Duke of York, nor Earl of March, to soil
Their hands in kindred's blood, whom they did foil; 70
No need of Tudor, roses to unite,
None knows which is the red, or which the white.
Spain's braving fleet a second time is sunk;
France knows, how of my fury she hath drunk,
By Edward third and Henry fifth of fame, 75
Her lilies in mine arms avouch the same.
My sister Scotland hurts me now no more,
Though she hath been injurious heretofore;
What Holland is, I am in some suspense,
But trust not much unto his excellence. 80
For wants, sure some I feel, but more I fear,
And for the pestilence, who knows how near?
Famine and plague, two sisters of the sword,
Destruction to a land doth soon afford;
They're for my punishments ordained on high, 85
Unless thy tears prevent it speedily.
But yet, I answer not what you demand:
To show the grievance of my troubled land.
Before I tell th'effect, I'll show the cause,
Which are my sins, the breach of sacred laws. 90
Idolatry, supplanter of a nation
With foolish superstitious adoration,
And liked and countenanced by men of might,
The gospel trodden down, and hath no right;
Church offices were sold and bought for gain, 95
That Pope had hope to find Rome here again;

69] *No Duke of York, nor Earl of March*: Edmund Plantagenet (1341–1402), usurper
and founder of the House of York. Roger Mortimer, lover of Queen Isabella, was
the Earl of March (see note to line 39).

75] *Edward third and Henry fifth*: Edward III (1312–1377) controlled a number of
French territories, and laid claim to the French throne, in the early decades of the
Hundred Years War; Henry V (1386–1422) defeated the French at the Battle of
Agincourt in 1415.

76] *lilies*: The *fleur-de-lis* (lily flower) is an enduring emblem of France; here, French-born
queens of England such as Henry V's wife, Catherine of Valois (1401–1437), and
her elder sister Isabella, child bride to Richard II from 1396 to 1399.

89–108] This passage (from 'the cause') outlines a Nonconformist perspective on the
English church, focusing on the perceived 'popish' influences and corruption that
had caused Nonconformists such as Bradstreet and her family to leave for New
England.

96] *That*: so that.

For oaths and blasphemies, did ever ear
From Belzebub himself such language hear?
What scorning of the saints of the most high?
What injuries did daily on them lie? 100
What false reports, what nicknames did they take
Not for their own, but for their master's sake?
And thou, poor soul, wast jeered among the rest,
Thy flying for the truth I made a jest.
For Sabbath-breaking, and for drunkenness, 105
Did ever land profaneness more express?
From crying bloods yet cleansèd am not I,
Martyrs, and others, dying causelessly.
How many princely heads on blocks laid down
For nought but title to a fading crown? 110
'Mongst all the cruelties which I have done,
O, Edward's babes, and Clarence hapless son!
O Jane, why didst thou die in flow'ring prime?
Because of royal stem, that was thy crime.
For bribery, adultery, for thefts, and lies, 115
Where is the nation I can't paralyse
With usury, extortion, and oppression?
These be the hydras of my stout transgression.
These be the bitter fountains, heads, and roots
Whence flowed the source, the sprigs, the boughs, and fruits 120
Of more than thou canst hear or I relate,
That with high hand I still did perpetrate:
For these were threatenèd the woeful day
I mocked the preachers, put it far away;
The sermons yet upon record do stand 125
That cried destruction to my wicked land.

98] *Belzebub*: Beelzebub, one of the names of Satan.
112] *Edward's babes, and Clarence hapless son*: Richard III is believed to have had his two nephews, sons of Edward IV, murdered in the Tower in 1483 in order to succeed to the throne. Edward, Earl of Warwick, the son of Richard's other brother George, Duke of Clarence, was beheaded in 1499.
113] *Jane*: Lady Jane Grey (1537–54) reigned for nine days in 1553 at the nomination of Edward VI, before being deposed by Edward's half-sister Mary Tudor (Queen Mary I). Jane was beheaded six months later.
118] *hydras*: many-headed monsters in Greek mythology, whose heads grow again as fast as they are cut off.

These prophet's mouths (alas the while) was stopped
Unworthily, some backs whipped, and ears cropped;
Their reverent cheeks did bear the glorious marks
Of stinking, stigmatising, Romish clerks.   130
Some lost their livings, some in prison pent,
Some grossly fined, from friends to exile went:
Their silent tongues to heaven did vengeance cry,
Who heard their cause, and wrongs judged righteously,
And will repay it sevenfold in my lap;   135
This is forerunner of my afterclap.
Nor took I warning by my neighbours' falls.
I saw sad Germany's dismantled walls,
I saw her people famished, nobles slain,
Her fruitful land, a barren heath remain.   140
I saw, unmoved, her armies foiled and fled,
Wives forced, babes tossed, her houses calcinèd.
I saw strong Rochel yielding to her foe,
Thousands of starvèd Christians there also.
I saw poor Ireland bleeding out her last,   145
Such cruelty as all reports have passed;
My heart, obdurate, stood not yet aghast.
Now sip I of that cup, and just't may be
The bottom dregs reservèd are for me.

New England

To all you've said, sad Mother, I assent: 150
Your fearful sins great cause there's to lament,
My guilty hands, in part, hold up with you,

127–30] These vivid lines describing the treatment of Nonconformist preachers were
cut in the 1670 version of the poem (see 'Textual notes').

131] *livings*: church benefices.

138] *sad Germany's dismantled walls*: the defeat of German Protestant forces in the
Palatinate during the Thirty Years War (1618–48).

142] *calcinèd*: turned to ashes.

143] *Rochel*: La Rochelle, a Huguenot stronghold during the sixteenth and seventeenth
centuries. The Huguenots, French Protestant followers of Calvin, were defeated
after a fourteen-month siege at La Rochelle in 1627–28.

145] *poor Ireland bleeding out her last*: A massacre of English Protestant settlers in
Ireland took place in the winter of 1641. Bradstreet later described it in lines added
to *The Four Ages of Man* (1678 edition): 'Three hundred thousand slaughtered
innocents, / By bloody popish, hellish miscreants'.

A sharer in your punishment's my due.
But all you say amounts to this effect,
Not what you feel, but what you do expect.   155
Pray, in plain terms, what is your present grief?
Then let's join heads and hands for your relief.

Old England

Well, to the matter then: there's grown of late
'Twixt king and peers a question of state.
Which is the chief: the law, or else the king?   160
One says it's he, the other no such thing.
My better part, in court of parliament,
To ease my groaning land, show their intent
To crush the proud, and right to each man deal,
To help the church, and stay the commonweal.   165
So many obstacles come in their way,
As puts me to a stand what I should say;
Old customs, new prerogatives stood on,
Had they not held law fast, all had been gone;
Which by their prudence stood them in such stead,   170
They took high Strafford lower by the head;
And to their Laud be't spoke, they held i'th'Tower
All England's metropolitan that hour.
This done, an act they would have passèd fain,
No prelate should his bishopric retain;   175
Here tugged they hard, indeed, for all men saw
This must be done by gospel, not by law.
Next the militia they urged sore,
This was denied, I need not say wherefore.
The king, displeased, at York himself absents,   180

165] *stay*: support, sustain. *commonweal*: the common good, and also the whole body
of the people; the state.
171] *Strafford*: Thomas Wentworth, Earl of Strafford, a chief minister of Charles I and
supporter of Archbishop William Laud. Strafford was arraigned by parliament, and
tried and executed in 1641.
172] *Laud*: William Laud, Archbishop of Canterbury, imprisoned in 1641 and executed
in 1645.
173] *metropolitan*: archbishop.
174–77] The Root and Branch Petition was presented to parliament in December
1640, demanding the abolition of episcopacy.
180] *York*: Charles I left London and Windsor for York in March 1642.

They humbly beg return, show their intents;
The writing, printing, posting to and fro,
Shows all was done, I'll therefore let it go.
But now I come to speak of my disaster:
Contention's grown 'twixt subjects and their master;   185
They worded it so long, they fell to blows,
That thousands lay on heaps, here bleeds my woes.
I that no wars so many years have known
Am now destroyed and slaughtered by mine own;
But could the field alone this cause decide,   190
One battle, two, or three I might abide;
But these may be beginnings of more woe,
Who knows, the worst, the best may overthrow.
Religion, gospel, here lies at the stake,
Pray now dear child, for sacred Zion's sake.   195
O pity me in this sad perturbation,
My plundered towns, my houses' devastation,
My ravished virgins, and my young men slain;
My wealthy trading fall'n, my dearth of grain.
The seed-time's come, but ploughman hath no hope   200
Because he knows not, who shall in his crop;
The poor they want their pay, their children bread,
Their woeful mothers' tears unpitièd.
If any pity in thy heart remain,
Or any childlike love thou dost retain,   205
For my relief, now use thy utmost skill,
And recompense me good, for all my ill.

New England

Dear Mother, cease complaints and wipe your eyes,
Shake off your dust, cheer up, and now arise.
You are my mother nurse, I once your flesh,   210
Your sunken bowels gladly would refresh;

186] *they fell to blows*: the outbreak of open conflict in August 1642.
195] *sacred Zion*: one of the hills of Jerusalem, on which the city of David was built; allusively, the 'true' church.
201] *in*: gather, harvest.

Your griefs I pity much, but should do wrong,
To weep for that we both have prayed for long.
To see these latter days of hoped-for good,
That Right may have its right, though't be with blood.   215
After dark popery the day did clear,
But now the sun in's brightness shall appear.
Blessed be the nobles of thy noble land,
With ventured lives for truth's defence that stand.
Blessed be thy commons, who for common good   220
And thine infringèd laws have boldly stood.
Blessed be thy counties, which do aid thee still,
With hearts and states to testify their will.
Blessed be thy preachers, who do cheer thee on,
O cry, 'the sword of God and Gideon';   225
And shall I not on them wish Mero's curse
That help thee not with prayers, arms, and purse?
And for myself, let miseries abound,
If mindless of thy state I e'er be found.
These are the days, the church's foes to crush,   230
To root out prelates, head, tail, branch, and rush.
Let's bring Baal's vestments out to make a fire,
Their mitres, surplices, and all their 'tire,
Copes, rochets, crosiers, and such trash,
And let their names consume, but let the flash   235
Light Christendom, and all the world to see
We hate Rome's whore, with all her trumpery.

212–15: These stirring lines are moderated in 1678 (see 'Textual notes').

225] Judges 7:18: 'When I blow with a trumpet, I and all that are with me, then blow you the trumpets also on every side of all the camp, and say, "The Sword of the Lord, and of Gideon"'; and see Judges 7:19–20.

226] Judges 5:23: 'Curse you Meroz, said the angel of the Lord, curse you bitterly the inhabitants thereof; because they came not to the help of the Lord, to the help of the Lord against the mighty'.

231] *prelates*: clerics of high authority, such as bishops and archbishops.

232] *Baal*: a Levantine god, associated in Judaism, Islam, and Christianity with false deity. *vestments*: ceremonial clothing, a particular point of contention between Laudian Anglicans and puritans.

233–34] vestments and ritual objects of the Laudian Church of England.

237] *Rome's whore*: the Christian church under the influence of Rome and Roman Catholic forms of worship.

Go on brave Essex, show whose son thou art,
Not false to king nor country in thy heart;
But those that hurt his people and his crown 240
By force expel, destroy, and tread them down.
Let gaols be filled with th'remnant of that pack
And sturdy Tyburn loaded till it crack,
And you, brave nobles, chase away all fear,
And to this blessèd cause closely adhere. 245
O Mother, can you weep, and have such peers?
When they are gone, then drown yourself in tears.
If now you weep so much, that then no more
The briny ocean will o'erflow your shore.
These, these are they, I trust, with Charles our King, 250
Out of all mists such glorious days will bring,
That dazzled eyes beholding much shall wonder
At that thy settled peace, thy wealth and splendour.
Thy church and weal, established in such manner
That all shall joy, that thou displayed'st thy banner, 255
And discipline erected, so I trust,
That nursing kings shall come and lick thy dust.
Then justice shall in all thy courts take place,
Without respect of person, or of case;
Then bribes shall cease, and suits shall not stick long, 260
Patience and purse of clients for to wrong;
Then high commissions shall fall to decay,
And pursivants and catchpoles want their pay,
So shall thy happy nation ever flourish,
When truth and righteousness they thus shall nourish. 265
When thus in peace thine armies brave send out
To sack proud Rome, and all her vassals rout,
There let thy name, thy fame, thy valour shine,
As did thine ancestors in Palestine;
And let her spoils, full pay with interest be, 270
Of what unjustly once she polled from thee.

238] *brave Essex*: Robert Devereux, third Earl of Essex (1591–1646), commander of
the main parliamentary army during the First Civil War (1642–46). His father, also
Robert, the second Earl of Essex (1565–1601), was a favourite of Queen Elizabeth
I and an important Protestant military leader.
243] *Tyburn*: the public gallows in London.
263] *pursivants and catchpoles*: royal or state messengers with power to execute warrants;
warrant officers who arrest for debt.

Of all the woes thou canst let her be sped,
Execute to th'full the vengeance threatenèd;
Bring forth the beast that ruled the world with's beck,
And tear his flesh, and set your feet on's neck,   275
And make his filthy den so desolate,
To th'stonishment of all that knew his state.
This done, with brandished swords to Turkey go,
For then what is't, but English blades dare do?
And lay her waste, for so's the sacred doom,   280
And do to Gog as thou hast done to Rome.
O Abraham's seed lift up your heads on high,
For sure the day of your redemption's nigh;
The scales shall fall from your long blinded eyes,
And him you shall adore, who now despise.   285
Then fullness of the nations in shall flow,
And Jew and Gentile to one worship go;
Then follows days of happiness and rest;
Whose lot doth fall to live therein is blessed.
No Canaanite shall then be found i'th'land,   290
And holiness on horses' bells shall stand.
If this make way thereto, then sigh no more,
But if at all, thou didst not see't before.
Farewell dear Mother, parliament prevail,
And in a while you'll tell another tale.   295

Note

Composed (according to its title) in 1642, this dialogue poem speaks
directly to the religious and political conflicts that led to the outbreak
of Civil War in England in August of that year. The dialogue poem was

---

272] *sped*: discharged.
274] *beck*: command. The beast of the biblical book of Revelation was frequently
associated by puritans with the papacy.
281] *Gog*: the enemy of God's people (Ezekiel 38–39; Revelation 20:9).
282] *Abraham's seed*: God's chosen people (Galatians 3:29).
284] 'And immediately there fell from his [Saul's] eyes as it had been scales: and he
received sight forthwith, and arose, and was baptised' (Acts 9:18). See also Isaiah
25:8, Revelation 7:17.
290] *Canaanite*: a native of Canaan, 'a non-Israelite'.
291] 'In that day shall there be upon the bells of the horses, HOLINESS UNTO THE
LORD' (Zechariah 14:20).

a popular civil war genre, with its capacity to put two voices in conversation or contention with each other; and it is often, as here, closely related to the complaint mode. Bradstreet's clear and at times rousing support of Nonconformist religion and of parliament was to some extent softened and sanitised in the later printing of this poem, in 1678. See the notes and 'Textual notes' for details.

An Elegy upon that Honourable and Renowned Knight, Sir
Philip Sidney, who was Untimely Slain at the Siege of
Zutphen, Anno 1586 [1650]

By A.B. in the year 1638

When England did enjoy her halcyon days,
Her noble Sidney wore the crown of bays,
No less an honour to our British land,
Than she that swayed the sceptre with her hand.
Mars and Minerva did in one agree,   5
Of arms, and arts, thou should'st a pattern be;
Calliope with Terpsichore did sing,
Of poesy and of music thou wert king;
Thy rhetoric, it struck Polymnia dead,
Thine eloquence made Mercury wax red;   10
Thy logic from Euterpe won the crown,
More worth was thine than Clio could set down.
Thalia and Melpomene, say th'truth
(Witness *Arcadia*, penned in his youth):
Are not his tragic comedies so acted,   15
As if your ninefold wit had been compacted
To show the world, they never saw before
That this one volume should exhaust your store?
I praise thee not for this: it is unfit.
This was thy shame, o miracle of wit!   20
Yet doth thy shame (withal) purchase renown,
What do thy virtues then? O, honour's crown!
In all records, thy name I ever see,
Put with an epithet of dignity,

1] *halcyon days*: days of perfect calm.
2] *crown of bays*: In ancient Greece and Rome, bay laurel wreaths were awarded as an emblem of military victory or of distinction in poetry.
4] *she*: Elizabeth I (see also Bradstreet's elegy on her).
5] *Mars; Minerva*: the Roman god of war, and the goddess of wisdom and crafts.
7] *Calliope; Terpsichore*: the Greek muse of epic poetry, and the muse of dancing.
9] *Polymnia*: Polyhymnia, the Greek muse of sacred poetry.
10] *Mercury*: the Roman god of eloquence.
11] *Euterpe*: the Greek muse of lyric poetry and the flute.
12] *Clio*: the Greek muse of history, associated with poetic inspiration.
13] *Thalia; Melpomene*: the Greek muses of comedy and of tragedy.
14] *Arcadia*: Sidney's long prose romance *The Countess of Pembroke's Arcadia* (1590).
19] *unfit*: The more severe puritans disapproved of romances. Sidney later turned to divine poetry, paraphrasing the biblical Psalms with his sister Mary Sidney.

Which shows thy worth was great, thine honour such,   25
The love thy country ought thee, was as much.
Let then none disallow of these my strains,
Which have the self-same blood yet in my veins,
Who honours thee for what was honourable,
But leaves the rest, as most unprofitable;   30
Thy wiser days condemned thy witty works;
Who knows the spells that in thy rhetoric lurks?
But some infatuate fools soon caught therein;
Fond Cupid's dam had never such a gin,
Which makes severer eyes but scorn thy story,   35
And modest maids and wives blush at thy glory.
Yet he's a beetle-head that can't descry
A world of treasure in that rubbish lie,
And doth thy self, thy work, and honour wrong
(O brave refiner of our British tongue);   40
That sees not learning, valour, and morality,
Justice, friendship, and kind hospitality,
Yea, and divinity within thy book;
Such were prejudicate, and did not look.
But to say truth, thy worth I shall but stain: 45
Thy fame and praise is far beyond my strain.
Yet great Augustus was content (we know)
To be saluted by a silly crow;
Then let such crows as I thy praises sing,
A crow's a crow, and Caesar is a king.   50
O brave Achilles, I wish some Homer would

26] *ought*: owed.

28] *the self-same blood*: Anne Dudley Bradstreet believed herself to be related to Sidney through his mother, a sister to Robert Dudley, Earl of Leicester. The claim is removed from the 1678 version of the poem (see 1678, line 38: 'English blood').

34] *Cupid's dam*: Venus, the Roman goddess of love (and Cupid's mother). *gin*: trap.

37] *beetle-head*: a common contemptuous epithet, indicating stupidity.

40] Sidney's *Apology for Poetry* (published in 1595) was an influential piece of early literary criticism, exploring poetic traditions and commenting on contemporary English poetics.

44] *prejudicate*: prejudiced.

47–48] Augustus (63 BC–14 AD) was the founder and first Emperor of the Roman Empire, said to have been much pleased when presented with a crow who had been taught to say 'Greetings to Caesar, our victorious commander'.

50] *Caesar*: the name given to Roman rulers from Augustus onwards, and here a reference to Augustus himself, who was adopted by Gaius Julius Caesar.

51] *Achilles*; *Homer*: Achilles, the greatest of the Greek heroes in the Trojan War, as told by Homer in the *Iliad*.

Engrave on marble, in characters of gold,
What famous feats thou didst on Flanders coast,
Of which, this day, fair Belgia doth boast.
O Zutphen, Zutphen, that most fatal city,   55
Made famous by thy fall, much more's the pity.
Ah! In his blooming prime, Death plucked this rose
Ere he was ripe, his thread cut Atropos.
Thus man is born to die, and dead is he;
Brave Hector by the walls of Troy we see.   60
O, who was near thee, but did sore repine
He rescued not with life that life of thine?
But yet impartial death this boon did give:
Though Sidney died, his valiant name should live.
And live it doth, in spite of death, through fame;   65
Thus being overcome, he overcame.
Where is that envious tongue, but can afford
Of this, our noble Scipio, some good word?
Noble Bartas, this to thy praise adds more:
In sad, sweet verse, thou didst his death deplore.   70
Illustrious Stella, thou didst thine full well,
If thine aspect was mild to Astrophel.
I fear thou wert a comet, did portend
Such prince as he, his race should shortly end;
If such stars as these, sad presages be,   75
I wish no more such blazers we may see.
But thou art gone, such meteors never last,

53–54] Sidney's military exploits in the Low Countries. Sidney was made governor of Flushing, on Walcheren island, facing the Flemish coast, in 1585.
55] Sidney's death was caused by a wound incurred at the Battle of Zutphen in 1586.
58] *Atropos*: one of the three Fates in Greek mythology, she who cut the thread of mortal life.
60] *Hector, Troy*: Hector, the greatest Trojan warrior, was killed by Achilles while defending the city
68] *Scipio*: Publius Cornelius Scipio Africanus (236–183 BC), a renowned Roman republican general.
69–70] The French Protestant poet Guillaume de Saluste Du Bartas praised Sidney, before his death, in *La Seconde Semaine* (1584). Bradstreet must have encountered the passage in Josuah Sylvester's English translation, completed after Sidney's death, which refers to the 'world-mourned' Sidney (*Bartas: His Divine Weeks and Works*, 1605, p. 433).
71] *Stella*: the female addressee in Sidney's sonnet sequence *Astrophel and Stella*. The following passage puns on the meaning of her name ('star'). Stella was widely identified with Penelope Rich, *née* Devereux (1563–1607). See the 1678 version of this poem (p. 76) for a significant recasting of these lines on Stella.

And as thy beauty, so thy name would waste,
But that it is record by Philip's hand,
That such an omen once was in our land.   80
O princely Philip, rather Alexander,
Who wert of honour's band, the chief commander,
How could that Stella so confine thy will?
To wait till she, her influence distil,
I rather judged thee of his mind that wept   85
To be within the bounds of one world kept,
But Omphala set Hercules to spin,
And Mars himself was ta'en by Venus' gin;
Then wonder less, if warlike Philip yield,
When such a Hero shoots him out o'th'field;   90
Yet this preeminence thou hast above,
That thine was true, but theirs adult'rate love.
Fain would I show, how thou fame's path didst tread,
But now into such labyrinths am I led,
With endless turns, the way I find not out;   95
For to persist, my Muse is more in doubt,
Calls me ambitious fool, that durst aspire;
Enough for me to look, and so admire,
And makes me now with Sylvester confess,
But Sidney's Muse can sing his worthiness.   100
Too late my error see, that durst presume
To fix my falt'ring lines upon his tomb,
Which are in worth, as far short of his due,
As Vulcan is, of Venus' native hue.

81] *Alexander*: Alexander the Great (356–323 BC), one of history's most successful military commanders. Alexander succeeded his father, Philippus II, as ruler of the ancient Greek kingdom of Macedonia.

87] *Omphala*: in Greek mythology, Omphale kept Heracles (Roman: Hercules) a slave.

88] *Mars*; *Venus*: Mars, the Roman god of war, and Venus, the Roman goddess of love, who were often depicted as a couple. *gin*: in Ariosto's *Orlando Furioso*, Vulcan sets a trap to catch Venus, his wife, and Mars in the act of adultery.

90] *Hero*: in Greek mythology, a priestess of Aphrodite, who lived in a tower in Sestos, on the European side of the Hellespont. Leander fell in love with her, and swam the strait every night to be with her.

100] *But*: no one but. Josuah Sylvester's introductory sonnet to his 'Elegiac Epistle for Sir William Sidney' (for the nephew of Philip) describes: 'I know none, but a Sidney's Muse, / Worthy to sing a Sidney's Worthinesse' (see Wade White, *Anne Bradstreet*, p. 146).

104] *Vulcan*; *Venus*: Vulcan was the Roman god of fire and metalworking and the husband of Venus; he lacked the physical perfection of the other gods, suffering from deformed feet.

Goodwill did make my headlong pen to run, 105
Like unwise Phaethon his ill-guided son,
Till taught to's cost, for his too hasty hand,
He left that charge by Phoebus to be manned.
So proudly foolish I with Phaethon strive,
Fame's flaming chariot for to drive, 110
Till terror-struck for my too-weighty charge,
I leave't in brief, Apollo do't at large.
Apollo laughed to patch up what's begun,
He bade me drive, and he would hold the sun,
Better my hap, than was his darling's fate, 115
For dear regard he had of Sidney's state,
Who in his deity had so deep share,
That those that name his fame, he needs must spare;
He promised much, but th'Muses had no will
To give to their detractor any quill. 120
With high disdain, they said they gave no more,
Since Sidney had exhausted all their store,
That this contempt it did the more perplex,
In being done by one of their own sex.
They took from me the scribbling pen I had; 125
I to be eased of such a task was glad.
For to revenge his wrong, themselves engage,
And drove me from Parnassus in a rage,
Not because sweet Sidney's fame was not dear,
But I had blemished theirs, to make't appear. 130
I, pensive for my fault, sat down, and then
Errata, through their leave, threw me my pen,
For to conclude my poem; two lines they deign,
Which writ, she bade return't to them again.
So Sidney's fame, I leave to England's rolls; 135
His bones do lie interred in stately Paul's.

106–14] In Greek myth, Phaethon is the son of Phoebus (also called Helios or Apollo),
who insists on driving his father's chariot of the sun. He loses control, threatening
to set the earth on fire.

128] *Parnassus*: in Greek mythology, Mount Parnassus is the home of the nine muses.

132] *Errata*: Erato, the muse of lyric poetry, is here named punningly: 'errata' are errors
in writing or a printed book.

136] *stately Paul's*: St Paul's Cathedral, London, where Sidney was buried.

His Epitaph

Here lies, entombed in fame, under this stone,
Philip and Alexander both in one.
Heir to the Muses, the son of Mars in truth,
Learning, valour, beauty, all in virtuous youth: 140
His praise is much, this shall suffice my pen,
That Sidney died the quintessence of men.

Note

Sir Philip Sidney (1554–86) was a Protestant English poet, soldier, and courtier from one of England's most eminent families. Sidney died at the age of thirty-one from a wound incurred while fighting with Protestant forces in the Battle of Zutphen in the Netherlands; his early death contributed to his place in the English imagination as the epitome of the Renaissance courtier, skilled in arts as well as arms. Sidney's death prompted an outpouring of elegiac literature, and textual echoes suggest that Bradstreet was familiar with the elegies gathered at the end of Edmund Spenser's *Colin Clout's Come Home Again* (1595) (see Wade White, *Anne Bradstreet*). Bradstreet's much later poem, written in 1638, is the first in her series of retrospective elegies on long-dead Elizabethan poets and political figures, conjuring up a kind of 'ghostly coterie' of ideal Protestants. See Gray, *Women Writers and Public Debate*. See p. 76 for the heavily revised 1678 version of this poem.

138] See line 81.

In Honour of Du Bartas, 1641

Amongst the happy wits this age hath shown,
Great, dear, sweet Bartas, thou art matchless known;
My ravished eyes and heart with faltering tongue,
In humble wise have vowed their service long,
But knowing the task so great, and strength but small,   5
Gave o'er the work before begun withal.
My dazzled sight of late reviewed thy lines,
Where art, and more than art in nature shines;
Reflection from their beaming altitude
Did thaw my frozen heart's ingratitude,   10
Which rays, darting upon some richer ground,
Had caused flowers and fruits soon to abound;
But barren I my daisy here do bring,
A homely flower in this my latter spring.
If summer, or my autumn age, do yield   15
Flowers, fruits, in garden, orchard, or in field,
They shall be consecrated in my verse,
And prostrate offered at great Bartas' hearse.
My Muse unto a child I fitly may compare,
Who sees the riches of some famous fair;   20
He feeds his eyes, but understanding lacks
To comprehend the worth of all those knacks;
The glittering plate and jewels he admires,
The hats and fans, the plumes and ladies' tires,
And thousand times his mazèd mind doth wish   25
Some part, at least, of that brave wealth was his;
But seeing empty wishes nought obtain,
At night turns to his mother's cot again,
And tells her tales (his full heart over-glad)
Of all the glorious sights his eyes have had,   30
But finds too soon his want of eloquence,
The silly prattler speaks no word of sense,
And seeing utterance fail his great desires,

14] *homely flower*: see Bradstreet, 'The Prologue', line 46.
18] *hearse*: tomb, grave.
22] *knacks*: tricks or crafty devices, often specifically literary ones.
24] *tires*: ornaments for women's heads, head-dresses.
25] *mazèd*: stupefied or dazed.
28] *cot*: bed.

Sits down in silence, deeply he admires.
Thus weak-brained I, reading thy lofty style,   35
Thy profound learning, viewing other while
Thy art, in natural philosophy,
Thy saint-like mind in grave divinity,
Thy piercing skill in high astronomy,
And curious insight in anatomy,   40
Thy physic, music, and state policy,
Valour in war, in peace good husbandry;
Sure liberal Nature did with art not small,
In all the arts make thee most liberal.
A thousand, thousand times my senseless senses,   45
Moveless, stand charmed by thy sweet influences,
More senseless than the stones to Amphion's lute,
Mine eyes are sightless, and my tongue is mute,
My full astonished heart doth pant to break,
Through grief it wants a faculty to speak;   50
Volleys of praises could I echo then,
Had I an angel's voice, or Bartas' pen,
But wishes can't accomplish my desire;
Pardon if I adore, when I admire.
O France, in him thou didst more glory gain,   55
Than in thy Pepin, Martel, Charlemagne,
Than in Saint Louis, or thy last Henry great,
Who tamed his foes, in blood, in scars and sweat.
Thy fame is spread as far, I dare be bold,
In all the zones, the temperate, hot and cold.   60
Their trophies were but heaps of wounded slain,
Thine, the quintessence of an heroic brain.
The oaken garland ought to deck their brows,
Immortal bays, all men to thee allows,

47] *Amphion's lute*: Amphion built a wall around Thebes by enchanting the stones with his lyre-playing.

56] *Pepin, Martel, Charlemagne*: three generations of Frankish leaders from the eighth century to the ninth century. Charles Martel restored Francia's former supremacy in Gaul. His son Pepin the Short became King of the Franks in 751. Charlemagne, his more famous son, became 'emperor of the Romans', the first Holy Roman Emperor, in 800.

57] *Saint Louis*: Louis IX of France (1226–1270), who led the Seventh Crusade and was canonised in 1297. *thy last Henry great*: Henry II of France (reigned 1547–59), who attempted to suppress Protestant elements, such as the Huguenots.

63–64] *oaken garland ... bays*: in ancient Greece or Rome, wreaths of oak or laurel bays were emblems of military or poetic distinction. See 'The Prologue', line 46.

Who in thy triumphs (never won by wrongs)   65
Lead millions chained by eyes, by ears, by tongues.
Oft have I wondered at the hand of heaven,
In giving one what would have served seven.
If e'er this golden gift was showered on any,
Thy double portion would have served many.   70
Unto each man his riches are assigned
Of name, of state, of body or of mind;
Thou hast thy part of all, but of the last,
O pregnant brain, o comprehension vast
Thy haughty style, and rapted wit sublime,   75
All ages wond'ring at, shall never climb.
Thy sacred works are not for imitation,
But monuments for future admiration.
Thus, Bartas' fame shall last while stars do stand,
And whilst there's air, or fire, or sea or land;   80
But lest my ignorance should do thee wrong,
To celebrate thy merits in my song,
I'll leave thy praise to those shall do thee right,
Good will, not skill, did cause me bring my mite.

His Epitaph

Here lies the pearl of France, Parnassus' glory,   85
The world rejoiced at's birth, at's death was sorry;
Art and Nature joined, by Heaven's high decree,
Now showed what once they ought, humanity;
And Nature's law, had it been revocable,
To rescue him from death, Art had been able.   90
But Nature vanquished Art, so Bartas died;
But Fame outliving both, he is revived.

Note

Guillaume de Saluste Du Bartas (1544–90) was a very influential French
Huguenot poet, a writer of extended verses based on biblical material.

70] *double portion*: a biblical phrase often indicating a blessing or reward; see, for
    example, Isaiah 61:7.
75] *rapted*: rapt, enraptured.
84] *mite*: small amount, and one of the smallest Roman coins.

His hexameral poems on the creation of the world, *La Semaine* (1578) and *La Seconde Semaine* (1584), were translated into English by Josuah Sylvester as *Bartas: His Divine Weeks and Works* (1605), and were enormously popular with seventeenth-century readers. Bradstreet is one of Du Bartas's most devoted followers: she expresses admiration for him and compares her poetic skill to his in several of her poems, including 'The Prologue'.

In Honour of that High and Mighty Princess, Queen Elizabeth, of Most Happy Memory

The Proem

Although, great Queen, thou now in silence lie,
Yet thy loud herald Fame doth to the sky
Thy wondrous worth proclaim in every clime,
And so has vowed while there is world or time.
So great's thy glory and thine excellence,   5
The sound thereof rapts every human sense,
That men account it no impiety
To say thou wert a fleshly deity.
Thousands bring offerings (though out of date)
Thy world of honours to accumulate;   10
'Mongst hundred hecatombs of roaring verse,
Mine bleating stands before thy royal hearse.
Thou never didst, nor canst thou now, disdain
T'accept the tribute of a loyal brain.
Thy clemency did erst esteem as much   15
The acclamations of the poor as rich,
Which makes me deem my rudeness is no wrong,
Though I resound thy greatness 'mongst the throng.

The Poem

No phoenix pen, nor Spenser's poetry,
No Speed's, nor Camden's learned history,   20
Eliza's works, wars, praise, can e'er compact;
The world's the theatre where she did act.
No memories nor volumes can contain
Th'eleven Olympiads of her happy reign,

Proem: a preface.
6] *rapts*: enraptures.
11] *hecatombs*: great public sacrifices or offerings, or simply large numbers.
12] *hearse*: tomb.
20] John Speed (1552–1629) wrote a history of Great Britain, and William Camden
    (1551–1623) a history of Elizabeth's reign.
24] *eleven Olympiads*: a period of forty-five years, the length of Queen Elizabeth's reign.
    An Olympiad was to the period of four years between Olympic Games and was
    used, in ancient Greece, as a means of dating.

Who was so good, so just, so learned, so wise;   25
From all the kings on earth she won the prize.
Nor say I more than duly is her due,
Millions will testify that this is true;
She hath wiped off th'aspersion of her sex,
That women wisdom lack to play the rex.   30
Spain's monarch says not so, nor yet his host;
She taught them better manners to their cost.
The Salic law had not in force now been,
If France had ever hoped for such a queen;
But can you, doctors, now this point dispute,   35
She's argument enough to make you mute.
Since first the sun did run his ne'er-run race,
And earth had, once a year, a new old face,
Since time was time, and man unmanly man,
Come show me such a phoenix if you can.   40
Was ever people better ruled than hers?
Was ever land more happy, freed from stirs?
Did ever wealth in England so abound?
Her victories in foreign coasts resound;
Ships more invincible than Spain's, her foe,   45
She wracked, she sacked, she sunk his armado;
Her stately troops advanced to Lisbon's wall,
Don Anthony in's right for to install.
She frankly helped Frank's brave distressèd king,
The states united now her fame do sing;   50
She their protectrix was; they well do know
Unto our dread virago, what they owe.
Her nobles sacrificed their noble blood,
Nor men, nor coin she spared, to do them good.

30] *rex*: king.
33] *The Salic law*: the ancient Frankish civil law code, which contained a passage forbidding female succession.
37] *ne'er-run race*: Helios drove the chariot of the sun in a never-ending cycle.
38] *earth had, once a year, a new old face*: refers to the annual arrival of spring.
40] *phoenix*: a person or thing of unique excellence or matchless beauty; a paragon.
48] *Don Anthony*: António, Prior of Crato (1531–1595), a claimant to the throne of Portugal used by Elizabeth I against Philip II of Spain.
52] *virago*: a warrior woman.

The rude, untamed Irish she did quell;   55
Before her picture the proud Tyrone fell.
Had ever prince such counsellors as she?
Herself Minerva caused them so to be.
Such soldiers and such captains never seen,
As were the subjects of our Pallas queen: 60
Her seamen through all straits the world did round,
Terra incognita might know her sound;
Her Drake came laden home with Spanish gold;
Her Essex took Cádiz, their Herculean hold.
But time would fail me, so my wit would too,   65
To tell of half she did, or she could do.
Semiramis to her is but obscure,
More infamy than fame she did procure;
She placed her glory but on Babel's walls,
World's wonder for a time, but yet it falls.   70
Fierce Tomris (Cyrus' headsman, Scythians' Queen)
Had put her harness off, had she but seen
Our Amazon in the camp at Tilbury,
Judging all valour, and all majesty,
Within that princess to have residence,   75
And prostrate yielded to her excellence.
Dido, first foundress of proud Carthage walls

55–56] Elizabethan England fought Irish resistance in the bloody Nine Years War (1594–1603). Though England won the military conflict, and in spite of what Bradstreet's formulation suggests, the adroit Irish rebel and second Earl of Tyrone, Hugh O'Neill (c. 1550–1616), managed to secure very favourable terms. This generous settlement, which was rushed because of Elizabeth's failing health, dismayed many in England.

58] *Minerva*: the Roman goddess of wisdom, often associated with Athena.

60] *Pallas*: an epithet for Athena, the Greek goddess of war and female work.

64] In 1596, the Earl of Essex, Robert Devereux, captured Cádiz, an important Spanish port city.

67] *Semiramis*: Assyrian queen and protagonist of ancient, medieval, and modern legends. See *The Four Monarchies*, line 59.

71] *Fierce Tomris (Cyrus' headsman, Scythians' Queen)*: Queen of the (Scythian) Massagetes, who, having defeated her enemy Cyrus, reportedly immersed his severed head in human blood, satiating his bloodthirst.

73] *Amazon ... at Tilbury*: In Greek myth, the Amazons were a nation of female warriors, famed for their bravery. On horseback and armoured with a silver breastplate, Elizabeth gave a rousing speech to English forces at Tilbury on the eve of the Spanish Armada.

77] *Dido*: the mythical founder of Carthage who burned herself to death on a pyre in order to save her city.

(Who living consummates her funerals),
A great Eliza, but compared with ours,
How vanishes her glory, wealth, and powers.   80
Proud, profuse Cleopatra, whose wrong name
Instead of glory, proved her country's shame;
Of her what worth in stories to be seen,
But that she was a rich Egyptian queen.
Zenobia, potent empress of the East,   85
And of all these without compare the best
(Whom none but great Aurelius could quell),
Yet for our queen is no fit parallel.
She was a phoenix queen, so shall she be,
Her ashes not revived, more phoenix she.   90
Her personal perfections, who would tell,
Must dip his pen in th'Heliconian well,
Which I may not, my pride doth but aspire
To read what others write, and then admire.
Now say, have women worth? Or have they none?   95
Or had they some, but with our queen is't gone?
Nay masculines, you have thus taxed us long,
But she, though dead, will vindicate our wrong;
Let such as say our sex is void of reason
Know 'tis a slander now, but once was treason.   100
But happy England, which had such a queen,
O happy, happy had those days still been.
But happiness lies in a higher sphere,
Then wonder not, Eliza moves not here.
Full fraught with honour, riches, and with days,   105
She set, she set, like Titan in his rays.
No more shall rise or set such glorious sun

81] *Cleopatra*: Cleopatra VII, the last Ptolemaic queen (c. 69–30 BC), who aligned
with Mark Antony and was heralded as 'queen of kings'. However, following Mark
Antony's defeat, she committed suicide, and Egypt became a province of the Roman
Empire.

85–87] Zenobia, widow of the former Palmyrene ruler Odaenathus, became queen of
the Palmyrene Empire following his death. Zenobia defied the Roman Empire, but
was vanquished by Emperor Aurelianus (Aurelius) in 272 AD.

89] *phoenix queen*: The mythical phoenix was an emblem used by Elizabeth I in reference
to its uniqueness (only one phoenix was reputed to live at a time). The phrase
'phoenix queen', by extension, upholds her as a rare paragon. See line 40.

92] *Heliconian*: In Greek myth, Helicon is the mountain residence of the muses.

98] *our wrong*: Eve tasting the forbidden fruit; original sin.

Until the heavens' great revolution;
If then new things their old forms must retain,
Eliza shall rule Albion once again.   110

Her Epitaph

Here sleeps the queen, this is the royal bed
Of th'damask rose, sprung from the white and red,
Whose sweet perfume fills the all-filling air.
This rose is withered, once so lovely fair.
On neither tree did grow such rose before,
The greater was our gain, our loss the more.

Another

Here lies the pride of queens, pattern of kings,
So blaze it, Fame, here's feathers for thy wings,
Here lies the envied, yet unparalleled prince
Whose living virtues speak (though dead long since).
If many worlds, as that fantastic framed,
In every one be her great glory famed.
                    1643

Note

The poem is dated 1643, indicating its composition as the Civil War in
England became increasingly bloody and protracted. Bradstreet's retrospec-
tive elegies on Queen Elizabeth, along with her those on Sir Philip Sidney,
look back to a golden age of English Protestantism and, in the case of
this poem, female rule. Retrospective elegies and poem of praise for
Elizabeth and her reign were common across political divides, and they
commonly tended towards hagiography (see Gray, *Women Writers and
Public Debate*). Bradstreet combines a chronicle of statecraft with a history
of women, finding Elizabeth the superlative embodiment of both and
using her success to lodge a defence of her sex, though not of her own
poetic abilities.

110] *Albion*: England.

David's Lamentation for Saul and Jonathan, 2 Samuel 1:19

Alas, slain is the head of Israel,
Illustrious Saul, whose beauty did excel;
Upon thy places mountainous and high,
How did the mighty fall, and falling die?
In Gath let not this thing be spoken on,   5
Nor published in the streets of Ashkelon,
Lest daughters of the Philistines rejoice,
Lest the uncircumcised lift up their voice.
O! Gilbo Mounts, let never pearled dew
Nor fruitful showers your barren tops bestrew,   10
Nor fields of off'rings ever on you grow,
Nor any pleasant thing e'er may you show;
For there the mighty ones did soon decay,
The shield of Saul was vilely cast away;
There had his dignity so sore a foil,   15
As if his head ne'er felt the sacred oil.
Sometimes from crimson blood of ghastly slain,
The bow of Jonathan ne'er turned in vain:
Nor from the fat and spoils of mighty men
Did Saul with bloodless sword turn back again.   20
Pleasant and lovely were they both in life,
And in their deaths was found no parting strife.
Swifter than swiftest eagles so were they,
Stronger than lions ramping for their prey.
O Israel's dames, o'erflow your beauteous eyes   25
For valiant Saul who on Mount Gilbo lies,
Who clothed you in cloth of richest dye,
And choice delights full of variety;
On your array put ornaments of gold,
Which made you yet more beauteous to behold.   30
O! how in battle did the mighty fall
In midst of strength not succourèd at all?
O! lovely Jonathan, how wert thou slain?
In places high, full low thou didst remain.
Distressed I am for thee, dear Jonathan,   35

1–40] The poem paraphrases 2 Samuel 1:19–27.
5–6] *Gath*; *Ashkelon*: Philistine cities.
9] *Gilbo Mounts*: Mount Gilboa, where Saul and Jonathan died.

Thy love was wonderful, surpassing man,
Exceeding all the love that's feminine,
So pleasant hast thou been, dear brother mine.
How are the mighty fall'n into decay?
And warlike weapons perished away?   40

Note

Saul, the first King of Israel, and his sons Jonathan, Abinadab, and
Malchishua died at Mount Gilboa when Israel was attacked by the
Philistines (1 Samuel 28–31). Bradstreet adopts here the voice of the
David, Saul's former servant and his successor as King of Israel. The
poem has been read as a lament for the death of Charles I or, alternatively,
as 'a reminder of Charles's role in bringing about his own destruction',
Saul having repeatedly attempted to assassinate David, God's anointed
as the rightful king of Israel. See Wade White, *Anne Bradstreet*; Suzuki,
'What's Political?', p. 935; and for Saul in a Civil War context, see
Prescott, 'A Year in the Life'.

From *Several Poems* (1678)

**An Elegy upon that Honourable and Renowned Knight, Sir
Philip Sidney, who was Untimely Slain at the Siege of
Zutphen, Anno 1586 [1678]**

When England did enjoy her halcyon days,
Her noble Sidney wore the crown of bays,
As well an honour to our British land,
As she that swayed the sceptre with her hand.
Mars and Minerva did in one agree,   5
Of arms, and arts, he should a pattern be;
Calliope with Terpsichore did sing,
Of poesy and of music he was king;
His rhetoric struck Polymnia dead,
His eloquence made Mercury wax red;   10
His logic from Euterpe won the crown,
More worth was his than Clio could set down.
Thalia and Melpomene, say truth
(Witness *Arcadia*, penned in his youth):
Are not his tragic comedies so acted,   15
As if your ninefold wit had been compacted
To show the world, they never saw before
That this one volume should exhaust your store?
His wiser days condemned his witty works;
Who knows the spells that in his rhetoric lurks?   20
But some infatuate fools soon caught therein;
Fond Cupid's dam had never such a gin,
Which makes severer eyes but slight that story,

1] *halcyon days*: days of perfect calm.
2] *crown of bays*: In ancient Greece and Rome, bay laurel wreaths were awarded as an emblem of military victory or of distinction in poetry.
4] *she*: Elizabeth I (see also Bradstreet's elegy on her).
5] *Mars*; *Minerva*: the Roman god of war, and the goddess of wisdom and crafts.
7] *Calliope*; *Terpsichore*: the Greek muse of epic poetry, and the muse of dancing.
9] *Polymnia*: Polyhymnia, the Greek muse of sacred poetry.
10] *Mercury*: the Roman god of eloquence.
11] *Euterpe*: the Greek muse of lyric poetry and the flute.
12] *Clio*: the Greek muse of history, associated with poetic inspiration.
13] *Thalia*; *Melpomene*: the Greek muses of comedy and of tragedy.
14] *Arcadia*: Sidney's long prose romance *The Countess of Pembroke's Arcadia* (1590).
22] *Cupid's dam*: Venus, the Roman goddess of love (and Cupid's mother). *gin*: trap.

Anne Bradstreet

And men of morose minds envy his glory.
But he's a beetle-head that can't descry   25
A world of wealth within that rubbish lie,
And doth his name, his work, his honour wrong,
The brave refiner of our British tongue;
That sees not learning, valour, and morality,
Justice, friendship, and kind hospitality,   30
Yea, and divinity within his book;
Such were prejudicate, and did not look.
In all records his name I ever see
Put with an epithet of dignity,
Which shows his worth was great, his honour such,   35
The love his country ought him, was as much.
Then let none disallow of these my strains
Whilst English blood yet runs within my veins.
O brave Achilles, I wish some Homer would
Engrave in marble, with characters of gold,   40
The valiant feats thou didst on Flanders coast,
Which at this day fair Belgia may boast.
The more I say, the more thy worth I stain:
Thy fame and praise is far beyond my strain.
O Zutphen, Zutphen, that most fatal city,   45
Made famous by thy death, much more the pity.
Ah! In his blooming prime, Death plucked this rose
Ere he was ripe, his thread cut Atropos.
Thus man is born to die, and dead is he;
Brave Hector by the walls of Troy we see.   50

25] *beetle-head*: a common contemptuous epithet, indicating stupidity.
28] Sidney's *Apology for Poetry* (published in 1595) was an influential piece of early literary criticism, exploring poetic traditions and commenting on contemporary English poetics.
32] *prejudicate*: prejudiced.
36] *ought*: owed.
38] English blood: Bradstreet here modifies her claim that the 'self-same' blood as Sidney's runs in her veins (see 1650, line 28).
39] *Achilles*; *Homer*: Achilles, the greatest of the Greek heroes in the Trojan War, as told by Homer in the *Iliad*.
41–42] Sidney's military exploits in the Low Countries. Sidney was made governor of Flushing, on Walcheren island, facing the Flemish coast, in 1585.
45] Sidney's death was caused by a wound incurred at the Battle of Zutphen in 1586.
48] *Atropos*: one of the three Fates in Greek mythology, she who cut the thread of mortal life.
50] *Hector*; *Troy*: Hector, the greatest Trojan warrior, was killed by Achilles while defending the city.

77

O, who was near thee, but did sore repine
He rescued not with life that life of thine?
But yet impartial Fates this boon did give:
Though Sidney died, his valiant name should live.
And live it doth, in spite of death, through fame;   55
Thus being overcome, he overcame.
Where is that envious tongue, but can afford
Of this, our noble Scipio, some good word?
Great Bartas, this unto thy praise adds more:
In sad, sweet verse, thou didst his death deplore.   60
And phoenix Spenser doth unto his life
His death present in fable to his wife;
Stella the fair, whose streams from conduits fell
For the sad loss of her dear Astrophel.
Fain would I show, how he fame's paths did tread,   65
But now into such labyrinths I am led,
With endless turns, the way I find not out;
How to persist, my Muse is more in doubt,
Which makes me now with Sylvester confess,
But Sidney's Muse can sing his worthiness.   70
The Muses' aid I craved, they had no will
To give to their detractor any quill.
With high disdain, they said they gave no more,
Since Sidney had exhausted all their store.
They took from me the scribbling pen I had   75
(I to be eased of such a task was glad),

58] *Scipio*: Publius Cornelius Scipio Africanus (236–183 BC), a renowned Roman
republican general.
59–60] The French Protestant poet Guillaume de Saluste Du Bartas praised Sidney,
before his death, in *La Seconde Semaine* (1584). Bradstreet must have encountered
the passage in Josuah Sylvester's English translation, completed after Sidney's death,
which refers to the 'world-mourned' Sidney (*Bartas: His Divine Weeks and Works*,
1605, p. 433).
61–64] Edmund Spenser's 'Astrophel: A Pastoral Elegy upon the Death of the Most
Noble and Valorous Knight, Sir Philip Sidney' (1595) was dedicated to Sidney's
widow Frances Walsingham (c.1568–1632), then Countess of Essex. Spenser's poem
works to construct Sidney's widow as the Stella of Sidney's sonnet sequence *Astrophel
and Stella* (first published 1591), rather than Lady Penelope Rich, to whom Sidney
wrote the sonnets in his youth. Bradstreet here follows his lead, modifying her lines
on Stella in the 1650 version of this poem.
70] *But*: no one but. Josuah Sylvester's introductory sonnet to his 'Elegiac Epistle for
Sir William Sidney' (for the nephew of Philip) describes: 'I know none, but a Sidney's
Muse, / Worthy to sing a Sidney's Worthinesse' (see Wade White, *Anne Bradstreet*,
p. 145).

Then to revenge this wrong, themselves engage,
And drove me from Parnassus in a rage.
Then wonder not if I no better sped,
Since I the Muses thus have injurèd.   80
I, pensive for my fault, sat down, and then
Errata, through their leave, threw me my pen,
My poem to conclude; two lines they deign,
Which writ, she bade return't to them again.
So Sidney's fame, I leave to England's rolls;   85
His bones do lie interred in stately Paul's.

His Epitaph

Here lies in fame under this stone,
Philip and Alexander both in one.
Heir to the Muses, the son of Mars in truth,
Learning, valour, wisdom, all in virtuous youth: 90
His praise is much, this shall suffice my pen,
That Sidney died 'mong most renowned of men.

Note

See p. 59 for the version of this poem that was published in *The Tenth Muse* (1650). That is Bradstreet's earliest dated poem (it is described as being written in 1638), and it is the most extensively revised in *Several Poems* (1678). In 1678, it is shortened and tightened, 142 lines being reduced to 92. Sidney is no longer addressed in the second person in this later version; the long description of Sidney's Stella in the earlier version is truncated and altered; and Bradstreet's rhetoric of her own poetic inadequacy as a woman writer is much reduced.

78] *Parnassus*: In Greek mythology, Mount Parnassus is the home of the nine muses.
82] *Errata*: Erato, the muse of lyric poetry, is here named punningly: 'errata' are errors in writing or a printed book.
86] *stately Paul's*: St Paul's Cathedral, London, where Sidney was buried.
88] *Alexander*: Alexander the Great (356–323 BC), one of history's most successful military commanders. Alexander succeeded his father, Philippus II, as ruler of the ancient Greek kingdom of Macedonia.

The Flesh and the Spirit

In secret place where once I stood,
Close by the banks of lachrym flood,
I heard two sisters reason on
Things that are past, and things to come.
One Flesh was called, who had her eye   5
On worldly wealth and vanity;
The other Spirit, who did rear
Her thoughts unto a higher sphere.
'Sister', quoth Flesh, 'what liv'st thou on,
Nothing but meditation?   10
Doth contemplation feed thee so
Regardlessly to let earth go?
Can speculation satisfy
Notion without reality?
Dost dream of things beyond the moon,   15
And dost thou hope to dwell there soon?
Hast treasures there laid up in store
That all in th'world thou count'st but poor?
Art fancy sick, or turned a sot
To catch at shadows which are not?   20
Come, come, I'll show unto thy sense,
Industry hath its recompense.
What canst desire, but thou mayst see
True substance in variety?
Dost honour like? Acquire the same,   25
As some to their immortal fame,
And trophies to thy name erect
Which wearing time shall ne'er deject.
For riches dost thou long full sore?
Behold enough of precious store.   30
Earth hath more silver, pearls and gold,
Than eyes can see, or hands can hold.
Affect's thou pleasure? Take thy fill,
Earth hath enough of what you will.
Then let not go, what thou mayst find,   35
For things unknown, only in mind'.
Spirit: 'Be still thou unregenerate part,

2] *lachrym*: lachrymal, of tears, here figured as a river

Disturb no more my settled heart,
For I have vowed (and so will do)
Thee as a foe still to pursue,   40
And combat with thee will and must,
Until I see thee laid in th'dust.
Sisters we are, yea, twins we be,
Yet deadly feud 'twixt thee and me;
For from one father are we not,   45
Thou by old Adam was begot,
But my arise is from above,
Whence my dear father I do love.
Thou speak'st me fair but hatest me sore,
Thy flatt'ring shows I'll trust no more.   50
How oft thy slave hast thou me made,
When I believed what thou hast said,
And never had more cause of woe
Than when I did what thou badest do.
I'll stop mine ears at these thy charms,   55
And count them for my deadly harms;
Thy sinful pleasures I do hate,
Thy riches are to me no bait,
Thine honours do nor will I love,
For my ambition lies above.   60
My greatest honour it shall be
When I am victor over thee,
And triumph shall with laurel head
When thou my captive shalt be led.
How I do live, thou need'st not scoff,   65
For I have meat thou know'st not of;
The hidden manna I do eat,
The word of life it is my meat.
My thoughts do yield me more content
Than can thy hours in pleasure spent.   70
Nor are they shadows which I catch,
Nor fancies vain at which I snatch,
But reach at things that are so high,
Beyond thy dull capacity.
Eternal substance I do see,   75
With which enriched I would be:

67] *manna*: a nutritious substance supplied by God when the Israelites were lost in
   the wilderness (Revelation 2:17).

Mine eye doth pierce the heavens, and see
What is invisible to thee.
My garments are not silk nor gold,
Nor such like trash which earth doth hold,   80
But royal robes I shall have on,
More glorious than the glistering sun;
My crown not diamonds, pearls, and gold,
But such as angels' heads enfold.
The city where I hope to dwell,   85
There's none on earth can parallel.
The stately walls both high and strong,
Are made of precious jasper stone;
The gates of pearl, both rich and clear,
And angels are for porters there;   90
The streets thereof transparent gold,
Such as no eye did e'er behold;
A crystal river there doth run,
Which doth proceed from the Lamb's throne.
Of life, there are the waters sure,   95
Which shall remain forever pure;
Nor sun, nor moon, they have no need,
For glory doth from God proceed.
No candle there, nor yet torchlight,
For there shall be no darksome night.   100
From sickness and infirmity,
For evermore they shall be free,
Nor withering age shall e'er come there,
But beauty shall be bright and clear.
This city pure is not for thee,   105
For things unclean there shall not be:
If I of heaven may have my fill,
Take thou the world and all that will'.

Note

This spiritual dialogue poem is in medieval tradition of dialogues between body and soul, rather than the more contentious mode of many Civil War dialogue poems (including Bradstreet's own *A Dialogue between Old England and New*). See Margaret Cavendish, 'A Dialogue between the Body and the Mind' and Cavendish's several uses of the dialogue form.

94] *Lamb's throne*: Jesus is referred to as the Lamb of God; see John 1:29.

The Author to her Book

Thou ill-formed offspring of my feeble brain,
Who after birth didst by my side remain,
Till snatched from thence by friends, less wise than true,
Who thee abroad, exposed to public view,
Made thee in rags, halting to th'press to trudge,   5
Where errors were not lessened (all may judge).
At thy return my blushing was not small,
My rambling brat (in print) should mother call,
I cast thee by as one unfit for light,
Thy visage was so irksome in my sight;   10
Yet being mine own, at length affection would
Thy blemishes amend, if so I could:
I washed thy face, but more defects I saw,
And rubbing off a spot, still made a flaw.
I stretched thy joints to make thee even feet,   15
Yet still thou runst more hobbling than is meet;
In better dress to trim thee was my mind,
But nought save home-spun cloth i'th'house I find.
In this array 'mongst vulgars mayst thou roam;
In critics' hands beware thou dost not come,   20
And take thy way where yet thou are not known;
If for thy father asked, say thou hadst none,
And for thy mother, she alas is poor,
Which caused her thus to send thee out of door.

Note

Appearing only in the second edition of Bradstreet's work, *Several Poems*
(1678), this poem responds to the publication of *The Tenth Muse* in 1650,
and describes a process of making subsequent amendments to the poems
that had been 'exposed to public view'. Bradstreet's poems had been
taken to London in the late 1640s and published there as *The Tenth Muse*
(1650), apparently against Bradstreet's wishes. See 'Textual introduction'.

15] *feet*: a pun on metrical feet.
16] *meet*: fit, proper.

A Letter to her Husband, Absent upon Public Employment

My head, my heart, mine eyes, my life, nay more,
My joy, my magazine of earthly store;
If two be one, as surely thou and I,
How stayest thou there whilst I at Ipswich lie?
So many steps, head from the heart to sever,   5
If but a neck, soon should we be together.
I, like the earth this season, mourn in black,
My sun is gone so far in's zodiac,
Whom whilst I'joyed, nor storms, nor frosts I felt;
His warmth such frigid colds did cause to melt.   10
My chilled limbs now numbed lie forlorn;
Return, return sweet Sol from Capricorn.
In this dead time, alas, what can I more
Than view those fruits which through thy heat I bore?
Which sweet contentment yield me for a space,   15
True living pictures of their father's face.
O strange effect now thou art southward gone;
I weary grow, the tedious day so long.
But when thou northward to me shalt return,
I wish my sun may never set, but burn   20
Within the Cancer of my glowing breast,
The welcome house of him my dearest guest,
Where ever, ever stay, and go not thence,
Till nature's sad decree shall call thee hence.
Flesh of thy flesh, bone of thy bone,   25
I here, thou there, yet both but one.

Note

Bradstreet's husband Simon (1604–97) was a businessman who held
numerous public offices in the Massachusetts Bay colony, including posts
as the secretary of the colony and, from 1679, as governor. From the
1640s onwards, he served as a commissioner to the New England

---

2] *magazine*: storehouse.
12] *Sol*: the sun. *Capricorn*: the sign of the zodiac for December–January, the winter
   figured in the poem.
21] *Cancer*: the sign of the zodiac for June–July, the summer for which the speaker
   wishes.
25] *Flesh of thy flesh*: see Genesis 2:23–24.

Confederation, travelling as a representative of Massachusetts to other New England colonies and to London. This poem indicates that Simon had travelled south, probably to Boston, and perhaps literally during the winter figured in the poem. Through her imagery of the zodiacal signs, Bradstreet begs him to return northward and to bring with him the summer that is the time of Cancer. See Wade White, *Anne Bradstreet*, pp. 202–07.

Another ['As loving hind']

As loving hind that (hartless) wants her deer
Scuds through the woods and fern with harkening ear,
Perplexed, in every bush and nook doth pry,
Her dearest deer might answer ear or eye,
So doth my anxious soul, which now doth miss   5
A dearer dear (far dearer heart) than this.
Still wait with doubts, and hopes, and failing eye,
His voice to hear, or person to descry.
Or as the pensive dove doth all alone
(On withered bough) most uncouthly bemoan   10
The absence of her love and loving mate,
Whose loss hath made her so unfortunate,
E'en thus do I, with many a deep sad groan
Bewail my turtle true, who now is gone,
His presence and his safe return still woos,   15
With thousand doleful sighs and mournful coos.
Or as the loving mullet, that true fish,
Her fellow lost, nor joy nor life do wish,
But launches on that shore, there for to die,
Where she her captive husband doth espy,   20
Mine being gone, I lead a joyless life,
I have a loving fere, yet seem no wife.
But worst of all, to him can't steer my course;
I here, he there, alas, both kept by force.
Return my dear, my joy, my only love,   25
Unto thy hind, thy mullet, and thy dove,
Who neither joys in pasture, house, nor streams,
The substance gone, o me, these are but dreams.
Together at one tree, o let us browse,
And like two turtles roost within one house,   30

1–6] The hart or deer was a common image of the beloved. See Pulter, 'On the Death
   of my Dear and Lovely Daughter, J.P.' and Emblem 22 for a spiritual application.
2] *scuds*: moves swiftly or nimbly.
8] *descry*: catch sight of.
14] *turtle true*: Turtle-doves were renowned for their monogamous affection for their
   mate, and are an image of the beloved in the Song of Songs (2:12). See Pulter,
   'Why must I thus forever be confined' and Emblem 20.
22] *fere*: companion, consort, spouse.

And like the mullets in one river glide,
Let's still remain but one, till death divide.
> *Thy loving love and dearest dear,*
> *At home, abroad, and everywhere.*
> *A.B.*

Note

In this second occasional poem on her husband's absence, Bradstreet expands on common images of amorous loyalty from the natural world: the hart or deer (with common puns on 'heart' and 'dear'), the turtle-dove, and, here, the mullet.

In Memory of my Dear Grandchild Elizabeth Bradstreet, who Deceased August 1605, Being a Year and Half Old

Farewell dear babe, my heart's too much content,
Farewell sweet babe, the pleasure of mine eye,
Farewell fair flower that for a space was lent,
Then ta'en away unto eternity.
Blessed babe why should I once bewail thy fate,   5
Or sigh the days so soon were terminate,
Since thou art settled in an everlasting state.

By nature trees do rot when they are grown,
And plums and apples thoroughly ripe do fall,
And corn and grass are in their season mown,   10
And time brings down what is both strong and tall.
But plants new set to be eradicate,
And buds new blown to have so short a date,
Is by His hand alone that guides nature and fate.

Note

This is one of several elegies on grandchildren included in *Several Poems* (1678).

6] *terminate*: terminated.
12] *eradicate*: eradicated.
13] *blown*: blossomed. See Shakespeare's Sonnet 18.

Hester Pulter (c. 1605–1678)

Hester Pulter was born in or around 1605 in Dublin, into a well-connected and literary English family. Her father Sir James Ley, first Earl of Marlborough, was at the time Chief Justice of the King's Bench in Ireland; he went on to become the Lord Chief Justice and Lord High Treasurer of England, and he was also a writer, described as 'that old man eloquent' by Milton in a sonnet addressed to Hester's sister Margaret in 1642. Hester's mother, Mary Petty, was a first cousin of the Oxford antiquarian Anthony à Wood. Hester was apparently married at an early age, around thirteen, to Arthur Pulter, a Cambridge-educated man, and she moved to the Pulter estate of Broadfield in Hertfordshire at some point before the birth of their daughter Jane in 1625. Jane was the first of at least fifteen children born to the couple, only one of whom outlived Pulter, although a number of children lived into adulthood. Pulter's manuscript volume includes poems written to her daughters Margaret, Penelope, and Anne; a melancholic poem on her pregnancy with John, her fifteenth child, in 1648; and elegies on the death of Jane at the age of twenty in 1645.

Pulter was based at Broadfield for the rest of her life, and it was here that she composed her poems, her emblems, and the prose romance entitled *The Unfortunate Florinda*, all of which are contained in the sole surviving manuscript of her work. She appears to have written the poems from the mid-1640s onwards, and her royalist sympathies are clear. A number of poems and elegies on King Charles I and other royalist heroes (including Margaret Cavendish's brother Sir Charles Lucas and Arthur Pulter's first cousin Sir Arthur Capel) chart the sorry fortunes of the royalist cause during the last years of the Civil War, and her emblems articulate a stance of devout fortitude against the conditions of the English republic. Likely to have been composed in the 1650s, these emblems are nominally addressed to her children as didactic or advice pieces. Like her occasional and devotional poems, however, the emblems are more broadly addressed to an imagined community of royalist readers.

In her poems, Pulter construes Broadfield as a place of unwelcome isolation: she describes herself as 'shut up in a country grange', 'tied to one habitation', and 'buried, thus, alive'. There are, however, records of Pulter having visited London in the years of these poems' composition. Her sister Dionysia was married to the moderate parliamentarian Sir John Harington of Kelston, whose diary includes records of Pulter visiting the Haringtons in London in 1647 and 1652, and interacting while she was there with William Dugard, the printer of (among other things) the *Eikon Basilike*, and with James Ussher, Church of Ireland Archbishop of Armagh. Like so many other families, including those of Katherine Philips and Lucy Hutchinson, Pulter's was divided along political lines during the 1640s and 1650s, but these records suggest that parliamentarian and royalist sisters continued to interact with each other. Another of Hester and Dionysia's sisters is the addressee of Milton's Sonnet 10, 'To the Lady Margaret Ley', and Edward Phillips asserts that Milton spent much time in her company in the autumn and winter of 1643–44, after the departure of his wife Mary Powell. Little is known about the political affiliations of Pulter's husband, Arthur, but his patronage of a Presbyterian minister, Thomas Gardiner, at the local parish church in Cottered, Hertfordshire, may be an indication that his religious and political allegiances differed from his wife's.

Pulter's poetry engages in a number of the governing tropes of royalist literary culture in the 1640s and 1650s, including the conventions of royalist pastoral and retreat, elegy (especially for the king and for royalist heroes), the chorographical (or landscape) poetry practised by Sir John Denham and reaching back to Michael Drayton and Spenser, and the emblem poem. She may have had access to the poetry in manuscript of Andrew Marvell, but her coterie associations and networks, if any, are unclear. Interestingly, she writes a gently satirical poem on the royalist dramatist Sir William Davenant, whose major patron was William Cavendish, husband to Margaret; but she states that she is not known to Davenant, suggesting that she was not connected to the large and important literary coterie associated with William Cavendish and his family. Her poetry also reveals interests in natural history (relying especially on Pliny), alchemy, and natural philosophical advances in astronomical theory.

One of many intriguing aspects of Pulter's literary career is that there is, to date, no evidence of anyone having read her manuscript, other than those who have annotated it. Her poems did not appear in print, and she was unknown to literary history until her manuscript was uncovered in 1996. While there is no reception history for Pulter's verse, however, the content of her poems and their engagement in the tropes and conventions also evident in the poetry of Philips, Cavendish, and Hutchinson make her a notable woman poet of the English Civil War.

**The Invitation into the Country, to my Dear Daughters,
M.P., P.P., 1647, when his Sacred Majesty was at
Unhappy Hour**

Dear daughters come make haste away,
From that sad place make no delay;
He's gone that was the city's grace,
Five hydras now usurp his place;
The planes are overgrown with moss,   5
With shedding tears for England's loss;
Hard hearts insensible of woe
Whom marble walls in grief outgo.
Then come sweet virgins, come away,
What is it that invites your stay?   10

What can you learn there, else but pride,
And what your blushes will not hide?
There virgins lose their honoured name,
Which doth forever blur their fame;
There husbands look with jealous eyes,   15
And wives deceive them and their spies;
To Inns of Court and armies go
Wise children their own dads to know;
There shepherds, that no flocks do keep,
Like butchers' mastiffs, worry sheep.   20
Then come sweet children, come away,
What can allure you yet to stay?

Hyde Park, a place of chief delight,
Her bushes mourn like Jews in white,

Title] M.P. and P.P. are likely to be Pulter's daughters Margaret Pulter (1629–86) and
   Penelope Pulter (1633–55), who were apparently living in London while Pulter
   remained at Broadfield in rural Hertfordshire. Charles I was imprisoned at Holmby
   (or Holdenby) House in Northamptonshire between 7 February and 4 June 1647,
   before being moved to various other locations.
3] *He's gone*: refers to Charles I.
4] *hydras*: The Hydra is a many-headed monster in Greek mythology, whose heads
   grow again as fast as they are cut off; a common emblem of corruption and/or the
   unruly mob. See Bradstreet, 'A Dialogue between Old England and New', line 118.
5] *planes*: plane trees, common in London as ornamental and parkland trees.
17] *Inns of Court*: institutions in central London where men trained to become barristers.
23] *Hyde Park*: a London pleasure garden, a fashionable spot. See Pulter's Emblem
   20 and Philips, 'A Country Life'.
24] White clothing is traditional for Yom Kippur, the Jewish festival of atonement and
   repentance, although it is not a traditional Jewish colour of mourning.

The stately deer do weeping stray,   25
Anticipating their last day;
Spring Garden that such pleasures bred
Looks dull and sad since Chloris fled.
The crystal Thames her loss deplores,
And to the sea her grief out roars;   30
The swans upon her silver breast,
Though dying, yet can find no rest,
But full of grief cry 'welladay' –
And, singing, sigh their breath away.
Ay me, then come make haste away,   35
From that sad place make no delay.

Here's flowery vales and crystal springs,
Here's shady groves, here ever sings
The bullfinch, linnet, striving which
The auditors shall most bewitch.   40
The early lark, long ere the morn
With roses can her head adorn,
Sings cheerfully a roundelay,
Telling this lower world 'tis day.
Here thrushes, wrens, and red breasts sing   45
To welcome in the gladsome spring.
Then come sweet maidens, come away,
To this sweet place make no delay.

Here careful shepherds view their sheep,
They him, and he their souls doth keep;   50
Blessings flow on them from above
That are reciprocal in love.
He in his bosom bears the lambs,
And gently leads the heavy dams;
He whistles those that go astray,   55
By which means none runs quite away.
Here husbands free from jealous eye
Have wives as full of modesty;

27] *Spring Garden*: like Hyde Park, a fashionable London social spot.
28] *Chloris*: Queen Henrietta Maria (a common pastoral name, frequently paired with
    Amintas).
33] *welladay*: an exclamation of sorrow.
39] *bullfinch, linnet*: common songbirds.
43] *roundelay*: a bird's song.
54] *heavy dams*: pregnant mothers.

They in their children both rejoice,
Commending still their happy choice; 60
Most kind, and free from all debate,
That no true love can ever hate.
Then come my children, come away,
To this sweet place make no delay.

Here virgins sit in flow'ry vales, 65
Refreshed by sweet favorious gales,
Making them anadems and posies,
Crowning their heads with new blown roses.
In woods and dales fair maidens may,
Unfrighted, freely gather May. 70
Then lovely lasses, come away,
To cheer my heart make no delay.

But o, those times now changèd be;
Sad metamorphosis we see,
For since Amintas went away 75
Shepherds and sheep go all astray.
Those that deserved whole groves of bays,
In sighs consume their youthful days,
And that fair fleecy flocks did keep,
Despised in corners sit and weep. 80
Since Chloris went both wife and maid
In love and beauty hath decayed.
Where maypoles showed their feathered head,
There coloured ensigns now are spread;
Instead of music's pleasant sound 85
And lively lasses dancing round,
Tumultuous drums make deaf our ears
And trumpets fill our hearts with fears.
In shades where nymphs did use to walk,
There sons of Mars in armour stalk. 90

66] *favorious*: favourous, pleasing.
67] *anadems*: wreaths for the head.
70] *gather May*: the gathering of hawthorn blossom or flowers and young foliage to celebrate May Day. Maying rituals were fiercely attacked by puritans, and so became strongly associated with royalist culture.
75] *Amintas*: Charles I (a common pastoral name, frequently paired with Chloris).
77] *bays*: bay trees or bay laurel, a classical emblem for poets or to denote military victory.
84] *ensigns*: military banners or flags.
90] *Mars*: Roman god of war.

Enamelled vales and crystal streams
Prove now alas poor Broadfield's dreams.
Lea's drooping swans now sadly sing,
And Beane comes weeping from her spring;
Mimram and Stort in mourning weeds,   95
Showing their hearts for grief e'en bleeds;
All run to Lea for some relief
And in her bosom pour their grief;
Thus she and they all weeping go
To tell the Thames their grievous woe.   100
Ver looks and sees this shire look sad;
She whirls about as she were mad,
Round Verulam, his ruined stones
She runs, and tells to Colne her moans;
For since her saint his blood was shed   105
She never grieved so, as she said.
Colne sympathised with her in woe
And to the Thames resolved to go;
Clear Purwell too came bubbling out,
But long she did not stand in doubt;   110
Seeing our halcyon days were done,
She loathed (she said) to see the sun
As he pursued the cheerful day,
But turned her course another way,
And sighing shed forth tears as clear   115
As pearls, and ran to Bedfordshire;
To Ouse, who was so full of grief
That she herself did want relief,
And said, would any place receive
Her tears, she would her channel leave,   120

93] *Lea*: the river Lea; this and all the rivers described in lines 93–116 are in Hertfordshire, the county in which Broadfield is situated.
101] *Ver*: the river on which the Romans built Verulamium; it runs into the Colne (line 104).
102] *as*: as if.
103] *Verulam*: Verulamium, a ruined Roman town in Hertfordshire, near St Albans.
105] *her saint*: St Alban, a British martyr.
109] *Purwell*: The river Purwell flows from Hertfordshire to Buckinghamshire.
111] *halcyon days*: days of perfect calm.
117] *Ouse*: a large river in Bedfordshire.

As when King Richard's reign had date,
But this she was denied by fate.
Gray's Spring, too, sadly makes her moan
And with her tears turns moss to stone,
And, seeing delight with Chloris fled,   125
She sighed and, murmuring, hid her head
Within her womb that gave her birth,
Venting her grief below the earth.
The naiades here sit in ranks,
Forlorn upon our withered banks,   130
And garlands make of willow boughs
To hide their tears and shade their brows.
Since Chloris went our flowers fade,
No pleasure is in hill or shade;
Poor Philomel doth sit alone,   135
To senseless trees now makes her moan;
Our woods their choristers now lack,
The woozles whistle, clad in black,
And the forsaken turtle-dove
Bewails her own and Chloris' love.   140
The hamadryades invokes
The goddesses enshrined in oaks,
Who fold their yielding arms across
And weep with them Amintas' loss.
Some trees drop gum from their sad eyes   145
T'immortalise ambitious flies;
Though they can give us no relief
They'll sympathise with us in grief.
The oreads sport and play no more
But great Amintas' loss deplore;   150
Instead of roses, cypress boughs

121] probably a reference to 'Buckingham's Flood', extraordinary flooding of the rivers
Severn and Wye in 1483, towards the end of the reign of Richard III (see Eardley,
Lady Hester Pulter).
123] *Gray's Spring*: a petrifying spring at Broadfield.
129] *naiades*: naiads, nymphs who live in streams and rivers as their guardian spirits.
131] *willow*: a symbol of grief and of lost love.
135] *Philomel*: the nightingale.
138] *woozles*: ouzels, blackbirds.
139] The turtle-dove was renowned for its constant affection for its mate; see also
Pulter's Emblem 20.
141] *hamadryades*: hamadryads, wood nymphs.
149] *oreads*: mountain nymphs.
151] *cypress boughs*: used at funerals or as a symbol of mourning.

Pearled o'er with tears doth shade their brows,
Dishevelled, torn, neglected hair
Hangs o'er their throbbing bosom bare.
Nay, the Napaeae, from their hills   155
Dissolve with tears, weep crystal rills.
Those flowers which the valleys crown,
O'ercharged with grief their heads hang down:
Since lovely Chloris frightened fled,
The crown imperial hangs his head,   160
His princely breast o'erwhelmed with fears,
Weeping at once six crystal tears;
To lovely shades pale violets creep
And there unpitied sit and weep;
The royal rose that ne'er would yield,   165
But strove for mastery in the field
And Chloris' cheek, neglected fades
In silent, solitary shades.
The lily and the July flower
Do wish it were within their power   170
To sleep forever in their caves,
But 'tis denied by Nature's laws;
Th'auricula that cures the giddy brain,
Dizzy with grief, hangs down her head again.
Then shall not we with grief o'erflow?   175
Shall vegetables us outgo?
Thus neither woods, nor fields, nor hills,
Enamelled vales, nor crystal rills,
Nor birds, nor trees, nor flowers of scent,
But do this kingdom's loss resent.   180

155] *Napaeae*: nymphs who inhabit woods; also occasionally mountain and/or water nymphs.
156] *rills*: small streams, rivulets.
160] *crown imperial*: a flower consisting of several 'bells', each of which contains six droplets of water (see Eardley, *Lady Hester Pulter*).
165–67] The rose is associated with factions of royalty striving for mastery (in the Wars of the Roses, the house of Lancaster and its red rose fought the house of Lancaster and its white rose), and with the red and white of a lady's cheek (in a trope common to love poetry).
169] *July flower*: a gillyflower, a type of wallflower.
173] *auricula*: a flower, a species of primula; its root was thought to prevent dizziness when climbing to high altitudes (Eardley, *Lady Hester Pulter*).
176] *vegetables*: plants.

Then let us still lament and grieve
Till heaven in mercy doth relieve.
'Tis neither sight nor odour's scent
Can my afflicted heart content,
Until I see them both restored   185
Whose absence hath been so deplored.
Just Heaven, hear our prayers and tears,
And place them in their shining spheres.
Then come sweet daughters, come away,
To comfort me make no delay.   190

Note

This lengthy and meandering poem participates in several common Civil
War genres, and uses a number of prevailing royalist tropes. The opening
stanzas, with their recurring 'come away' refrain, tap into a long tradition
of secular and sacred invitation poetry. From line 73, there is a marked
structural shift, and Pulter's royalist pastoral here resembles that of Herrick
in his *Hesperides*, with maypoles and maying rituals standing for pastimes
prohibited by Puritans (see Marcus, 'Herrick's "Hesperides"' and *The
Politics of Mirth*). Lines 93–128 echo the river poems of Spenser and the
chorographical poetry of Michael Drayton, whose *Poly-Olbion* (1612)
charts the rivers of every county in Britain and gives them voice. These
lines also stand in a close relationship with Pulter's 'The Complaint of
Thames, 1647', written in the same year and with many images in common.
See Ross, *Women, Poetry, and Politics*.

185] *them both*: i.e. Charles I and Henrietta Maria.

The Complaint of Thames, 1647, when the Best of Kings was Imprisoned by the Worst of Rebels at Holmby

Late in an evening as I walked alone,
I heard the Thames most sadly make her moan.
As she came weeping from her western spring,
She thus bewailed the learnèd shepherd king:
'Amintas, sad Amintas, sits forlorn   5
And his fair Chloris now's become the scorn
Of Troynovant's ingrate, licentious dames;
No marvel then if poor afflicted Thames
With salt, abortive tears does wash this city,
As full of blood and lies as void of pity.   10
Perfidious town, know thou the power of fate;
Thy long felicity shall find a date,
And I may live to see another turn
When thy proud fabric shall unpitied burn.
Then heaven, just heaven, withhold thy rain,   15
And I will leave my channel once again,
As when my holy Albian's blood was spilt,
Seeing to wash away thy horrid guilt
Is more impossible than 'tis to change
The skins of Negros that in Afric range.   20
Then when thou fryest in vengeful flames of fire,
Thy scorched genius ready to expire,

Title] Charles I was imprisoned at Holmby (or Holdenby) House in Northamptonshire between 7 February and 4 June 1647, before being moved to various other locations.

3] *western spring*: The source of the Thames is in Gloucestershire, and the river flows from the west to the south-east.

5] *Amintas*: Charles I (a common pastoral name, frequently paired with Chloris).

6] *Chloris*: Queen Henrietta Maria (also a common pastoral name).

7] *Troynovant's*: London's. Pulter's description of London as Troynovant or 'New Troy' echoes Spenser in *The Ruins of Time* (1591) and in *The Faerie Queene* (1590).

7] *ingrate*: ungrateful.

9] *salt, abortive tears*: see Pulter, 'The Weeping Wish'.

14] This reference to London burning is oddly prescient, or may suggest that Pulter's poem was revised after the Great Fire of London in 1666.

17] *Albian*: St Alban, a British martyr who parted the waters of the Thames. St Albans, in Hertfordshire, is the site of Verulamium, the ruined city that features in Spenser's *The Ruins of Time*.

19–20] See Jeremiah 13:23: 'Can the Ethiopian change his skin, or the leopard his spots?'

22] *genius*: a spirit of a place, institution, or thing. Spenser's *The Ruins of Time* features the genius of the 'brent' (burned) city of Verulamium (line 19).

Thy tongue and mouth sable as salamander
With speaking 'gainst thy king and queen such slander,
Then not a drop of my cool crystal wave   25
To cool thy sulphurous tongue, or life to save,
But when I have of thee seen all my lust
And all thy pride and glory turned to dust,
Then I, triumphant with my watery train,
Will make this city quagmires once again.   30
But o, thy blood and perjuries repent,
Then heaven, I hope, in mercy will relent,
Thy king restore, call home his queen again,
Or all thy prayer and fasting is in vain.
Hast thou forgot (ay me), so have not I,   35
Those halcyon days, the sweet tranquillity
That we enjoyed under his happy reign,
Which heaven will once restore to us again,
Unless the dismal line of dissolution
(Which, o forbid) be drawn upon this nation.   40
Oft have I borne upon my silver breast
His lovely Chloris, like Aurora dressed
With youth and beauty, with her princely spouse;
Envied I was by Severn, Humber, Ouse.
The sacred Dee said she no more would boast   45
Her showing conquest on the conquering coast,
Though Edgar's glory from her river springs,
When he in triumph by eight captive kings
Was rowed upon her famous crystal stream,

23] *sable*: black.
23] *salamander*: a lizard-like animal, supposed to live in fire.
27] *all my lust*: all my desire; i.e. all that I wish to see.
36] *halcyon days*: days of perfect calm.
42] *Aurora*: Roman goddess of the dawn (and the subject of several poems by Pulter).
44–110] Pulter's Thames compares herself to rivers around Britain, the world, and the underworld.
44] *Severn, Humber, Ouse*: rivers in Wales, Yorkshire, and the south-east of England.
45] *sacred Dee*: a river running across north Wales and north-east England; 'Dee' means 'goddess' (Latin: *dea, deae*).
45–50] Edgar, an Anglo-Saxon king, had eight Scottish, Welsh, and Scandinavian kings row him up and down the river Dee in a gesture of submission in AD 793 (Eardley, *Lady Hester Pulter*).
46] *showing conquest*: Pulter's meaning is unclear; she may mean a show of conquest (see also 'Textual notes').

Those former honours showed now like a dream.   50
Nay, the Danube said, she'd ne'er rehearse
Her being biggest in the universe.
Even Tagus would not brag of golden sands
But said she envied more my happy strands;
So said the Loire. In envy Po looked on,   55
Though she were honoured by a Phaethon;
And Egypt's glory, Nilus, stately stream,
Said her felicities were but a dream
When on her o'erflowing waves were seen
The Roman eagles and her black-eyed queen;   60
And silver Ganges said the sacrifice
The Banians brought with elevated eyes,
Though all their carcasses by fire calcined
Were in her purifying waves refined,
Though all their wealth and treasure in they hurled   65
And she were lady of the eastern world,
Yet all that glory she did count a toy
Compared, she said, with happy Thames her joy.
Tiber said, of Horatius' valour brave
She ne'er would speak, but I the praise should have.   70

51] *Danube*: actually only the second longest river in Europe.

53] *Tagus*: the longest river on the Iberian peninsula, famous in classical poetry for its gold-bearing sands.

55] *Loire*; *Po*: the longest rivers in France and Italy.

56] *Phaethon*: in Greek myth, the son of Helios, who insists on driving his father's chariot of the sun. He loses control, threatening to set the earth on fire. Zeus strikes him down with a bolt of lightning so that he plunges into the river Eridanus (Po).

57] *Nilus*: the Nile, the longest river in the world.

60] *Roman eagles*; *queen*: the eagle was a symbol of ancient Rome. The black-eyed queen is Cleopatra, who escorted Julius Caesar along the Nile.

61] *Ganges*: river in northern India, sacred to Hindus.

62] *Banians*: Hindu traders.

63–64] *calcined*; *purifying waves*: Hindu dead are cremated (*calcined*: turned to ashes), and their ashes are thrown into the water of the Ganges.

69] *Tiber*; *Horatius' valour*: The Tiber is the river on which Rome stands. Horatius Cocles (530–500 BC) defended the Sublician bridge against invasion, and swam back across the Tiber in full armour once it had been demolished (Eardley, *Lady Hester Pulter*).

Crystal Euphrates never did envy
The glory of no other flood but I,
Though from a thousand founts her stream doth spring,
Yet did she never bear so good a king.
Through lofty Babylon her river flows,   75
And earthly Paradise she doth enclose;
Though brave Semiramis enlarge her fame,
Yet doth she envy still the English Thame.
But now, alas, they envy me no more
But with their tears my heavy loss deplore.   80
Oft have I born my sacred sovereign's barge,
Being richly gilt, most proud of such a charge.
My waves would swell to see his princely face,
Each billow loath to give his fellow place;
Sometimes they'd rise to kiss his royal hand   85
And hardly would give back at my command;
Billow with billow strive, and ruffling roar,
Scorning the blow of either hand or oar.
But now, insulting, on my billows ride
The kingdom's scourges and this city's pride,   90
Which make my trembling stream lamenting roar,
And her sad loss with troubled breast deplore.
Come, kind Charybdis, come, o come and help's,
Sweet lovely Scylla bring thy barking whelps;
Then should they need no monument nor tomb,   95
But Oceanus' dark and horrid womb
Should them involve. But wishes are in vain:
I will roar out my grief unto the main.
Now all the beauty that my waves adorn
Are snowy swans that sadly swim forlorn,   100

71–76] The Euphrates is the longest river in western Asia, and Babylon is the ancient
   city on its banks. The Hanging Gardens of Babylon were irrigated by water from
   the Euphrates.
77] *Semiramis*: legendary Assyrian queen who constructed monumental buildings in
   Babylon.
81] *my sacred sovereign's barge*: that of Charles I.
93] *help's*: help us.
93–94] *Charybdis*; *Scylla*: in Greek mythology, a whirlpool and a rock on either side
   of the strait of Messina. Scylla was depicted as a six-headed sea-monster surrounded
   by dogs.
96] *Oceanus*: Greek god of the sea.
98] *main*: open sea.

Nor do they in the sun their feathers prune
As they were wont, nor yet their voices tune,
But in despair hanging their head and wing,
This kingdom's dirges they expiring sing.
O that it in my power were to refuse   105
To see this town, like crystal Arethuse
Below this cursed earth would hide my head
And run amongst the caverns of the dead,
Where my pure wave with Acheron should mix
With Lethe, Phlegethon, Cocytus, Styx;   110
Then would I waft them to the stygian shade,
Examples unto rebels to be made.
O my sad heart these are but foolish dreams,
For they triumph upon my conquered streams.
Yet this I'll do while sighs breathe up my spring: 115
I'll trickle tears for my afflicted king
And look how far one drop of crystal Thames
Doth run, so far I'll memorise their fames,
So shall my grief immortalise their names'.
I hearing these complaints, though time to sleep,   120
Sat sadly down and with her 'gan to weep.

Note

This poem is in the tradition of the 'female complaint', a popular and
diverse mode that uses a female voice to utter complaint of various kinds,
from amorous woe, to political lament, to complaint against the times
(see Kerrigan, *Motives of Woe*). Pulter's poem echoes most closely Edmund
Spenser's *The Ruins of Time*, and her personification of the Thames may
also be indebted to Spenser's description of the marriage of Thames and
Medway, in *The Faerie Queene*, Canto IV, and to Michael Drayton's
Poly-Olbion (1612). See also Pulter's 'The Invitation into the Country,
to my Dear Daughters', written in the same year and sharing many
images with this poem.

101] *prune*: preen.
106] *Arethuse*: Arethusa, a spring in Syracuse and a nymph in Greek mythology who,
    pursued by the river god Alpheius, is helped by Artemis to flee underground.
    Alpheius follows her and mingles his waters with those of the spring.
109–10] Acheron, Lethe, Phlegethon, Cocytus, and Styx are the rivers of the classical
    underworld.
111] *stygian*: hellish, infernal (relating to the river Styx).
116] See also Pulter, 'The Weeping Wish'.

On Those Two Unparalleled Friends, Sir George Lisle and Sir Charles Lucas

Is Lisle and Lucas slain? O say not so!
Who could kill love and valour at a blow?
Just as Minerva's darling closed his eyes,
Love, kissing, wept, and on his bosom dies.
Ah me, what horrid Hydra had the heart   5
Them in their deaths thus to unite and part?
Mars on the Areopagus once was tried;
His valour saved him or he else had died.
His judge and jury were the best of gods,
These, worst of men; o me what odds!   10
Had Jove's three sons of everlasting fame,
Born of a mortal and celestial flame,
Had they been here this business to decide,
Then these two noble gallants had not died.
Or had Astraeus (lover of the Morn,   15
Of whose bright womb her brighter babe was born),
Had he been here, he would have took delight
To save their lives, that for his child did fight.
Then had their judges been the gods eternal,
Or upright men, nay, or the powers infernal,   20
This unambiguous business to decide,
Then this unparalleled friendship had not died.
But Jews, Turks, atheists, Independents, all
That cursèd rabble, made these gallants fall.

3] *Minerva*: Roman goddess of wisdom and warfare; her 'darling' is Lucas, who was
  shot first, Lisle running forward to catch his body and kiss his face.
5] *Hydra*: a many-headed monster in Greek mythology; also in the Civil War period
  a common emblem of the unruly mob.
7] *Mars*: Roman god of war, often associated with Ares, the Greek god of war. The
  gods of the Areopagus council tried and acquitted Ares on the Areopagus hill in
  Athens for the killing of Halirrhothius, who had tried to rape his daughter.
10] *These*: the judge and jury of these men (Lucas and Lisle), who were tried by a
  council of war.
11] *Jove*: another name for Jupiter, the king of the gods and the Roman equivalent of
  Zeus. Three of Zeus' sons are judges of the dead in the underworld: Aeacus, Minos,
  and Rhadamanthys.
15–18] Astraeus is the husband of Aurora (here *the Morn*); together they are the parents
  of Astraea, who is associated with Dike, the goddess of human law and justice.
23] *Jews, Turks*: terms of abuse used by royalists for their opposition. *Independents*:
  religious independents or congregationalists, who advocated religious freedom and
  separation of church and state.

How could they do it? Were they not amazed,   25
Whenas the cruel Parcae sat and gazed
On their perfections, as Lachis drew the thread,
'What won't you part asunder?' then she said;
They striving in their lives t'embrace each other,
She twirled and twisted both of them together.   30
Then Clotho at their constant love did wonder,
And in mere pity pulled them not asunder;
She being, it seems, the tender'st-hearted lass,
'Go noble souls', she said, and let them pass.
But Atropos, enraged, began to chide,   35
Saying 'these true love's knots must be untied';
But, seeing their lives she could not stay to untwist,
'Let those sit idling here', she said, 'that list.
How can we give account unto those powers
That us employ, in trifling out our hours?'   40
Then, scolding at her sisters for their sloth,
She with her fatal scissors snipped them both;
She then cried out, 'alas', but hurrying Fate
Forced her, poor girl: her pity came too late.
Lycaon, Tantal, tender to this brood,   45
Who fed on hostages and infants' blood,
Why are they now more cruel than at first?
They're drunk with Christian blood, yet still they thirst.
Doth that old vulture and his preying brood
Think to grow young with sucking spritely blood?   50
O let them next suck Nessus' poisoned gore,
Like mad Alcides let them rave and roar,

25] *amazed*: terrified, alarmed.

26] *Whenas*: at the time at which.

26–44] The Parcae are the Roman version of the three Fates, who spin the threads of fate: Clotho the 'Spinning', Lachesis the 'Lot-Casting', and Atropos the 'Unturnable'.

38] *list*: desire, wish.

45] *Lycaon*: Lycaon served human flesh to Zeus as a test of his omniscience. *Tantal*: Tantalus, who served his dismembered son Pelops to the gods as part of a feast.

49] *that old vulture*: Oliver Cromwell, whose long nose led royalists to compare him to a vulture.

50] an allusion to the myth that eagles' beaks become so long in old age that they cannot eat, and must suck on blood to survive (Eardley, *Lady Hester Pulter*).

51–52] In Greek mythology, Nessus is a centaur who is shot by Heracles (known also as Alcides) with an arrow dipped in the poison of the Hydra. Before he dies, Nessus gives Heracles' wife Deianira some of his poisoned blood, telling her it is a love spell. She later uses this on Heracles' gown, causing him to burn to death.

And as they've been three kingdoms' sore annoyers,
Let them, like him, at last be self-destroyers.
Had these undaunted, loving heroes died   55
In former times, they had been deified;
Then their renown and love had spread as far
As those two famous thunderbolts of war;
Effigies, pyramids, columns, colosses,
Had been erect to memorise our losses.   60
But we are now denied our just desires;
True, grateful love in this our age expires.
Yet some sad swan, I know, there will be found
That for this only action shall be crowned:
That shall bear lovely Lisle and Lucas' name   65
Unto the temple of eternal fame.
When that black army after their short dream
Shall floating be on Styx, his sable stream,
They by the angry billows shall be tossed
Till in Oblivion's horrid womb they're lost.   70
If he that fired Diana's fane for fame
Lost both his expectation and his name,
If covetous Cambyses, who presumed
To rob the gods till sand his men consumed,
Or that fierce Gaul, who Delphi meant to plunder,   75

53] *three kingdoms*: England, Ireland, and Scotland.

58] *two famous thunderbolts*: Cornelius Scipio (Africanus Major) (236–183 BC) and Cornelius Scipio (c. 185–129 BC), two Roman generals who were known as the 'two thunderbolts of war' (Virgil, *The Aeneid*, VI.841–44).

59] *colosses*: colossuses, huge statues such as the Colossus of Rhodes.

63] *some sad swan*: In Ariosto's epic poem *Orlando Furioso* (1532), the lives of individuals are each represented by a metal tag with their name stamped on it. When the Fate Atropos cuts the thread on which the tag hangs, the old man Time throws the tag in the river Lethe (the river of forgetfulness and oblivion). Two swans carry the few tags they are able to carry to the temple of eternal fame. See Eardley, *Lady Hester Pulter*, and Ludovico Ariosto, *Orlando Furioso*, trans. John Harington (1591), 34.87–35.29.

67] *black army*: the parliamentarian army, in ascendance in 1648.

68] *Styx*: the principal river in Hades, the underworld.

71] *he*: Herostratus, who was so desperate for immortal fame that he set fire to the great temple (fane) of Diana at Ephesus, one of the wonders of the ancient world.

73] *Cambyses*: a King of Persia (530–522 BC), who lost fifty thousand men in a terrible sandstorm. Plutarch mentions this loss in his account of Alexander the Great's journey to destroy the temple of Jupiter Hammon (i.e. it was Alexander who sought to 'rob the gods'). See Eardley, *Lady Hester Pulter*.

75] *fierce Gaul*: Brennus, who invaded Delphi in 279 BC; in legend, his forces were repelled by lightning storms and an earthquake.

Till fiery Phoebus routed him with thunder,
If these live now in honour, then no doubt
Fame shall attend this sacrilegious rout
Who have our faith's defender over-powered,
And temples, altars, victims, all devoured.   80
But these victorious souls live now above,
And gloriously go on in endless love,
Whilst their fair frames, which here did close their lives,
Shall live in fame till they in glory rise.

Note

Sir George Lisle (d. 1648) and Sir Charles Lucas (1613–48) were royalist
commanders and military heroes, captured and executed at the fall of
the city of Colchester after a months-long siege, in August 1648. Lucas
was the brother of Margaret Cavendish, and is commemorated in her
'Upon the Funeral of my Dear Brother, Killed in these Unhappy Wars'.
Lisle and Lucas were executed by firing squad on 28 August, and an
immediate outpouring of royalist panegyrics and elegies (in which Pulter's
poem participates) transformed them into royalist martyrs. See also Pulter,
'On the Same ["Let none sigh more"]'; and for the literary response to
Lisle's and Lucas's deaths, see Brady, 'Dying with Honour'.

76] *Phoebus*: an epithet of Apollo, Greek god of the sun.
78] *rout*: crowd, mob; the parliamentarian opponents of Charles I.
79] *our faith's defender*: Charles I, as King of England and *fidei defensor* (Defender of
the Faith) from 1521. From 1534, the English monarch was head of the national
church, and the desire of religious Independents for separation of church and state
was a central issue in the Civil War.

Upon the Death of my Dear and Lovely Daughter, J.P.

All you that have indulgent parents been,
And have your children in perfection seen
Of youth and beauty, lend one tear to me;
And trust me I will do as much for thee,
Unless my own grief do exhaust my store;   5
Then will I sigh till I suspire no more.
Twice hath the earth thrown Chloris' mantle by,
Embroidered o'er with curious tapestry,
And twice hath seemed to mourn unto our sight
Like Jews, or Chinesses in snowy white,   10
Since she laid down her milky limbs on earth,
Which dying gave her virgin soul new birth;
Yet still my heart is overwhelmed with grief,
And tears (alas) give sorrow no relief.
Twice hath sad Philomel left off to sing   15
Her mortifying sonnets to the spring,
Twice at the sylvan choristers' desire
She hath lent her music to complete their choir,
Since all-devouring Death on her took seizure,
And Tellus' womb involved so rich a treasure;   20
Yet still my heart is overwhelmed with grief,
And time nor tears will give my woes relief.
Twelve times hath Phoebe hornèd seemed to fight,
As often filled them with her brother's light,
Since she did close her sparkling diamond eyes;   25
Yet my sad heart for her still pining dies.
Through the twelve houses hath the illustrious sun

Title] *J. P.*: Jane Pulter.

6] *suspire*: sigh forth, breathe out.

7] Chloris is the goddess of the spring; her 'mantle' is spring flowers. Two years have
   passed since Jane's death.

10] *Chinesses*: Chinese women, who (like Chinese men) traditionally wear white in
    mourning. White clothing is traditional for Yom Kippur, the Jewish festival of atonement
    and repentance, although it is not a traditional Jewish colour of mourning.

15] *Philomel*: the nightingale, which does not sing in the winter.

20] *Tellus*: in Roman mythology, the goddess of the earth. *involved*: enveloped.

23] *Phoebe*: the moon, which has the appearance of having horns when it is in its
    crescent form.

24] i.e. when the moon is full, the space between her horns is 'filled' with the light of
    her brother (the sun).

27] *twelve houses*: the twelve signs of the zodiac.

With splendency his annual journey run,
Twice hath his fiery furious horses hurled
His blazing chariot to the lower world, 30
Showing his lustre to the wondering eyes
Of our (now so well known) antipodes,
Since the brack of her spotless virgin story,
Which now her soul doth end in endless glory;
Yet my afflicted, sad, forsaken soul 35
For her in tears and ashes still doth roll.
O could a fever spot her snowy skin
Whose virgin soul was scarcely soiled with sin!
Ay me it did; so have I sometimes seen
Fair maidens sit encircled on a green, 40
White lilies spread when they were making posies,
Upon them scatter leaves of damask roses.
E'en so the spots upon her fair skin show,
Like lily leaves, sprinkled with damask rose,
Or as a stately hart to death pursued 45
By ravening hounds, his eyes with tears bedewed,
An arrow sticking in his trembling breast;
His lost condition to the life expressed.
So trips he o'er the lawns on trodden snow,
And from his side his guiltless blood doth flow; 50
So did the spots upon her fair skin show
Like drops of blood upon unsullied snow.
But what a heart had I, when I did stand,
Holding her forehead with my trembling hand;
My heart to heaven with her bright spirit flies, 55
Whilst she (ah me) closed up her lovely eyes;
Her soul being seated in her place of birth,
I turned a Niobe as she turned earth.

28] *splendency*: splendour.
33] *brack*: breach, violation.
37] Jane is likely to have died of smallpox (or possibly measles).
44–52] These lines have been added to the poem, apparently at a later date. See 'Textual notes' and Figures 2 and 3.
45–50] Charles I is frequently described in the royalist literature of the period as a stately deer pursued by hounds. The hunted, wounded hart is also a common spiritual image, deriving in part from Psalm 42:1: 'as the hart panteth after the water brooks, so panteth my soul after thee, O God'. See Pulter's Emblem 22 for a development of these implications.
55] *heart*: a play, via the homonym, on 'hart' (see note above).
58] *Niobe*: in Greek legend, supposed to have been turned into stone while weeping for her children.

Note

Jane Pulter was baptised on 1 May 1625 and buried on 8 October 1645 aged twenty, according to an antiquarian who has annotated Pulter's manuscript. Pulter addressed a number of poems to Jane and her sisters, and this is the first of two elegies on Jane's death. The lines on the hunted stag (44–52) are an interpolation and may postdate the original poem; see footnotes to the poem, 'Textual notes', and Figures 2 and 3. The images of the hunted stag and of Niobe have led to comparison with Marvell's 'A Nymph Complaining on the Death of her Fawn'. See also Pulter, 'On the Same ["Tell me no more"]', and see Ross, *Women, Poetry, and Politics*.

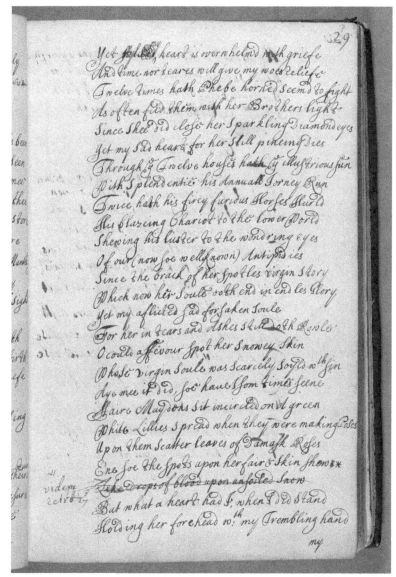

Figure 2 Hester Pulter, 'Upon the Death of my Dear and Lovely Daughter, J.P.', with an ideogram of a pointing finger indicating where new lines are to be added.

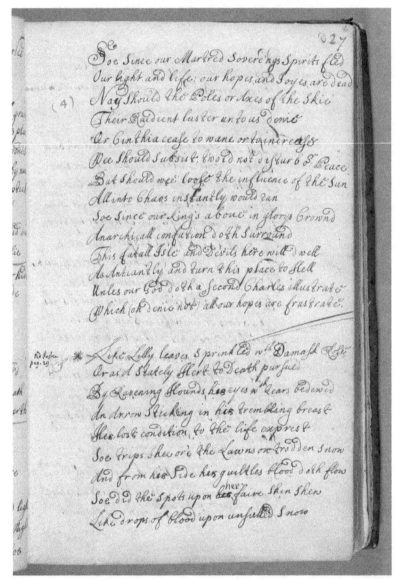

Figure 3 Hester Pulter, lines to be added to 'Upon the Death of my Dear and Lovely Daughter, J.P.', indicated with a matching ideogram, added at the end of an elegy on Charles I.

On the Same ['Tell me no more']

Tell me no more her hair was lovely brown,
Nor that it did in curious curls hang down,
Or that it did her snowy shoulders shroud
Like shining Cynthia in a sable cloud;
Tell me no more of her black diamond eyes,   5
Whose cheerful look made all my sorrows fly,
Like glittering Phoebus' influence and light
After a northern winter's half year's night;
Tell me no more her cheeks excelled the rose,
Though lily leaves did sweetly interpose,   10
Like ruddy Aurora rising from her bed,
Her snowy hand shading her Orient head;
Tell me no more of her white, even nose
Nor that her ruby lips when they disclose
Did so revive this drooping heart of mine,   15
Like golden apples on a silver shrine;
Tell me no more her breasts were heaps of snow,
White as the swans, where crystal Thames doth flow.
Chaste as Diana was her virgin breast;
Her noble mind can never be expressed: 20
This but the casket was of her rich soul
Which now doth shine above the highest pole.
Tell me no more of her perfection,
Because it doth increase my heart's dejection;
Nor tell me that she passed her happy days   25
In singing heavenly and the Muses' lays;
Nor like the swans on crystal Po
She sung her dirges ere she hence did go;
Nor never more tell my sad soul of mirth:
With her I lost most of my joys on earth.   30
Nor can I ever raise my drooping spirit
Until with her those joys I shall inherit,

Title] *On the Same*: i.e. on the death of Jane Pulter. The poem immediately follows
    'Upon the Death of my Dear and Lovely Daughter, J.P.' in Pulter's manuscript.
4] *Cynthia*: a literary epithet for Luna, the moon. *sable*: black.
7] *Phoebus*: an epithet of Apollo, Greek god of the sun.
11] *Aurora*: the dawn.
19] *Diana*: the virgin goddess of hunting.
27] *Po*: the river Po in northern Italy, renowned in classical times for its swans; this
    underscores the image of Jane's swansong.

Those glories which our finite thoughts transcend
Where we shall praises sing, world without end,
To him that made both her and me of earth,   35
And gave us spirits of celestial birth.
Tell me no more of her unblemished fame,
Which doth immortalise her virgin name,
Like fragrant odours, aromatic fumes,
Which all succeeding ages still perfumes;   40
Nor why I mourn for her ask me no more,
For all my life I shall her loss deplore,
Till infinite power her dust and mine shall raise,
To sing in Heaven his everlasting praise.

Note

This is the second of two elegies on Pulter's daughter Jane, who died at
the age of twenty in 1645. The 'tell me no more' refrain and its 'ask me
no more' variant are popular in lyrics of the period; see Nixon, '"Aske
me no more"' and Henry King's 'Sonnet' opening 'Tell me no more
how fair she is'. See also Pulter's use of the 'ask me no more' phrase in
'Upon the Imprisonment of his Sacred Majesty, that Unparalleled Prince,
King Charles the First'.

Upon the Imprisonment of his Sacred Majesty, that Unparalleled Prince, King Charles the First

Why I sit sighing here ask me no more:
My sacred sovereign's thralldom I deplore.
Just Nemesis (whom they pretend to adore),

Put on thy sable, blood-besprinkled gown,
And thy o'erflowing vengeance thunder down   5
On these usurpers of our Caesar's crown.

They have his sacred person now in hold,
They have their king and country bought and sold,
And hope of glory, all for cursèd gold.

Then seeing they eternity thus slight,   10
Let Acheron's fierce issue them affright
Till endless horror doth their souls benight.

Then let our Job-like saint rise from the ground,
For piety and patience so renowned,
That for the best of kings he may be crowned.   15

Then ask no more why I'm in tears dissolved:
Whilst our good king with sorrow is involved,
To pray and weep for him I am resolved.

Note

Between 1647 and 1649 Pulter wrote several poems on the trials of
Charles I, culminating in her three elegies on his death. Charles was
imprisoned by parliamentarian forces at Holmby (or Holdenby) House

---

1, 16] *ask me no more*: like her second elegy on the death of her daughter Jane ('On the Same ["Tell me no more"]'), this poem works with a refrain popular in seventeenth-century lyric culture (see Nixon, '"Aske me no more"').
3] *Nemesis*: Greek goddess and personification of retribution.
4] *sable*: black.
6] *our Caesar*: Charles I, in a common royalist association of the king with the assassinated Roman statesman Julius Caesar (100–44 BC).
8–9] See Matthew 26:14–16, in which Judas agrees to betray Jesus for thirty pieces of silver.
11] *Acheron*: one of the rivers of the underworld which marks its borders, or (as here), the underworld itself. *issue*: offspring.
13] *Job*: Charles I, in a common royalist association with the biblical Job, known for his patience and fortitude in prolonged suffering.

in Northamptonshire between 7 February and 4 June 1647, before being moved to various other locations. He was executed on 30 January 1649. See also Pulter's 'The Complaint of Thames, 1647'. The imagery of sighs and tears in this poem is common across many of Pulter's poems on the royalist defeat.

On the Horrid Murder of that Incomparable Prince, King Charles the First

Let none presume to weep: tears are too weak,
Such an unparalled loss as this to speak.
Poor village girls do so express their grief,
And in that sad expression find relief
When such a prince in such a manner dies.   5
Let us (ay me) no more drop tears but eyes;
Nor let none dare to sigh or strike their breast
To show a grief that so transcends the rest:
Plebeians so each vulgar loss deplore,
We do too little if we do no more.   10
When such a king in such a manner dies,
Let us suspire our souls, weep out our eyes.

Note

This is the shortest of Pulter's elegies on Charles I, who was executed outside Whitehall Palace on 30 January 1649.

2] *unparalled*: unparalleled.
12] *suspire*: sigh forth, breathe out.

On the Same ['Let none sigh more']

Let none sigh more for Lucas or for Lisle,
Seeing now the very soul of this sad isle
(At which trembling invades my soul) is dead,
And with our sacred sovereign's spirit's fled
To heaven, where smiling he looks down,   5
And sees these monsters struggling for his crown,
Whilst his illustrious brows, adorned with glory,
Expects the *finis* of their tragic story.
How could they do it? Sure they were afraid,
And therefore called in Jews unto their aid,   10
Who their redeemer and their king betrayed.
O horrid villains! Could they do this deed,
To wound that heart for whom all should bleed.
And noble Capel, let it be thy glory,
Though dead, to live in his unparalled story;   15
Take it not ill that we could scarce deplore
This kingdom's loss in thee, when full before.
Thy loss, heroic kinsman, wounded deep,
Had we had power left to sigh or weep;
Senseless we were of private desolation,   20
Just like a flood after an inundation.
Thus Nile doth proudly swell to lose her name,
And be involvèd in the ocean's fame;
Thus stately Volga's in the Caspian tossed,
And Nature's great design in thee is lost.   25
So mercury surrounds the purest gold,

8] *finis*: 'end' (Latin), as frequently used at the end of printed books.

10] *Jews*: an allusion to the role of Jews in the crucifixion of Christ, a common comparison in royalist writings on the execution of Charles I.

13] *heart*: a homonym for 'hart', one of Pulter's recurring images for the king. See 'On the Death of my Dear and Lovely Daughter, J.P.', 'The Weeping Wish', and Emblem 22.

15] *unparalled*: unparalleled.

17] *when full before*: when already full of grief.

18] *heroic kinsman*: Capel was a first cousin of Pulter's husband, Arthur, on his mother's side.

19] *Had*: if only had.

22–24] *Nile … Volga*: Africa's and Europe's longest rivers, running into the Mediterranean and the Caspian seas respectively and losing themselves in larger bodies of water.

23] *involvèd*: enveloped.

26] *mercury*: an essential element in alchemical processes, the aim of which was to turn baser metals into gold.

And Phoebus' beams doth Hermes' light infold,
Hiding his radiant fulgour from our sight;
So is thy splendency outshined by light.
Thy pardon, greatest soul, grant; I presume   30
Not to add odours to thy choice perfume;
I only do it to illustrate forth,
By his great virtue, thy transcendent worth,
Heroic prince, now raised above their hate,
Thou tramplest over death and adverse fate,   35
And as one fate your bodies did dissolve,
So immortality shall both involve;
Just as our martyred king his spirit fled,
The spouse of Christ hung down her virgin head,
And sighing said, 'my faith's defender's dead',   40
Then trickling tears down on her trembling breast,
She said (ay me) 'when shall I safely rest?'
At which a voice from heaven said, 'weep no more,
Nor my heroic champion's death deplore;
A second Charles shall all thy joys restore'.   45

Note

This elegy for Charles I takes as its starting point the executions of the
royalist commanders Sir George Lisle and Sir Charles Lucas, after they
were captured at Colchester at the end of a months-long siege from 14
June to 27 August 1648. Lisle's and Lucas's executions by firing squad
on 28 August generated a flurry of royalist panegyrics and elegies that
rapidly transformed them into martyrs; see Pulter's earlier poem 'On
Those Two Unparalleled Friends, Sir George Lisle and Sir Charles Lucas',

27] *Phoebus*: an epithet of Apollo, Greek god of the sun. *Hermes*: Mercury, the planet
closest to the sun.
28] *fulgour*: dazzling brightness, splendour.
29] *splendency*: splendour.
30] *greatest soul*: Charles I, whom the speaker now addresses.
33] *his*: Capel's.
39] *spouse of Christ*: the individual believer and/or the church, a multivalent trope
deriving from the biblical canticles (Song of Songs). See also Ephesians 5:22–33.
40] *faith's defender*: Charles I, as king of England and *fidei defensor* (Defender of the
Faith) from 1521. From 1534, the English monarch was head of the national church;
and the desire of religious Independents for separation of church and state was a
central issue in the Civil War.
45] *a second Charles*: the son of Charles I, who was crowned Charles II at the restoration
of the monarchy in 1660.

and see Margaret Cavendish's poem on Lucas, 'Upon the Funeral of my Dear Brother, Killed in these Unhappy Wars'. Pulter also references here the later execution of Sir Arthur Capel, who was captured with Lisle and Lucas but not executed until 9 March 1649. Capel was the first cousin of Pulter's husband, Arthur, on his mother's side. This poem, likely to date from soon after Capel's execution, echoes the river imagery of her poems on the king's imprisonment in 1647; see 'The Invitation into the Country, to my Dear Daughters' and 'The Complaint of Thames, 1647'.

The Circle ['In sighs and tears there is no end']

In sighs and tears there is no end;
My soul, on heaven alone depend.
Sighs like the air doth clouds condense,
Which tears from our sad eyes dispense.
Trust me, in sighs there is no ease,   5
No more than wind doth calm the seas,
And tears (ah me) descend in vain;
To sighs they rarefy again.
In this sad circle I run round
Till, giddily, I tumble down.   10
But should poor I suspire to air,
I know the sad fruits of despair;
Or should I into tears dissolve,
What horror would my soul involve.
Then, gracious God, in thee I'll trust,   15
Although thou crumble me to dust;
No grief shall so emergent be
To separate my soul from thee.
Of nothing thou didst me create,
And should thou now annihilate,   20
Abrupt, or consummate my story,
O let it be unto thy glory.

Note

This is one of four Pulter poems entitled 'The Circle'. It is an image with alchemical implications (see 'The Circle ["Those that the hidden chemic art profess"]'), but in this devotional poem it is an emblem of speaker's earthly emotions, an endless cycle of tears and grief, which can be escaped only through a turn to trust in God.

8] *rarefy*: make thin or less substantial (here, by evaporation).
11] *suspire*: sigh forth, to breathe out.
14] *involve*: envelop.
16] *dust*: See Genesis 3:19: 'for dust thou art, and unto dust shalt thou return'.
17] *emergent*: pressing, urgent.
19] Genesis 2:7: 'And the Lord God formed man of the dust of the ground, and breathed into his nostrils the breath of life; and man became a living soul'.
21] *abrupt*: break off. *consummate*: bring to completion.

'Dear God turn not away thy face'

Dear God turn not away thy face,
Desert me not, in such a case
As I am in, without thy grace,
Involved with death and night.

O that the spirits of life and love   5
Would leave his glorious throne above,
And deign on my dark soul to move,
To illuminate me with light.

Though I no offering fit can bring,
Yet I will hallelujahs sing   10
To my eternal God and king,
Whilst here I pass my story.

And when the elements are agreed
On my mortality to feed,
And neither faith, nor hope shall need,   15
I'll shine with love in glory.

O then turn not thy face away,
Let love and light bear all the sway;
They'll soon create eternal day.
O do it but explore.   20

Then shall thy blessèd influence
Triumph o'er Death her impotence,
Whilst I enrobed with innocence
Am crowned forever more.

1–2] See Psalm 27:9: 'Hide not thy face far from me … leave me not, neither forsake me, O God'.
4] *Involved*: enveloped.
7–8] See Genesis 1:2–3: 'And the spirit of God moved upon the face of the waters … And God said, let there be light: and there was light'.
15–16] See 1 Corinthians 13:13 for the three theological virtues: faith, hope, and love (charity).
17–18] See lines 1–2 and 7–8.

Note

This is one of many simple devotional lyrics in Pulter's manuscript, reminiscent of the lyrics of George Herbert. Pulter's insistence that she is 'Involved with death and night' could be a reference to her religious and political isolation; or it could simply be a stock description of the earthly state of the devout Christian.

The Circle ['Those that the hidden chemic art profess']

Those that the hidden chemic art profess
And visit Nature in her morning dress,
To mercury and sulphur philtres give
That they consumed with love may live
In their posterity, and in them shine,   5
Though they their being unto them resign,
Glorying to shine in silver and in gold,
Which fretting vermil poison doth enfold,
Forgetting quite that they were once refined.
By time and state to dust are all calcined,   10
Lying obliviated in their urn
Till they to their great ancestors return;
So man the universe's chiefest glory,
His primitive's dust (alas) doth end his story.

Note

This poem draws on ideas and images of alchemy, the medieval and early Renaissance 'chemic art' by which the alchemist attempted to concoct the elixir (or philosopher's stone) which would transmute base metals into gold and/or prolong life indefinitely. The density of alchemical imagery in this poem attests to Pulter's close knowledge of alchemical philosophy; however, she uses this imagery to critique the alchemist, who seeks eternal life and forgets that true riches are to be found in the spiritual realm. See Archer, 'A "Perfect Circle"?'

1] *chemic*: of alchemy (and, in more modern uses, of chemistry).
2] *morning dress*: a woman's dress intended for informal day wear.
3] *mercury and sulphur*: not the two metallic elements in modern chemistry but, in alchemy, the two basic and idealised principles in all matter. In alchemical symbolism, mercury is a white woman (or queen) and sulphur a red man (or king), and these come together in sexual union, the 'chymical wedding' (see Archer, 'A "Perfect Circle"?'). *philtres*: love potions.
5] *posterity*: offspring.
7] *silver, gold*: metallic elements used in alchemy, and also another version of the two idealised alchemical principles in all matter. Gold (Sol, the sun) is the masculine principle, and silver (Luna, the moon) is the feminine.
8] *fretting*: corrosive. *vermil*: vermilion, mercuric sulphide, a bright red poison.
9] *refined*: pure, i.e. morally and spiritually pure and elevated.
10] *calcined*: reduced to ash by burning. Calcination is the oxidation of metals; here, figuratively, calcination to dust is death.
11] *obliviated*: forgotten, committed to oblivion. *urn*: perhaps a reference to the limbeck, the alchemist's vessel.
14] *primitive's*: ancestor's, i.e. that of Adam, who was created from dust (Genesis 2:7).

On the King's Most Excellent Majesty

Victorious palm, triumphing laurel boughs
Encircles round illustrious Caesar's brows,
Whose valour fills with wonder future story,
Whilst virtue crowns him with immortal glory.
Let bright Minerva's olive tree still grow   5
To shade his throne, whence truth and peace may flow
Down to our humble orbs. O let him live,
Still to receive from heaven, to us to give;
And let his lovely, loyal, royal queen
To all succeeding ages still be seen   10
A most unparalled pattern of true love,
Begun on earth, ending in heaven above.
O let them in their shining spheres be fixed,
And never with prodigious meteors mixed,
But by the *primum mobile* turned round,   15
Lasting as Delia's let their race be found;
And when those glitt'ring globes are all dissolved,
Let them in endless glory be involved;
Till when let grace and blessing from above
Descend on them and all that do them love.   20

1] Palm trees and bay laurels were Roman and Greek symbols of victory and triumph.

2] *Caesar*: Charles I, in a common royalist association of the king with the Roman statesman Julius Caesar (100–44 BC).

5] Minerva is associated with Athena, the Greek goddess of war, crafts, and female work. Athena won ownership and naming rights over Athens by planting an olive tree.

9] *queen*: Queen Henrietta Maria.

11] *unparalled*: unparalleled.

13] *fixed*: The stars were traditionally described as 'fixed', to distinguish them from the 'wandering' planets (Eardley, *Lady Hester Pulter*).

14] *prodigious*: abnormal.

15] *primum mobile*: In the Ptolemaic model of the solar system, the outermost sphere encircling all the planets and stars; the 'prime mover'.

16] *Delia's*: possibly a reference to Delius, an epithet of Apollos (who was born on the island of Delos); alternatively, Apollo's sister Artemis, who is occasionally referred to as Delia.

18] *involved*: enveloped.

Note

It is unclear whether this panegyric on King Charles I and Queen Henrietta Maria dates from before or after the execution of Charles I on 30 January 1649. Either way, it celebrates the heavenly qualities of Charles and his queen, focusing on their immortality in reputation and in heaven as a kind of victory without end.

To my Dear J.P., M.P., P.P., they Being at London, I at Broadfield

Come, my dear children, to this lonely place
Where Gray's cool, stupefying spring doth trace;
Trust me, I think I of this fount partake,
I am so dull, and such sad fancies make.
Nor can the quintessence of Bacchus' liquor,   5
Nor the elixir, make my spirit quicker;
Those gross extractions doth my thoughts annoy,
'Tis fasting fancies are my soul's sole joy.
When my freed soul flies to her place of birth,
Then am I brave, my foot then spurns this earth;   10
My mind being raised above these worldly jars,
Me thinks I play at football with the stars.
Condemning all these garish, empty toys,
My thoughts are fixed on true celestial joys.
Come then, exhilarate my drooping spirit   15
So may you those eternal joys inherit;
So may there ever in your happy breast
Those blessèd gems, joy and peace, still rest.
Then when Astraea, with her sacred charms,
Hath thrown you in mild Mercy's downy arms,   20
O'erlooked by Providence, allured by Love
To those immortal mansions above,
Then when each element its part shall claim,
May you all live in glory and in fame.

Title] *J.P., M.P., P.P.*: Pulter's daughters Jane (1625–45), Margaret (1629–86), and
Penelope (1633–55), who were apparently living in London while Pulter lived at
Broadfield.
2] *Gray's ... spring*: a petrifying spring at Broadfield.
4] *fancies*: imaginings, and also poems.
5] *Bacchus' liquor*: In Greek mythology, Bacchus is the god of wine.
6] *elixir*: an essence capable of indefinitely prolonging life (a supposed product of
alchemy).
7] *gross*: material (not spiritual).
11] *jars*: conflicts.
19] *Astraea*: in Roman mythology, the goddess of truth or justice. Her name means
'starry maiden'.

Note

Like 'The Invitation into the Country, to my Dear Daughters', this poem invites Pulter's daughters to join her in the country, at the rural family home of Broadfield Hall, Hertfordshire. Broadfield is construed here as a lonely place, and the poem's turn to devout consolation parallels Pulter's advice to female readers in her Emblem 20.

Hester Pulter

A Solitary Complaint

Must I be still confined to this sad grove
Whenas those vast and glorious globes above
Eternally in treble motions move?
Thrice happy Hermes moves in endless day,
Being underneath the sun's illustrous ray;   5
Next, lovely Venus swiftly hurries round
The sun's bright throne, with equal lustre crowned;
Next Tellus, to whom Sol his light extends,
Runs round his orb; fair Cynthia her attends,
Whom he irradiates with constant light   10
Though she appears so various to our sight.
Mars, soldier-like, no sabbath ever knows
For round the fount of light he ever goes.
Then Jupiter, attended like a king,
Four radiant moons he in his train doth bring;   15
Saturn, as many following his huge sphere,
At least no more to our dim sight appear;
All these encircle Phoebus' glorious mound
By whom, with splendour, all these stars are crowned.
But whether this sun his influence doth owe   20
Unto some other sun, none sure doth know;
But every orb his fellow doth illustrate,
For none the ends of nature dares to frustrate.
Thus all those suns and stars forever move
About the fount of life, and light, and love.   25
Then, o my God, irradiate my sad soul,

2] *Whenas*: while. *globes*: planets.
3] *treble motions*: a reference to the Copernican theory of astronomy, in which the planets, including the earth, orbit around the sun. The 'treble motions' are the daily rotation of the earth, the yearly orbit of the earth around the sun, and the conical motion of the earth's axis (Eardley, *Lady Hester Pulter*).
4] *Thrice happy*: extremely fortunate. *Hermes*: Mercury, the planet closest to the sun.
8] *Tellus*: the earth (Tellus is the Roman goddess of the earth). *Sol*: the sun (the Titan god of light).
9] *Cynthia*: the moon.
14] *Jupiter*: the largest planet; the Roman equivalent of Zeus, king of the gods.
16] *as many*: as many moons.
18] *Phoebus*: Apollo, Greek god of the sun.
19] *stars*: planets.
22] *illustrate*: illuminate.
23] *ends*: aims, purposes.
26] *irradiate*: illumine with spiritual light.

That I about thy glorious throne may roll;
Let me the meanest of these stars attend,
Then all my rays in praise shall reascend.
For thee, and only thee, I will adore;   30
My God, my God for ever, ever more.

Note

This is one of many poems that construes Pulter's residence at Broadfield as one of sad isolation, its title indicating its engagement in the mode of complaint (see also 'The Complaint of Thames, 1647'). The extended astronomical references illustrate Pulter's interest in natural philosophy, and in particular a striking understanding of the 'new' astronomy: Copernicus' heliocentric view of the solar system, as confirmed by Galileo. For extended discussion of Pulter's astronomy (including this poem), see Hutton, 'A Woman Poet'.

'Must I thus ever interdicted be?'

Must I thus ever interdicted be?
My gracious God, to thee and only thee
I will complain; pardon and pity me.

Have I thy sacred pledges took in vain,
Or heard thy blessed word applause to gain,   5
That thou dost thus thine ordinances restrain?

If it be so, thy mercy I implore
To lay my sins upon my Saviour's score,
And me unto thy church again restore.

The wanton sparrow and the chaster dove   10
Within thy sacred temple freely move,
But I, ay me, am kept from what I love.

O let thy spirit my sad soul sustain
Until those comforts I do reattain,
Then let me never part with them again   15

Until my captivated soul takes wing,
Then will I hallelujahs ever sing
To thee, my gracious God and glorious king.

Note

This is another of Pulter's simple devotional lyrics, reminiscent of the lyrics of George Herbert. Pulter's insistence that she is 'interdicted' – that is, precluded from religious ceremonies – may mean that she was not taking part in religious worship at her local parish church at Cottered, Hertfordshire, where a Presbyterian minister was in place in the 1650s (see Clarke, 'Women in Church'). Pulter's husband, Arthur, was a patron

1] *interdicted*: prohibited, debarred, precluded.
6] *ordinances*: decrees of God or providence; or, more specifically, religious or ceremonial observances.
8] *Saviour's score*: Christ's account of her sins
10] *sparrow; dove*: The sparrow was associated with lechery, while turtle-doves were renowned for constancy and devotion in love. See Pulter's Emblem 20.
11] *thy sacred temple*: a place of divine worship, a church; also, any place occupied by the divine presence, including the person or body of a Christian. The title of George Herbert's enormously popular volume of devotional poems *The Temple* (1633) refers to the church, the individual, the community of believers, and the volume of poetry itself.

of the minister, Thomas Gardiner, which may also suggest differences in religious opinion between Hester and Arthur Pulter. Alternatively, the poem may simply be exploring a sense of being out of God's favour, a common starting point for the devotional poet (see Pulter, 'Dear God turn not away thy face').

'Why must I thus forever be confined'

Why must I thus forever be confined
Against the noble freedom of my mind?
Whenas each hoary moth, and gaudy fly,
Within their spheres enjoy their liberty.
The virgin bee her luscious cell forsakes,   5
And on a thousand flowers pleasure takes.
The glist'ring beetle casts her stag-like horns;
The next year, new her stately front adorns.
She rolls her unctuous embryo east and west
To call great Nature, who hears her behest.   10
The silk worm feeds, then works, then she involves
Herself, then breeds, then flies till she dissolves.
The basilisk that kills by fascination
Is not, like me, tied to one habitation;
No, nor the catablepe, whose poisonous eye   15
Where'er she goes, makes grass and flowers die;
Though these destroy, yet may they freely range,
Whilst I am shut up in a country grange.
My looks, though sad, would make my friend revive;
Why must I then be buried, thus, alive?   20
The amphisbaena that at both's ends kill
Doth freely slide about where'er she will;
The dipsas that doth make men lie with quaffing,
And the tarantula that kills with laughing,
With that bold worm which killed th'Egyptian queen,   25

3] *Whenas*: at the time at which. *hoary*: greyish white. *fly*: butterfly.
7] *glist'ring*: glittering.
8] *new*: i.e. new horns. Pulter's image conflates Pliny's descriptions of stag beetles and dung beetles.
9] *unctuous*: oily, greasy.
11] *involves*: envelops.
13] *basilisk*: a reptile, also called a cockatrice; ancient authors stated that its breath, and even its look, was fatal. *fascination*: casting a spell, a faculty attributed to serpents.
15] *catablepe*: a legendary creature whose eyes kill on sight but whose head is so heavy that it always hangs down, hence killing the grass and flowers.
21] *amphisbaena*: a mythical serpent with a head at each end of its body.
23] *dipsas*: a serpent whose bite was fabled to produce a raging thirst.
24] *tarantula*: The venom of this spider was believed to cause people to die laughing.
25] Cleopatra reportedly committed suicide by allowing asps to bite her.

All freely crawling 'bout the world are seen.
Thus insects, reptiles, that spontaneous breed,
From such a solitude as mine are freed,
And I (o my sad heart), and only I,
Must in this sad confinement living, die.   30
The swiftest dolphin and the vastest whale
Are not immured, as I, in wall or pale,
But every sort of fish, e'en as they please,
Do dive and swim about the spacious seas.
Though the dull oyster from a rock is torn,   35
Yet she with sails, and wind, and tide, is borne
O'er all the swelling billows at her pleasure,
Until the cunning crab on her takes seizure.
The flying fish, though she doth oft despair,
Yet she commands the seas and vaster air;   40
And those fair birds which hover still above,
Which are so far indulgent to their love
To let their females lay upon their back,
No noble freedom surely they can lack,
Nor do they fear the terriblest tyrant's lour   45
Should shut them in a bastille, or a tower,
For they disdain to touch this dunghill earth;
Thus they enjoy the freedom of their birth.
But I to solitude am still confined,
The cruellest curb unto a noble mind.   50
The halcyon that calms the ruffling seas
Is not restrained, but flies where'er she please;
Nor doth the swan on Thames, her silver breast,
Ask leave to rise off from her downy nest;
The rav'nous ravens, deaf to their young ones' cry,   55
May in the spacious air most freely fly;

27] *that spontaneous breed*: refers to the idea of spontaneous generation, the development
of living organisms out of air or water (thought particularly to apply to serpents).

31] Pliny emphasises the speed of the dolphin.

32] *immured*: shut up or enclosed. *pale*: a wooden stake used to create a boundary or
a fence.

41] *fair birds*: manucodes, or birds of paradise.

45] *lour*: frown, scowl.

46] *bastille*: a fortified tower, a small prison.

51] *halcyon*: kingfisher, believed to breed on days of perfect calm.

55] *rav'nous ravens*: In the Bible, God provides food for young ravens abandoned by
their mothers (Psalm 147:9).

But I above my life my children love,
Yet I to comfort them cannot remove.
The foolish ostrich doth her eggs expose
To thousand dangers, ere they do disclose,   60
Yet proudly she by wind and wing is borne,
The swiftest horse and rider she doth scorn;
But I for mine would willingly dissolve,
Yet sad obscurity doth me involve.
The mild and tender-hearted turtle-dove,   65
That was so constant to her only love,
Though she resolves to have no second mate,
Yet she her flight about the air doth take;
But I, that am more constant than this dove,
Unto my first, and last, and only, love   70
Cannot from this sad place (ay me) remove.
The cuckoo that doth put her eggs to nurse,
Then eats their foster brothers, which is worse;
Yet this cursed emblem of ingratitude
Is not, like me, enslaved to solitude.   75
All volatiles, from the eagle to the dove,
Their freedom freely both enjoy and love;
But I no liberty expect to have
Until I find my freedom in my grave.
The swiftest su no liberty can lack,   80
That bears her spritely offspring on her back;
The canibal, when she the huntsman hears,

59] *foolish ostrich*: The ostrich 'leaveth her eggs in the earth, and warmeth them in dust,
   And forgetteth that the foot may crush them' (Job 39:14–15). Pliny also emphasises
   the ostrich's stupidity.
60] *disclose*: hatch.
61–62] also deriving from the biblical book of Job: 'What time she lifteth up herself
   on high, she scorneth the horse and his rider' (Job 39:18).
63] *dissolve*: disintegrate, die.
64] *involve*: envelop.
65–67] Turtle-doves were renowned for their monogamous affection for their mate,
   and are an image of the beloved in the Song of Songs (2:12); see also Pulter's
   Emblem 20.
72–73] The cuckoo deposits eggs in the nests of other birds, sometimes at the cost of
   the host's own eggs.
76] *volatiles*: birds, winged creatures.
80] *su*: a sensationalised creature, said to live in Patagonia, that carried its young on
   its back.
82] *canibal*: an animal resembling a kangaroo, with a pouch in which she keeps her
   young.

Her pretty younglings in a wallet bears;
Thus from pursuers they are all secure;
But these sad shades doth me, ay me, immure,   85
That I cannot assist mine in their sorrow,
Which makes me sigh and weep both eve and morrow.
The lion, tiger, elephant, and bear,
And thousands more, do no confinement fear;
Thus beasts, birds, fishes, equivocal worm, and fly,   90
Enjoy more liberty (woe's me) than I.
Were't for my God, king, country, or my friend,
My love, my children, 'twere a noble end;
Or were't for sin, my guilty head I'd hide,
And patiently the stroke of death abide;   95
Or were't my venial slips to expiate,
Then my restraint would have a happy date;
Or were't for debt, I soon could pay that score;
But 'tis, o my sad soul, I'll say no more;
To God alone my suff'rings I'll deplore.   100

Note

This is one of many poems in which Pulter dwells on her isolation, 'shut up in a country grange' at Broadfield. It is unclear how real this 'sad confinement' was, but her felt isolation defines her depiction of rural retirement. This poem contrasts her own condition with the freedom of various real, sensationalised, and mythologised creatures. The descriptions and associations of these creatures illustrate her keen interest in natural history, particularly via Pliny in Philemon Holland's translation, *The History of the World: Commonly Called the Natural History of C. Plinius Secundus* (1601). Very many of the creatures referred to in this poem are subjects of Pulter's emblem poems (see, for example, Emblem 20 on the turtle-dove).

85] *immure*: shut up.
90] *equivocal*: unclassifiable (because of spontaneous or 'equivocal' generation).
96] *venial slips*: pardonable missteps, as opposed to deadly sins.

To Sir William Davenant, upon the Unspeakable Loss of the Most Conspicuous and Chief Ornament of his Frontispiece

Sir,
Extremely I deplore your loss;
You're like Cheapside without a cross,
Or like a dial and no gnomon.
In pity (trust me) I think no man
But would his leg or arm expose   5
To cut you out another nose.
Nor of the female sex there's none
But'ld be one flesh, though not one bone.
I, though unknown, would slight the pain
That you might have so great a gain.   10
Nay any fool, did he know it,
Would give his nose to have your wit,
And I myself would do the same,
Did I not fear t'would blur my fame;
I, as once said a gallant dame,   15
My nose would venture, not my fame;
For who but that bright eye above
Would know 'twere charity, not love.
Then Sir, your pardon I must beg,
Excuse my nose, accept my leg;   20
But yet be sure both night and day
For me, as for yourself, you pray,
For if I first should chance to go
To visit those sad shades below,
As my frail flesh there putrefies,   25
Your nose no doubt will sympathise.
But this I fear, lest that blind boy

2] *Cheapside*: once the site of a stone cross erected by King Edward I in the thirteenth century; the cross at Cheapside was destroyed in May 1643, shortly after the start of the Civil War, under an order of parliament.

3] *gnomon*: the upright arm on a sundial.

5–6] A method for reconstructing noses out of flaps of skin cut from a patient's arm was published by the Italian surgeon Gaspare Tagliacozzi in 1597.

8] Women would be willing to share their flesh with him, but not their bones (with an allusion to Genesis 2:23–24).

14] *fame*: reputation. That is, people might think she had lost her nose to syphilis, too.

15] *gallant*: fine-looking, splendid.

20] *accept my leg*: possibly a reference to a curtsy, as well as to line 5.

27] *blind boy*: Cupid, the Roman god of desire and erotic love.

Which Fate descend (yet such a toy
May take the chit) should shoot again,
Then the next loss would be your brain.   30
Some coy young lass you might adore,
Which would prefer some base Medore,
And all your wit and titles slight,
Embrace a page before a knight.
Then should some noble-minded friend   35
Astolpho-like, to heaven ascend
And, having searchèd near and far,
And found your most capacious jar,
Then being with joy returned again,
You could not then snuff up your brain;   40
Though all your strength you should expose
You want the organ called a nose.
Prodigious the knight remains
Without or nose, or fame, or brains.
Then a bold ordinance struck the title off;   45
Thus the proud Parcae sit and at us scoff.
What now remains? The man at least?
No, surely nothing left but beast.
Then royal favour glued it on again,
And now the knight is bow-dyed and in grain.   50
Then trample not that honour in the dust;
In being a slave to those are slaves to lust.

Note

Sir William Davenant (1606–68), a royalist poet, playwright, and theatre manager, famously lost his nose to syphilis in the early 1630s. Davenant's

---

28] *descend*: will decree. *toy*: thing of little importance.
29] *chit*: brat.
32] *Medore*: a young soldier in Ariosto's epic poem *Orlando Furioso*. Orlando, the hero, falls in love with Angelica, who spurns him for Medore.
36] *Astolpho*: another character in *Orlando Furioso*. Orlando loses his wits after being rejected by Angelica, but Astolpho finds them in a jar on the moon and forces Orlando to snort them.
43] *Prodigious*: freakish, marvellous.
45] *bold ordinance*: probably an allusion to a parliamentary ordinance of 1646 that declared void any title conferred since May 1642 and not confirmed by both houses of parliament. Charles I had conferred a knighthood on Davenant in 1643.
46] *Parcae*: the Fates.
50] *bow-dyed and in grain*: dyed scarlet, and ingrained, permanent.

illness was widely satirised, in publications including poems published in *Certain Verses Written by Several of the Author's Friends* (1653). Davenant was supported by the literary patron and royalist military commander Sir William Cavendish (husband of Margaret Cavendish), but Pulter's poem makes explicit that she does not know Davenant personally; this suggests that she was not part of William Cavendish's royalist coterie of poets and dramatists. For a discussion of Pulter's poem in relation to other satires on Davenant's loss of his nose, see Nevitt, 'The Insults of Defeat'.

The Weeping Wish

O that the tears that trickle from mine eyes
Were placed as blazing comets in the skies,
Then would their numerous and illustrous rays
Turn my sad nights into the brightest days.
O that the sighs that breathe from my sad soul   5
Might fly above the highest star or pole
Unto that God that views my dismal story,
E'en He that crowns my dying hopes with glory.

O that my tears that fall down to the earth
Might give some noble unknown flower birth,   10
Then would Hadassah's more resplendent fame
Outlive the famous Artemisia's name.
The Iris trickles tears from her sad eyes,
And from their salt her offspring doth arise,
But my abortive tears descend in vain,   15
For I can never see those joys again.

Hart's briny tears a bezoar doth condense;
O let mine eyes whole floods of tears dispense,
That I a cordial to my friends may give;
Then though I die, yet I may make them live.   20
I gladly would this good to them impart,
Though, in the doing it, it breaks my heart.
Then let my dying tears a cordial prove,
Seeing I my friends above my life do love.

3] *illustrous*: illustrious.

6] *pole*: a point in the celestial sphere (north and south) about which the stars appear to revolve; the point at which the line of the earth's axis meets the celestial sphere.

11] *Hadassah*: Pulter as author, in a barely disguised pseudonym.

12] *Artemisia*: sister and wife of King Maussollus, ruler of Halicarnassus. After his death in 353 BC, she built for him the magnificent tomb that became one of the seven wonders of the world, the Mausoleum.

13] *Iris*: a flower said to be born from droplets of water shed by its parents.

17] *Hart*: a deer, in a possible homophone with 'heart'. See Pulter's 'Upon the Death of my Dear and Lovely Daughter, J.P.' and Emblem 22; and Bradstreet's 'Another'. *bezoar*: a concretion found in the stomach of a mountain goat that was believed to have medicinal properties as a counter-poison or antidote. See also Emblem 22.

19] *cordial*: restorative drink, an antidote.

Note

This poem, dated 1665, is likely to be one of the latest poems in Pulter's manuscript. The reference to Hadassah draws on her own self-construction as Hadassah in the titles to her poem sequences 'Hadassah's Chaste Fancies' and (for the emblems) 'The Sighs of a Sad Soul Emblematically Breathed Forth by the Noble Hadassah'. The name Hadassah is a variant of Esther (and Hester), the biblical Esther being renowned for her intercession with King Ahasuerus on behalf of her people. The poem's final stanza draws together images of regenerative condolence: the speaker's tears, the bezoar, and the cordial. For extended discussion, see Ross, 'Tears, Bezoars' and *Women, Poetry, and Politics*.

Emblem 4

Virtue once in the Olympics fought a duel,
Her second, Wisdom, that transcendent jewel;
Fortune courageously did her oppose,
And giddily for second, Folly chose.
The sad spectators grieved to see this fray,   5
Fearing that Virtue's side would win the day;
Thus pitying Fortune, and her fellow, Folly,
The city cockneys sat most melancholy.
But see the fate of war: Fortune was blind
And madly laid about her foes to find,   10
Nor cared on who, or where, her blows did light;
Folly as bravely did maintain the fight,
Not valuing what she did, or what she said,
And now the people that were so afraid
'Gan to rejoice. Then Virtue, she gave place,   15
Wisdom drew back with slow but modest pace;
Then acclamations made the welkin ring,
Paeans the people unto Fortune sing.
Folly with Fortune's help did wear the crown;
Virtue with Wisdom both were hissèd down.   20
Then let none by success judge of the cause,
For we have lived (ay me) to see the laws
Of God and Nature basely trampled on,
When bold impiety the vict'ry won;
And such a king killed at this isle before   25
Did never see, nor never will see more,
Unless our God his princely son restore.

2] *second*: in a duel, a person who acts as a representative of the principal, carrying the challenge, arranging locality, and loading weapons.

4] *giddily*: foolishly.

8] *city cockneys*: people born in the City of London, associated by royalists with opposition to the king and the monarchy.

9] Fortuna, the goddess of Fortune, was blind.

10] *laid about*: dealt violent and repeated blows on all sides.

15] *gave place*: yielded.

17] *welkin*: sky, heavens.

25] *such a king*: Charles I, executed on 30 January 1649.

27] *princely son*: Charles, son of Charles I, who became King Charles II of England on 29 May 1660.

Note

This is the fourth poem in Pulter's series of emblems, poems that take an image, text, or situation and draw a moral lesson from it (see the Introduction to this volume). Pulter's emblems date from the 1650s, and Emblem 4 typifies their bitter reflections on the defeat of Charles I and on the follies of Cromwell's supporters (in this poem, 'city cockneys'). The poem looks to consolation in the possible restoration of the monarchy in the form of Charles II, son of Charles I.

Emblem 20

Who can but pity this poor turtle-dove,
Which was so kind and constant to her love,
And since his death his loss she doth deplore;
For his dear sake she'll never couple more.
When others' wanton blood doth nimbly flow,   5
Warmed with the spring, hers then runs cool and slow;
Nor Valentine, though 'tis a tempting tide,
Can make her lay her chaste resolves aside.
Not like that wanton and licentious bird
Who, losing one, a second, and a third,   10
Like that prodigious, bedlam, Belgic beast,
Who had a score of husbands at the least;
A bitter thralldom she deserves to have
Who, being freed so oft, would be a slave.
Shame of her sex! O let her loathèd name   15
Be ne'er enrollèd in the book of fame.
But let Alcestis' and Artemisia's story
Be still remembered to her endless glory.
Some Deborahs, and Annas, sure have been,
But in this age of ours few such are seen.   20
Then ladies, imitate this turtle-dove
And constant be unto one only love;

1–4] Turtle-doves were renowned for their monogamous affection for their mate. See
also Pulter's 'Why must I thus forever be confined', lines 65–71.

9] *wanton and licentious bird*: possibly a sparrow (see Pulter's 'Must I thus ever interdicted
be?', line 10).

11] *prodigious, bedlam*: abnormal, mad. *Belgic*: of or pertaining to the Netherlands.

11–12] Annotations in the margin to the poem explain these lines: 'This monster lived
within 2 miles of Amsterdam. She survived 24 husbands. My uncle, Edward Pulter,
did know her'. Further marginal notes draw a comparison to a story told by St
Jerome (and recounted in a John Donne sermon) about the marriage of a man who
had had twenty wives and a woman who had had twenty-two husbands.

17] *Alcestis*: In Greek mythology, Alcestis was married to Admetus, and was prepared
to die for him. *Artemesia*: sister and wife of King Maussollus, ruler of Halicarnassus.
After his death in 353 BC, she built for him the magnificent tomb that became one
of the seven wonders of the world, the Mausoleum.

19] *Deborahs, and Annas*: Deborah, wife of Lapidoth, was a militant prophetess (Judges
4:4) and is here the model of a virtuous wife. Anna, a prophetess who recognised
the baby Jesus as the Messiah, remained a widow for eighty-four years after her
husband's death (Luke 2:36–37).

Then if your husbands rant it high and game,
Be sure you double not their guilt and shame.
Leave off Hyde Park, Hanes, Oxford John's, and Kate's,   25
Spring, Mulberry Garden, let them have a date;
Buy not these follies at so dear a rate.
These places I know only by their names,
But 'tis these places which do blast your fames.
Who would with their dear reputation part   30
To eat a scurvy cheesecake or a tart?
For such poor follies, who abroad would roam?
Have we not better every day at home?
They say to plays and taverns some do go;
I say no modest ladies will do so.   35
Though countess, duchess, or Protector's daughter
Those places haunt, their follies run not after.
Be modest then and follow mine advice;
You'll find that virtue's pleasanter than vice.
Yet anchorites I would not have you turn,   40
Nor halcyons, nor be your husband's urn,
But chastely live and rather spend your days
In setting forth your great creator's praise,

23] *rant*: to be jovial, boisterous, or uproariously merry; to lead a riotous or dissolute life. *high*: greatly, to excess. *game*: to gamble. (Pulter's previous Emblem 19 criticises men who 'drink, rant, throw the die'.)

25–26] *Hyde Park ... Mulberry Garden*: all parks and taverns popular for socialising and flirtation. Hyde Park was a notorious pleasure-garden in London. 'Hanes' has not been identified. 'Oxford Johns' may be St John's College, Oxford; or it may be a tavern similar to 'Oxford Kate's', which was a tavern by Covent Garden, London, popular with pleasure-seeking royalist women (Eardley, *Lady Hester Pulter*). Spring Garden and Mulberry Garden in London were known for excessive alcohol consumption and socialising. See also Philips, 'A Country Life', lines 66–68.

31] *scurvy*: worthless, contemptible. *cheesecake ... tart*: delicacies served at teahouses in London parks.

36] *Protector's daughter*: Bridget, the eldest daughter of Oliver Cromwell, Lord Protector of England, Scotland, and Ireland from December 1653 to September 1658. Bridget met her second husband, Charles Fleetwood, in St James's Park, and married him less than a year after the death of her first husband, Henry Ireton.

40] *anchorites*: recluses; women who retire from the world for religious reasons.

41] *halcyons*: In Greek mythology, Alcyone is married to Ceyx, who drowns in a shipwreck, leaving her distraught. The gods take pity on the couple and transform them into sea birds called halcyons. *husband's urn*: may be a further reference to Artemisia II, who was said to have drunk the ashes of Maussollus mixed with wine, hence becoming her husband's living urn.

And for diversion pass your idle times
As I do now, in writing harmless rhymes.   45
Then for your honours', and your fair souls' sake,
Both my examples and my counsel take.
In fine, love God, the fountain of all good,
Next those ahead by marriage, grace, and blood.
So let's live here in chaste and virtuous love,   50
As we'll go on eternally above;
Then, o my God, assist me with thy grace,
That when I die I may but change my place.

Note

This emblem moralises on the need for female constancy, beginning with the image of the faithful turtle-dove and comparing it with a series of 'wanton and licentious' birds and women. The poem reveals much about pleasure-seeking activities popular among women in the city. Pulter is highly critical of these activities, and advocates instead that women spend their time in writing godly rhymes.

48] *In fine*: in conclusion.

Emblem 22

The hunted hart when she begins to tire,
Before her vital spirits doth expire,
She every way doth roll her weeping eye;
At last she finds her longed-for dittany,
Which having eat, if she be but alive,   5
It doth her fainting spirit so revive
That she outruns all that her life pursue,
Though they their courage and their cries renew.
Yet she trips on; the hounds their yelping cease,
And she in those sweet shades doth rest in peace;   10
Thus if at any time she be oppressed,
In her loved dittany she findeth rest.
E'en so, a soul which is o'erwhelmed with grief,
And in this empty orb finds no relief,
Though present sorrows doth her heart oppress,   15
And future fears afflict her thoughts no less,
Though her sad soul with suff'rings 'gins to tire,
Her fainting spirit ready to expire,
Though she is pursued by her ghostly foes,
Who all her sins in their true colours shows,   20
Her soul being filled with horrid, hellish fears,
Her heart e'en broke with sighs, her eyes with tears
Being quite dissolved; e'en fainting then she goes
To him, who for her sake his life did lose.
Then, o my God, though sorrows do involve   25
My sinful soul, though I to tears dissolve,
Or though my spirit I suspire to air,
Yet let me trust in thee and not despair;
And when my sorrows and my sins do cease
Let me enjoy thy everlasting peace.   30

1] *The hunted hart*: The hunted, wounded hart is a common spiritual image in the
   literature of the period, deriving from Psalm 42:1: 'As the hart panteth after the
   water brooks, so panteth my soul after thee, O God'.
4] *dittany*: a herb famous for its alleged medicinal virtues and believed to draw arrows
   out of the body; these qualities were also frequently given a spiritual analogue.
14] *empty orb*: this world (a world of sin).
19] *ghostly*: spiritual.
24] *him*: Christ.
25] *involve*: envelop, especially with trouble and difficulties.
27] *suspire*: sigh forth, to breathe out.

Note

The hunted hart that features in this emblem is primarily a spiritual image, representing the soul that runs after Christ. In his *Natural History*, Pliny describes the hart eating the medicinal herb dittany to draw arrows out of its body, but the herb's qualities were often given a spiritual meaning, with the dittany of Christ's love having the power to draw out the shafts of sin. Elsewhere in Pulter's poems, the hart also has implications of the king being pursued by his foes; see the hart image in 'On the Death of my Dear and Lovely Daughter, J.P.'. See Ross, *Women, Poetry, and Politics*.

Katherine Philips (1632–1664)

Katherine Philips was born in London in 1632 to a family with puritan connections: her uncle was a puritan minister and friend of Marvell and Milton, and her aunt was married to a prominent parliamentary lawyer. She was an overtly religious child, able to recite sermons verbatim and committing to memory sections of the Bible, which she had apparently read by the age of four. She was educated at home until the age of eight, and then enrolled at a boarding school for girls in Hackney. Her father died just two years later, and with her mother's next marriage to Sir Richard Phillipps of Pembrokeshire, Katherine was taken to live with her step-family in Wales. At the age of sixteen, in 1648, she married a twenty-four-year old James Philips, a kinsman of her step-father and a substantial landowner in Cardiganshire. For most of her married life, Katherine lived in the small Welsh town of Cardigan, of which her husband was a leading citizen, with occasional visits to London. Her son, Hector, died in infancy in 1655, and a daughter, Katherine, was born in 1656.

Philips's politics were firmly royalist, and she maintained connections in the 1650s to royalist circles in London, including those of the musician Henry Lawes, who set several of her poems to music. Many of her poems express her royalist sympathies, including 'Upon the Double Murder of King Charles I' and 'To Antenor, on a Paper of Mine', a poem in which she is at pains to set her political leanings against those of her husband. James Philips (whom Katherine dubbed 'Antenor' in her poems and letters) supported the Cromwellian government, although he had a reputation among his contemporaries as a moderate, and he served as an MP in parliaments under both Cromwell and Charles II. She composed several poems celebrating rural retirement, imitating and developing the model of Horace and his seventeenth-century followers, including her associate Abraham Cowley. But she also composed a number of overtly political poems, including those in the early 1660s that celebrate the accession of Charles II to the throne.

As a poet, Katherine Philips is best known for poems on the theme of friendship, and for the establishment of a 'Society of Friendship' among her close associates, to whom she assigned pastoral coterie names (her own was 'Orinda'). The most intense expression of emotion in her writings can be found in poems addressed to women. Twenty-one poems are addressed to her 'dearest friend' Anne Owen ('Lucasia'), and nine to Mary Aubrey ('Rosania'), a friend since childhood. Six further poems celebrate the friendship between Rosania and Lucasia. Among Philips's poems, the theme of absence or separation is also especially prominent, partly because of the circumstances of her life in the isolation of rural Wales. Except in brief visits to London, she rarely saw Mary Aubrey after her friend's marriage in December 1651, and though she frequently exchanged visits with Anne Owen, who lived twenty-five miles away, after her second marriage in 1662 Anne, now Lady Dungannon, left Wales to reside in Ireland.

In June 1662 Katherine Philips accompanied her newly married friend to Dublin, where she remained for over a year. Nearly all of Philips's surviving letters date from this period of her life: forty-seven letters to her friend Sir Charles Cotterell, from December 1661 to May 1664, later published as *Letters from Orinda to Poliarchus* (1705), tell of her year in Dublin and her reluctant return to the 'desert' of rural Wales, 'to converse with the rocks and mountains, where Fate has allotted me my abode' (Thomas (ed.), *Collected Works*, vol. 1, pp. 84, 88). Several letters to Cotterell involve delicate negotiations to arrange a visit to London.

Philips actively circulated her poetry in manuscript, and was well known as a manuscript poet in a number of overlapping literary, musical, social, and political circles. Her poem 'To Antenor, on a Paper of Mine' illustrates the political nature of some of the exchanges; other poems, such as her encomium 'To the Right Honourable Alice, Countess of Carbery, on her Enriching Wales with her Presence', serve a more social purpose. Her poems were published by Richard Marriot in 1664, in a volume to which Philips objected in the strongest terms. It is not, however, entirely clear that she had no part in their publication.

Philips returned to London shortly after the publication of *Poems* (1664), but three months later she contracted smallpox. She died at her brother-in-law's house in Fleet Street on 22 June 1664, at the age of thirty-two. She was buried, along with her father, grandparents, and infant son, in the church of St Benet Sherehog in London on 23 June. A revised edition of her *Poems* was published in 1667 (see Figure 4), with an extensive collection of prefatory poems praising 'The Matchless Orinda'.

Figure 4 Frontispiece from Katherine Philips, *Poems by the Most Deservedly Admired Mrs Katherine Philips, the Matchless Orinda* (1667).

From the 'Tutin' manuscript

To my Dearest Antenor, on his Parting

Though it be just to grieve when I must part
With him that is the guardian of my heart,
Yet by a happy change, the loss of mine
Is with advantage paid, in having thine.
And I (by that dear guest instructed) find   5
Absence can do no hurt to souls combined,
And we were born to love; brought to agree
By the impressions of divine decree
So when united nearer we became,
It did not weaken but increase our flame.   10
Unlike to those who distant joys admire
But slight them when possessed of their desire
Each of our souls did its own temper fit
And in the other's mould so fashioned it
That now our inclinations both are grown   15
Like to our interests and persons, one.
And souls whom such a union fortifies
Passion can ne'er betray nor fate surprise.
        Now, as in watches, though we do not know
When the hand moves we find it still doth go,   20
So I by secret sympathy inclined
Will, absent, meet and understand thy mind.
And thou at thy return, shalt find thy heart
Still safe, with all the love thou did impart;
For though that treasure I have ne'er deserved   25
It shall with strong religion be preserved.
But besides this thou shalt in me survey
Thy self reflected while thou art away.
For what some forward arts do undertake
The images of absent friends to make,   30
And represent their actions in a glass
Friendship itself can only bring to pass:
That magic which both fate and time beguiles
And in a moment runs a thousand miles.
So in my breast thy picture drawn shall be,   35

Title] *Antenor*: Philips's coterie name for her husband, James Philips.

My guide, life, object, friend and destiny,
And none shall know, though they employ their wit,
Which is the right Antenor, thou or it.

Note

This poem demonstrates Philips's keen interest in the striking imagery characteristic of metaphysical poets, and especially that of John Donne, as here she deploys paradox and spatial imagery and compares marital love to the workings of a mechanical device (compare Donne's 'A Valediction: Forbidding Mourning', another poem about parting from a spouse or lover with similar features).

A Retired Friendship, to Ardelia, 23rd August 1651

1.

Come, my Ardelia, to this bower
Where, kindly mingling souls a while,
Let's innocently spend an hour
And at all serious follies smile.

2.

Here is no quarrelling for crowns   5
Nor fear of changes in our fate,
No trembling at the great ones' frowns
Nor any slavery of state.

3.

Here's no disguise, nor treachery,
Nor any deep concealed design,   10
From blood and plots this place is free
And calm as are those looks of thine.

4.

Here let us sit, and bless our stars
Who did such happy quiet give,
As that removed from noise of wars,   15
In one another's hearts we live.

5.

Why should we entertain a fear?
Love cares not how the world is turned;
If crowds of dangers should appear
Yet friendship can be unconcerned.   20

6.

We wear about us such a charm
No horror can be our offence,
For mischief's self can do no harm
To friendship and to innocence.

Title] *Ardelia*: this is the only poem by Philips that addresses Ardelia, whose identity
is unknown. *23rd August 1651*: some of Philips's poems have dates included in the
manuscript. See Coolahan, '"We live by chance"'.

7.

Let's mark how soon Apollo's beams   25
Command the flocks to quit their meat,
And not entreat the neighbour streams
To quench their thirst but cool their heat.

8.

In such a scorching age as this,   30
Whoever would not seek a shade
Deserve their happiness to miss,
As having their own peace betrayed.

9.

But we (of one another's mind
Assured) the boist'rous world disdain,   35
With quiet souls and unconfined,
Enjoy what princes wish in vain.

Note

As well as celebrating a (possibly erotic) friendship, this poem, like many by Philips, extols the virtues of retreat and withdrawal, though this position can also be seen as a political statement in itself, suggesting solidarity with other royalists during the political adversity of the 1650s. See Anderson, *Friendship's Shadows*; Chalmers, *Royalist Women Writers*; Barash, *English Women's Poetry*; and Shifflett, 'How Many Virtues'.

25] *Apollo*: Apollo is a sun god from Greek and Roman mythology, and a patron of music and poetry.
29] *scorching age*: For the political events of 1651, see Philips, 'On the 3rd September 1651'.
33–34] See John Donne, 'A Valediction Forbidding Mourning', line 19.

Friendship's Mysteries, to my Dearest Lucasia

Set by Mr H. Lawes

Come, my Lucasia, since we see
That miracles men's faith do move
By wonder and by prodigy,
To the dull, angry world let's prove
There's a religion in our love.   5

For though we were designed t'agree
That fate no liberty destroys,
But our election is as free
As angels' who, with greedy choice,
Are yet determined to their joys.   10

Our hearts are doubled by their loss,
Here mixture is addition grown,
We both diffuse, and both engross
And we, whose minds are so much one,
Never, yet ever, are alone.   15

We count our own captivity
Than thrones more great and innocent;
'Twere banishment to be set free
Since we wear fetters whose intent
Not bondage is, but ornament.   20

Divided joys are tedious found
And griefs united easier grow;
We are our selves but by rebound
And all our titles shuffled so
Both princes, and both subjects too.   25

Our hearts are mutual victims laid
While they (such power in friendship lies)
Are altars, priests, and offerings made
And each heart which thus kindly dies
Grows deathless by the sacrifice.   30

Title] *Lucasia*: the coterie name that Philips used for her friend Anne Owen. *Mr. H. Lawes*: Henry Lawes, a court composer who set to music poems by Philips as well as by prominent royalists such as Thomas Carew.
3] *prodigy*: an omen or sign.
13] *diffuse*: disperse, become less dense. *engross*: thicken, become more dense.

Note

As in 'Friendship in Emblem or the Seal, to my Dearest Lucasia', Philips evokes John Donne's imagery here. In 'The Sun Rising' Donne's speaker asserted 'She's all States, and all Princes, I', and this is evoked and perhaps rebuked by Philips's use of the same imagery but for equality rather than conquest: 'And all our titles shuffled so / Both princes, and both subjects too'. The imagery of mixing and dispersing in the third stanza also evokes metaphysical conceptions of friendship. Philips deploys paradoxes and hyperbole, common features of Cavalier poetry, in phrases such as 'Grows deathless by the sacrifice', ''Twere banishment to be set free', and 'doubled by their loss'. See Andreadis, 'Reconfiguring Early Modern Friendship'; Barash, *English Women's Poetry*; Chalmers, *Royalist Women Writers*.

Content, to my Dearest Lucasia

Content, the false world's best disguise,
The search, and faction of the wise,
Is so abstruse and hid in night
That, like that fairy Redcross knight
Who treacherous falsehood for clear truth had got,   5
Men think they have it, when they have it not.

For courts Content would gladly own
But she ne'er dwelt about a throne,
And to be flattered rich or great
Are things that do man's senses cheat   10
But grave experience long since this did see
Ambition and Content could ne'er agree.

Some vainer would Content expect
From what their bright outsides reflect,
But sure Content is more divine   15
Than to be digged from rock or mine,
And they that know her beauties will confess
She needs no lustre from a glittering dress.

In mirth some place her, but she scorns
Th'assistance of such crackling thorns   20
Nor owes herself to such thin sport
That is so sharp and yet so short,
And painters tell us they the same strokes place
To make a laughing and a weeping face.

Others there are that place Content   25
In liberty from government,
But who his passions do deprave
Though free from shackles is a slave;
Content and bondage differ only then
When we are chained by vices, not by men.   30

Title] *Content*: contentment. *Lucasia*: the coterie name that Philips used for her friend
     Anne Owen.
4] *fairy Redcross knight*: a character from Edmund Spenser's *The Faerie Queene*.
13] *Some vainer*: some vainer people.

Some think the camp Content does know
And that she sits o'th'victor's brow
But in his laurel there is seen
Often a cypress bough between
Nor will Content herself in that place give   35
Where noise and tumult and destruction live.

But the most discreet believe
The schools this jewel do receive,
And thus far true without dispute:
Knowledge is still the sweetest fruit.   40
But while men seek for truth they lose their peace
And who heaps knowledge, sorrow doth increase.

But now some sullen hermit smiles
And thinks he all the world beguiles,
And that his cell and dish contain   45
What all mankind do wish in vain;
But yet his pleasure's followed with a groan
For man was never made to be alone.

Content herself best comprehends
Betwixt two souls and they two friends   50
Whose either joys in both are fixed
And multiplied by being mixed,
Whose minds and interests are so the same
Their very griefs imparted lose that name.

These far removed from all bold noise   55
And – what is worse – all hollow joys,
Who never had a mean design
Whose flame is serious and divine,
And calm and even, must contented be
For they've both union and society.   60

31] *camp*: military camp.
34] *cypress bough*: a coniferous tree often associated with mourning; here it appears among the laurel, a plant associated with military victory as well as literary achievement.

Then, my Lucasia, we who have
Whatever love can give or crave,
With scorn or pity can survey
The trifles which the most betray.
With innocence and perfect friendship fired,   65
By virtue joined, and by our choice retired;

Whose mirrors are the crystal brooks
Or else each other's hearts, and looks,
Who cannot wish for other things,
Than privacy and friendship brings,   70
Whose thoughts and persons changed and mixed are one
Enjoy content, or else the world has none.

Note

This poem explores the ideal of contentment. Philips suggests the various proposed locales and sources of contentment: courts, physical beauty, mirth, autonomy, military victory, academic knowledge, hermit-like solitude. She rejects all these in favour of the friendship between Lucasia and herself, diverging from poets who champion solitude and placing her own take on Cavalier sociability by promoting female friendship rather than male friendship or heterosexual romantic companionship.

Katherine Philips

Friendship in Emblem, or the Seal, to my Dearest Lucasia

1.

The hearts thus intermixed speak
A love that no bold shock can break,
For joined and growing, both in one,
Neither can be disturbed alone.

2.

That means a mutual knowledge too,   5
For what is't either heart can do,
Which by its panting sentinel
It does not to the other tell?

3.

That friendship hearts so much refines
If nothing but itself designs   10
The hearts are free from lower ends
For each point to the other tends.

4.

They flame, 'tis true, and several ways
But still those flames do so much raise
That while to either they incline   15
They yet are noble and divine.

5.

From smoke or hurt those flames are free
From grossness or mortality,
The hearts (like Moses' bush presumed)
Warmed and enlightened, not consumed.   20

6.

The compasses that stand above
Express this great immortal love,
For friends like them can prove this true,
They are and yet they are not two.

Title] *Lucasia*: the coterie name that Philips used for her friend Anne Owen.
20] *not consumed*: The hearts do not burn up but are 'Warmed and enlightened'.

7.

And in their posture is expressed   25
Friendship's exalted interest;
Each follows where the other leans
And what each does, the other means.

8.

And as when one foot does stand fast,
And t'other circles seeks to cast,   30
The steady part does regulate
And make the wanderer's motion straight.

9.

So friends are only two in this
T'reclaim each other when they miss
For whosoe'er will grossly fall,   35
Can never be a friend at all.

10.

And as that useful instrument
For even lines was ever meant,
So friendship from good angels springs
To teach the world heroic things.   40

11.

As those are found out in design
To rule and measure every line,
So friendship governs actions best
Prescribing law to all the rest.

12.

And as in nature nothing's set   45
So just as lines and numbers met,
So compasses for these being made
Do friendship's harmony persuade.

13.

And like to them so friends may own
Extension, not division: 50
Their points, like bodies, separate,
But head, like souls, knows no such fate.

14.

And as each part so well is knit
That their embraces even fit,
So friends are such by destiny,   55
And no third can the place supply.

15.

There needs no motto to the seal
But that we may the mine reveal
To the dull eye it was thought fit
That friendship only should be writ.   60

16.

But as there is degrees of bliss
So there's no friendship meant by this
But such as will transmit to fame
Lucasia's and Orinda's name.

Note

Here Philips draws together several influences and allusions to create a
very original poem. The poem was not accompanied by an image but
alludes in its title to emblem books in which woodcut images (here
presumably a pair of flaming, interlinked hearts) were followed by poems
and mottos explaining their symbolism. Philips also alludes to John
Donne's 'A Valediction: Forbidding Mourning' which famously uses a
pair of compasses as an image for the lovers who are parted but never
fully separate. See Andreadis, 'Sapphic-Platonics'; Barash, *English Women's
Poetry*; Chalmers, *Royalist Women Writers*.

57] *motto ... seal*: 'seal' here refers to the emblem of the title, imagining it as used to
seal a letter or document. Emblem books would often have explanatory mottos but
Philips suggests this is not necessary as the seal's meaning is self-evident from
looking at the friends.

From the 'Tutin' manuscript, reverse

The World

We falsely think it due unto our friends
That we should grieve for their too early ends;
He that surveys the world with serious eyes
And strips her from her gross and weak disguise
Shall find 'tis injury to mourn their fate.   5
He only dies untimely who dies late.
For if 'twere told to children in the womb
To what a stage of mischief they must come,
Could they foresee with how much toil and sweat
Men court that gilded nothing, being great,   10
What pains they take not to be what they seem
Rating their bliss by others' false esteem,
And sacrificing their content to be
Guilty of grave, and serious vanity;
How each condition hath its proper thorns   15
And what one man admires another scorns.
How frequently their happiness they miss
And, so far from agreeing what it is,
That the same person we can hardly find
Who is an hour together in a mind;   20
Sure they would beg a period of their breath
And what we call their birth would count their death.
Mankind are mad; for none can live alone
Because their joys stand by comparison,
And yet they quarrel at society   25
And strive to kill they know not whom nor why.
We all live by mistake, delight in dreams,
Lost to our selves, and dwelling in extremes;
Rejecting what we have, though ne'er so good,
And prizing what we never understood.   30
Compared to our boisterous inconstancy
Tempests are calm, and discords, harmony.
Hence we reverse the world and yet do find
The God that made, can hardly please our mind.
We live by chance, and slip into events,   35
Have all of beasts except their innocence;

The soul, which no man's pow'r can reach, a thing
That makes each woman man, each man a king,
Doth so much lose and from its height so fall
That some continued to have no soul at all.   40
'Tis either not observed or (at the best)
By passion sought, withal by sin depressed;
Freedom of will, God's image, is forgot
And if we know it, we improve it not.
But thoughts (though nothing can be more our own),   45
Are still unguided, very seldom known.
Time 'scapes our hands as water in a sieve;
We come to die, e'er we begin to live.
Truth (the most suitable and noble prize),
Food of our spirits, yet neglected lies.   50
Errors and shadows are our choice, and we
Owe our perdition to our own decree.
If we search truth we make it more obscure
And when it shines we can't the light endure.
For most men who plod on, and eat and drink,   55
Have nothing less their business than to think,
And those few that inquire how small a share
Of truth they find! How dark their notions are;
That serious evenness that calms the breast,
And in a tempest can bestow a rest   60
We either not attempt, or else decline,
By every trifle snatched from our design.
(Others he must in his deceits involve,
Who is not true unto his own resolve)
We govern not ourselves, but loose the reins,   65
Counting our bondage to a thousand chains.
And with as many slaveries content,
As there are tyrants ready to torment.
We live upon a rack extended still
To one extreme or both, but always ill.   70
For since our fortune is not understood,
We suffer less from bad than from the good.
The sting is better dressed, and longer lasts,
As surfeits are more dangerous than fasts.
And, to complete the misery to us,   75
We see extremes are still contiguous,
And as we run so fast from what we hate

(Like squibs on ropes to know no middle state),
So (outward storms strengthened by us) we find
Our fortune as disordered as our mind.   80
But that's excused by this, it does its part:
A treacherous world befits a treacherous heart.
All ills our own; the outward storms we loathe
Receive from us their birth, or sting, or both.
And that our vanity be past a doubt,   85
'Tis one new vanity to find it out.
Happy are they to whom God gives a grave
And from themselves, as from his wrath, doth save.
'Tis good not to be born, but if we must
The next good is soon to return to dust,   90
When th'uncaged soul, fled to eternity,
Shall rest and live and sing and love and see
Here we but crawl and grope and play and cry,
Are first our own, then others' enemy.
But there shall be defaced both stain and score,   95
For time and death and sin shall be no more.

Note

'The World' turns against the pleasures of the world, developing the
conventional theme of *contemptus mundi*. Philips is often thought of as
a secular poet, writing about politics and friendship rather than religious
subjects, but this is one of several religious poems gathered at the back
of her Tutin manuscript.

78] *squibs on ropes*: fireworks.

The Soul

1.

How vain a thing is man, whose noblest part,
    That soul which through the world doth roam,
Traverses heav'n, finds out the depths of art,
    Yet is so ignorant at home!

2.

In every brook or mirror we can find   5
    Reflections of our face to be,
But a true optic to present our mind
    We hardly get, and darkly see.

3.

Yet in the search, after ourselves we run,
    Actions and causes we survey,   10
And when the weary chase is almost done
    From our own quest we slip away.

4.

'Tis strange and sad that, since we do believe
    We have a soul must never die,
There are so few that can a reason give   15
    How it obtains that life or why.

5.

I wonder not to find those that know most
    Profess so much their ignorance,
Since in their own souls greatest wits are lost
    And of themselves have scarce a glance.   20

6.

But somewhat sure doth here obscurely lie
    That above dross would fain advance,
And pants, and catches at eternity,
    As 'twere its own inheritance.

7] *optic*: a device aiding vision.
22] *dross*: scum produced in the process of smelting, and figuratively a waste product.
    fain: gladly.

7.

A soul self-moved which can dilate, contract,   25
    Pierces and judges things unseen;
But this gross heap of matter cannot act
    Unless impulsèd from within.

8.

Distance and quantity, to bodies due,
    The state of souls cannot admit,   30
And all the contraries which nature knew
    Meet there, nor hurt themselves nor it.

9.

God never made body so bright and clean
    Which good and evil could discern,
What these words, honesty and honour, mean,   35
    The soul alone knows how to learn.

10.

And though ('tis true) she is imprisoned here,
    Yet hath she notions of her own,
Which sense doth only jog, awake and clear,
    But cannot at the first make known.   40

11.

The soul her own felicity hath laid
    And, independent on the sense,
Sees the weak terrors which the world invade
    With pity or with negligence.

12.

So unconcerned, she lives so much above   45
    The rubbish of her clotty gaol
That nothing doth her energy improve,
    So much as when those structures fail.

27] *gross*: massive; material, bodily (rather than spiritual).
28] *impulsèd*: impelled.
46] *clotty*: describing a mass or lump.

13.

She's then a substance subtle, strong and pure,
      So immaterial, and refined,   50
As speaks her from the body's fate secure
      As wholly of a different kind.

14.

Religion for reward in vain would look,
      Virtue were doomed to misery;
All actions were like babbles in a brook   55
      Were't not for immortality.

15.

And, as that conqueror who millions spent
      Thought it too mean to give a mite,
So the world's judge can never be content
      To bestow less than infinite.   60

16.

Treason against eternal majesty
      Must have eternal justice too,
And since unbounded love did satisfy,
      He will unbounded mercy show.

17.

It is our narrow thoughts shortens these things   65
      By their companion flesh inclined
Which, feeling its own weakness, gladly brings
      The same opinion to the mind.

18.

We stifle our own sun, and live in shade;
      But where its beams do once appear   70
They make that person of himself afraid
      And to his own acts most severe.

55] *babbles*: incoherent noise; the murmur of flowing water.
58] *mite*: a little amount, a small coin of low value.

19.

For ways to sin close, and our breasts disguise
    From outward search we soon may find
But who can his own soul bribe or surprise   75
    Or sin without a sting behind?

20.

He that commands himself is more a prince
    Than he who nations keep in awe,
And those who yield to what their souls convince
    Shall never need another law.   80

Note

One of Philips's religious poems, this could be compared to Cavendish's poems such as 'Of Stars' and 'A Dialogue betwixt Man and Nature'. Where Cavendish stresses man's inadequacies in terms of knowledge and understanding of the natural world, Philips takes a more specifically Christian stance in stressing the narrowness of man's earthly existence compared with the immortal soul.

Invitation to the Country

Be kind, my dear Rosania, though 'tis true
Thy friendship will become thy penance too.
Though there be nothing can reward the pain,
Nothing to satisfy or entertain,
Though all be empty, wild, and like to me   5
Who make new troubles in my company,
Yet is the action more obliging great
'Tis hardship only makes desert complete.
But yet to prove mixtures all things compound
There may in this be some advantage found,   10
For a retirement from the noise of towns
Is that for which some kings have left their crowns,
And conquerors whose laurels pressed their brow
Have changed it for the quiet myrtle bough.
For titles, honours, and the world's address   15
Are things too cheap to make up happiness;
The easy tribute of a giddy race
And paid less to the person than the place.
So false, reflected, and so short, content,
Is that which fortune and opinion lent   20
That who most tried it, have of fate complained
With titles burdened and to greatness chained.
For they alone enjoyed what they possessed
Who relished most and understood it best
And yet that understanding made them know   25
The empty swift dispatch of all below;
So that what most can outward things endear
Is the best means to make them disappear.
And ev'n that tyrant sense doth these destroy
As more officious to our grief than joy.   30
Thus all the glittering world is but a cheat
Obtruding on our sense things gross, for great.
But he that can enquire and undisguise,
Will soon perceive the sting that hidden lies

1] *Rosania*: the coterie name that Philips used for her friend Mary Montagu (née Aubrey).

14] *myrtle*: a plant symbolising love (and sometimes also constancy and immortality) and contrasted with the laurel, here symbolising public achievement such as military victory or literary plaudits.

And find no joys merit esteem but those   35
Whose scene lies wholly at our own dispose,
Man unconcerned without, himself may be
His own both prospect and security.
Kings may be slaves by their own passions hurled
But who commands himself, commands the world.   40
A country life assists this study best
When no distractions doth the soul arrest:
There heav'n and earth lie open to our view,
There we search nature, and its author too,
Possessed with freedom and a real state   45
Look down on vice, on vanity, and fate.
There (my Rosania) will we, mingling souls,
Pity the folly which the world controls,
And all those grandeurs which the most do prize
We either can enjoy, or will despise.   50

Note

As in many of her poems, Philips here brings together praise of retreat
and praise of friendship. The poem draws on Stoicism in its focus on
self-control. Furthermore, it reacts to neo-Platonism in her rejection of
sense and the bodily ('gross', line 32) in favour of the mingling of souls.
See also Pulter's 'The Invitation into the Country, to my Dear
Daughters'.

Katherine Philips

On the 3rd September 1651

As when the glorious magazine of light
Approaches to his canopy of night,
He with new splendour clothes his dying rays
And double brightness to his beams conveys;
As if to brave and check his ending fate   5
Puts on his highest looks in's lowest state,
Dressed in such terror as to make us all
Be anti-Persians and adore his fall.
Then quits the world, depriving it of day,
While every herb and plant does droop away: 10
So when our gasping English royalty
Perceived her period now was drawing nigh
She summons her whole strength to give one blow
To raise herself, or pull down others too.
Big with revenge and hope she now spake more   15
Of terror than in many months before,
And musters her attendants or to save
Her from, or wait upon her to the grave.
Yet but enjoyed the miserable fate
Of setting majesty, to die in state.   20
Unhappy kings! who cannot keep a throne
Nor be so fortunate to fall alone!
Their weight sinks others: Pompey could not fly
But half the world must bear him company;
Thus captive Samson could not life conclude   25
Unless attended with a multitude.
Who'd trust to greatness now, whose food is air

1] *magazine of light*: the sun. *magazine*: storehouse.
8] *anti-Persians*: Persians were thought to be sun-worshippers.
12] *period*: end.
16] *many months before*: the period before the Battle of Worcester had seen smaller royalist uprisings.
17–18] *or ... or*: either ... or.
23] *Pompey*: The Roman leader Pompeius Magnus (106–48 BC) was deposed, exiled, and then decapitated, providing imaginative connections with both Charles I and Charles II in the period. Philips would later translate a French play about the Roman leader. Her translation of Corneille's *Pompey* was performed and printed in Dublin in 1663. See Chalmers, *Royalist Women Writers*, p. 88.
25] *captive Samson*: Blinded and imprisoned, Samson pulled down the temple filled with Philistines, killing them along with himself (Judges 16:25–30).
27] *whose food is air*: greatness feeds on nothing, is insubstantial.

173

Whose ruin sudden, and whose end despair?
Who would presume, upon his glorious birth
Or quarrel for a spacious share of earth   30
That sees such diadems become thus cheap
And heroes tumble in the common heap?
O! Give me virtue then, which sums up all
And firmly stands when crowns and sceptres fall.

Note

King Charles II and his largely Scottish army were defeated by Oliver
Cromwell's forces at the Battle of Worcester on 3 September 1651. Charles
fled, and the defeat ended royalist hopes for a restoration of the monarchy
by force. In this poem Philips explores the conventional monarchical
sun imagery and adapts it strikingly for the plight, and even failings, of
the royalist cause. See also Hutchinson's Elegy 2, 'To the Sun Shining
into her Chamber', and Dryden, *Astraea redux*.

2 Corinthians 5:19, God was in Christ reconciling the world
to himself, 8th April 1653

When God, contracted to humanity,
Could sigh and suffer, could be sick and die,
When all that heap of miracles combined
To form the greatest, which was, save mankind;
Then God took stand in Christ, studying a way   5
How to repair the ruined world's decay.
His love, power, wisdom must some means procure
His mercy to advance, justice secure;
And since man was in so much misery hurled
It cost him more to save, than make the world.   10
O what a desperate lump of sins had we
When God must plot, for our felicity;
When God must beg us that he may forgive;
And die himself before mankind could live?
And what still are we when our king in vain   15
Begs his lost rebels to be friends again!
What floods of love proceed from Heaven's smile
At once to pardon, and to reconcile!
O wretched men who dare your God confine
Like those who separate what he does join.   20
Go, stop the rivers with an infant's hand;
Or count with your arithmetic the sand;
Forbid the light! the fertile earth persuade
To shut her bosom from the lab'rer's spade!
And yield your God (if these cannot be done)   25
As universal as the sea, or sun.
What God hath made he therefore cannot hate,
For it's one act, to love and to create.
And he's too perfect: full of majesty
To need additions from our misery.   30
He hath a father's, not a tyrant's joy,
'Tis equal pow'r to save, as to destroy.
Did there ten thousand worlds to ruin fall:
One God would save, one Christ redeem them all.

Title] *2 Corinthians 5:19*: 'To wit, that God was in Christ, reconciling the world unto
    himself, not imputing their trespasses unto them, and hath committed unto us the
    word of reconciliation'.
33] *Did there*: if it were to happen that.

Be silenced then, you narrow souls, take heed   35
Lest you restrain the mercy you will need
But o! my soul, from these be different,
Imitate thou a nobler precedent.
As God with open arms the world does woo
Learn thou like him to be enlarged too;   40
As he begs thy consent to pardon thee
Learn to submit unto thy enemy;
As he stands ready thee to entertain
Be thou as forward to return again;
As he was crucified for, and by, thee,   45
Crucify thou what caused him agony;
And like to him be mortified to men,
Die to the world, as he died for it then.

Note

8 April 1653 was Good Friday, and Philips engages closely with a biblical passage focusing on God's reconciliation with mankind through the crucifixion of Christ. There may also be some political bite in Philips's use of the common characterisation of God as 'our king' (line 15), as she is writing in a king-less state (she notes the date of 1653). This same political acumen is apparent in her assertion that God has 'a father's, not a tyrant's joy' (line 31).

From *Poems* (1664)

Upon the Double Murder of King Charles I, in Answer to a Libellous Copy of Rhymes Made by Vavasor Powell

I think not on the state, nor am concerned
Which way soever the great helm is turned:
But as that son whose father's dangers nigh
Did force his native dumbness, and untie
The fettered organs; so here's a fair cause   5
That will excuse the breach of nature's laws.
Silence were now a sin, nay passion now
Wise men themselves for merit would allow.
What noble eye could see (and careless pass)
The dying lion kicked by every ass?   10
Has Charles so broke God's laws, he must not have
A quiet crown, nor yet a quiet grave?
Tombs have been sanctuaries, thieves lie there
Secure from all their penalty and fear.
Great Charles his double misery was this: 15
Unfaithful friends, ignoble enemies.
Had any heathen been this prince's foe,
He would have wept to see him injured so.
His title was his crime, they'd reason good
To quarrel at the right they had withstood.   20
He broke God's laws, and therefore he must die;
And what shall then become of thee and I?
Slander must follow treason; but yet stay,
Take not our reason with our king away.
Though you have seized upon all our defence,   25
Yet do not sequester our common sense.

1] *I think not on the state*: see Philips's 'A Country Life', line 46.
3] *that son*: in Herodotus, the mute son of King Croesus who, according to prophecy, would begin to speak only on an unlucky day. When Croesus is about to be killed by a Persian invader, his son calls for him to be spared.
10] In a fable by Phaedrus, the dying lion is attacked by his old adversaries, the boar and the bull, but 'seem[s] to die a second death' when kicked by the cowardly ass.
21] Thomas (ed.), *Collected Works*, vol. 1, suggests that this is likely to be a line from Powell's poem; it is the 'reason' of line 19.
26] *sequester*: confiscate. Sequestration of royalist lands was common during the English republic.

But I admire not at this new supply:
No bounds will hold those who at sceptres fly.
Christ will be King, but I ne'er understood
His subjects built his kingdom up with blood,   30
Except their own; or that he would dispense
With his commands, though for his own defence.
Oh! to what height of horror are they come
Who dare pull down a crown, tear up a tomb?

Note

Philips is replying here to verses written by Vavasor Powell (1617–70), a radical Fifth Monarchist and colleague of her husband, James Philips. The poem landed her in hot water, with her parliamentarian husband's adversary Jenkin Jones threatening to humiliate him by publishing his wife's royalist poem. This provoked Philips's subsequent poem 'To Antenor, on a Paper of Mine which J. Jones Threatens to Publish to Prejudice him'.

Katherine Philips

On the Numerous Access of the English to Wait upon the King in Flanders

Hasten, great prince, unto thy British Isles,
Or all thy subjects will become exiles.
To thee they flock, thy presence is their home,
As Pompey's residence made Afric Rome.
They that asserted thy just cause go hence   5
To testify their joy and reverence;
And those that did not, now, by wonder taught,
Go to confess and expiate their fault.
So that if thou dost stay, thy gasping land
Will itself empty on the Belgic sand: 10
Where the affrighted Dutchman does profess
He thinks it an invasion, not address.
As we unmonarched were for want of thee,
So till thou come we shall unpeopled be.
None but the close fanatic will remain,   15
Who by our loyalty his ends will gain:
And he th'exhausted land will quickly find
As desolate a place as he designed.
For England (though grown old with woes) will see
Her long-denied and sovereign remedy.   20
So when old Jacob could but credit give
That his so long-lost Joseph did still live,
(Joseph that was preserved to restore
Their lives that would have taken his before)
'It is enough', said he, 'to Egypt I   25
Will go, and see him once before I die'.

Note

This is one of Philips's many panegyrics on the restoration of Charles
II in 1660, exhorting Charles to hasten his journey back to Britain.
Charles left Brussels for the Netherlands on 30 March 1660.

Title] *Access*: going or coming into the presence of a person.
4] The Roman general Pompeius Magnus (106–48 BC) ruled unofficially in Africa.
15] *close*: secret.
21–26] Joseph, the favourite son of Jacob, was sold into slavery by his jealous brothers.
    Joseph rose out of slavery by saving Egypt from famine, and when Jacob was told
    that Joseph was still alive, he spoke the words in lines 25–26. See Genesis 45:25–28.

Arion on a Dolphin, to his Majesty at his Passage into England

Whom does this stately navy bring?
O! 'tis Great Britain's glorious king.
Convey him then, you winds and seas,
Swift as desire and calm as peace.
In your respect let him survey 5
What all his other subjects pay;
And prophesy to them again
The splendid smoothness of his reign.
Charles and his mighty hopes you bear:
A greater now than Caesar's here, 10
Whose veins a richer purple boast
Than ever hero's yet engrossed;
Sprung from a father so august,
He triumphs in his very dust.
In him two miracles we view: 15
His virtue and his safety too,
For when compelled by traitors' crimes
To breathe and bow in foreign climes,
Exposed to all the rigid fate
That does on withered greatness wait, 20
Had plots for life and conscience laid,
By foes pursued, by friends betrayed;
Then Heaven, his secret potent friend,
Did him from drugs and stabs defend;
And, what's more yet, kept him upright 25
'Midst flattering hope and bloody fight.
Cromwell his whole right never gained,
Defender of the Faith remained,
For which his predecessors fought
And writ, but none so dearly bought. 30
Never was prince so much besieged,

Title] *Arion*: a Greek lyric poet, borne to safe land on a dolphin after being thrown overboard by Corinthian sailors.
10] *greater*: Charles is a greater sovereign than Julius Caesar, who invaded England from Gaul in 55 and 54 BC.
12] *engrossed*: thickened, swollen.
28] *Defender of the Faith*: Pope Leo X granted Henry this title in 1521, and all subsequent English monarchs took it on. Cromwell refused the crown and so this title also.

At home provoked, abroad obliged;
Nor ever man resisted thus,
No not great Athanasius.
No help of friends could, or foes' spite,   35
To fierce invasion him invite.
Revenge to him no pleasure is,
He spared their blood who gaped for his;
Blushed any hands the English crown
Should fasten on him but their own.   40
As peace and freedom with him went,
With him they came from banishment.
That he might his dominions win,
He with himself did first begin:
And, that best victory obtained,   45
His kingdom quickly he regained.
Th'illustrious suff'rings of this prince
Did all reduce, and all convince;
He only lived with such success,
That the whole world would fight with less.   50
Assistant kings could but subdue
Those foes which he can pardon too.
He thinks no slaughter-trophies good,
Nor laurels dipped in subjects' blood,
But with a sweet resistless art   55
Disarms the hand, and wins the heart;
And, like a god, doth rescue those
Who did themselves and him oppose.
Go, wondrous Prince, adorn that throne
Which birth and merit make your own,   60
And in your mercy brighter shine
Than in the glories of your line;
Find love at home, and abroad fear,
And veneration everywhere.
Th'united world will you allow   65
Their chief, to whom the English bow;
And monarchs shall to yours resort,

34] *Athanasius*: St Athanasius (c. 296–373), Bishop of Alexandria, exiled from his see
    five times between 336 and 366 in the face of political persecution.
37–38] Charles is merciful to his enemies. On 4 April 1660, Charles offered a general
    pardon as part of the Declaration of Breda, and parliament then passed the Act of
    Indemnity and Oblivion in August. See also Dryden, *Astraea redux*, lines 260–61.

As Sheba's queen to Judah's court,
Returning thence, constrainèd more
To wonder, envy, and adore.   70
Disgusted Rome will hate your crown,
But she shall tremble at your frown.
For England shall (ruled and restored by you)
The suppliant world protect, or else subdue.

Note

This is one of a number of panegyric poems on Charles that Philips
wrote on his return to England in May 1660, his restoration, and his
coronation as Charles II. He had been in exile in Europe for almost nine
years. He was proclaimed king in London on 8 May 1660; he boarded
ship in the Netherlands on 23 May; and he arrived in London on 29
May.

68] See 1 Kings 10:1–13.

On the Fair Weather Just at Coronation

So clear a season, and so snatched from storms,
Shows heaven delights to see what man performs.
Well knew the sun, if such a day were dim,
It would have been an injury to him;
For then a cloud had from his eye concealed   5
The noblest sight that ever he beheld.
He therefore checked th'invading rains we feared,
And a more bright parenthesis appeared,
So that we knew not which looked most content,
The king, the people, or the firmament.   10
But the solemnity once fully past,
The storm returned with an impetuous haste,
And heaven and earth each other to outdo,
Vied both in canons and in fireworks too.
So Israel passed through the divided flood,   15
While in obedient heaps the ocean stood,
But the same sea (the Hebrews once on shore)
Returned in torrents where it was before.

Note

Charles II's coronation took place at Westminster Abbey on 23 April
1661. Philips's poem is one of a number of contemporary accounts
describing a thunderstorm that immediately followed the event and casting
it in auspicious terms. Samuel Pepys, the diarist, recounts: 'And strange
it is, to think that all is done and the King out of the hall; and then it
fell a-raining and thundering and lightening as I have not seen it do some
years – which people did take great notice of the blessing of the work of
these two days – which is a great foolery, to take too much notice of
such things' (23 April 1661).

7] *checked*: stopped in progress.
8] *parenthesis*: an interlude, a hiatus.
15–18] See Exodus 14:21–29.

On the Death of the Queen of Bohemia

Although the most do with officious heat
Only adore the living and the great,
Yet this queen's merits fame hath so far spread,
That she rules still, though dispossessed and dead.
For losing one, two other crowns remained: 5
Over all hearts and her own griefs she reigned.
Two thrones so splendid, as to none are less
But to that third which she does now possess.
Her heart and birth, Fortune so well did know,
That seeking her own fame in such a foe,   10
She dressed the spacious theatre for the fight,
And the admiring world called to the sight.
An army then of mighty sorrows brought,
Who all against this single virtue fought,
And sometimes stratagems, and sometimes blows,   15
To her heroic soul they did oppose;
But at her feet their vain attempts did fall,
And she discovered and subdued them all.
Till Fortune weary of her malice grew,
Became her captive and her trophy too,   20
And by too late a suit begged to have been
Admitted subject to so brave a queen.
But as some hero who a field hath won,
Viewing the things he had so bravely done,
When, by his spirit's flight, he finds that he   25
With his own life must buy the victory,
He makes the slaughtered heap that next him lies
His funeral pile, and then in triumph dies;
So fell this royal dame, with conquering spent,
And left in every breast her monument;   30
Wherein so high an epitaph is writ,
As I must never dare to copy it.
But that bright angel, which did on her wait,
In fifty years' contention with her fate,

4] *dispossessed*: Frederick V, her husband, was defeated by the Catholic imperial army
at the Battle of the White Mountain in November 1620, ending his short reign as
King of Bohemia. Frederick and Elizabeth fled to The Hague.
6] *Over all hearts*: Elizabeth was known as the 'Queen of Hearts'.
34] *fifty years*: approximately the number of years between her marriage and her death.

And in that office did with wonder see   35
How great her troubles, how much greater she;
How she maintained her best prerogative,
In keeping still the power to forgive;
How high she did in her devotion go,
And how her condescension stooped as low;   40
With how much glory she had ever been
A daughter, sister, mother, wife, and queen;
Will sure employ some deathless Muse to tell
Our children this instructive miracle,
Who may her sad illustrious life recite,   45
And after all her wrongs may do her right.

Note

Elizabeth Stuart, Queen of Bohemia, died in England on 13 February
1662. The eldest daughter of King James I, Elizabeth had married
Frederick, Elector Palatine, in 1613, in an important Protestant alliance.
Against the background of the Thirty Years War in Europe, her Protestant
husband's reign in Bohemia lasted just one year, from November 1619
to November 1620. She then lived for several decades in The Hague.
Philips's friend Sir Charles Cotterell had been in her service there from
1650 to 1655, perhaps prompting this panegyric on her death.

42] Elizabeth was the daughter of James VI and I, the sister of Charles I, and the
mother of thirteen children. Her daughter Sophia (1630–1714) became Electress
of Hanover and the mother of the future George I of Great Britain and Ireland.

To the Right Honourable Alice, Countess of Carbery, on her Enriching Wales with her Presence

1.

As, when the first day dawned, man's greedy eye
Was apt to dwell on the bright prodigy,
Till he might careless of his organ grow,
And so his wonder prove his danger too:
So when our country (which was deemed to be   5
Close-mourner in its own obscurity,
And in neglected chaos so long lay)
Was rescued by your beams into a day,
Like men into a sudden lustre brought,
We justly feared to gaze more than we ought.   10

2.

From hence it is you lose most of your right,
Since none can pay't, nor durst do't if they might.
Perfection's misery 'tis that Art and Wit,
While they would honour, do but injure it.
But as the deity slights our expense,   15
And loves devotion more than eloquence:
So 'tis our confidence you are divine,
Makes us at distance thus approach your shrine.
And thus secured, to you who need no art,
I that speak least my wit, may speak my heart.   20

3.

Then much above all zealous injury,
Receive this tribute of our shades from me,
While your great splendour, like eternal spring,
To these sad groves such a refreshment bring,
That the despisèd country may be grown,   25
And justly too, the envy of the town.
That so when all mankind at length have lost
The virtuous grandeur which they once did boast,
Of you like pilgrims they may here obtain
Worth to recruit the dying world again.   30

2] *bright prodigy*: the rising sun.
3] *organ*: the 'greedy eye' of line 1.

Note

Alice Vaughan (née Egerton), Countess of Carbery (1619–89), was the daughter of John Egerton, first Earl of Bridgewater, and his wife, Frances (née Stanley), and a celebrated musician. At the age of fifteen, she played the role of the Lady in Milton's masque *Comus*, performed at Ludlow Castle; and the records of the Bridgewater family contain songs performed by her in the 1640s. She was closely connected to the musician Henry Lawes and his circle through the 1650s, as was Katherine Philips. The poem celebrates the new countess's arrival in Wales, where Philips was also living, to take up residence at her husband's estate at Golden Grove in Carmarthenshire.

To Antenor, on a Paper of Mine which J. Jones Threatens to Publish to Prejudice him

Must then my crimes become his scandal too?
Why, sure the devil hath not much to do.
The weakness of the other charge is clear,
When such a trifle must bring up the rear.
But this is mad design, for who before   5
Lost his repute upon another's score?
My love and life I must confess are thine,
But not my errors, they are only mine.
And if my faults must be for thine allowed,
It will be hard to dissipate the cloud: 10
For Eve's rebellion did not Adam blast,
Until himself forbidden fruit did taste.
'Tis possible this magazine of hell
(Whose name would turn a verse into a spell,
Whose mischief is congenial to his life)   15
May yet enjoy an honourable wife.
Nor let his ill be reckoned as her blame,
Nor yet my follies blast Antenor's name.
But if those lines a punishment could call
Lasting and great as this dark lantern's gall;   20
Alone I'd court the torments with content,
To testify that thou art innocent.
So if my ink, through malice, proved a stain,
My blood should justly wash it off again.
But since that mint of slander could invent   25
To make so dull a rhyme his instrument,
Let verse revenge the quarrel. But he's worse
Than wishes, and below a poet's curse;
And more than this wit knows not how to give,
Let him be still himself, and let him live.   30

Title] *Antenor*: Philips's coterie name for her husband, James Philips.
1] *my crimes*: Philips's authorship of 'Upon the Double Murder of King Charles I'.
11–12] *For Eve's … did taste*: See Genesis 3:17, where Adam is cursed only because he himself ate from the tree of knowledge.
13] *magazine of hell*: storehouse or repository of evil.

Note

This poem provides insight into dangers of circulating politically sensitive poems in manuscript. Philips addresses her parliamentarian husband James Philips ('Antenor') in horror that his adversary Jenkin Jones is threatening to publish a paper of hers in order to damage his reputation. The paper that he is threatening to publish is Philips's royalist poem 'Upon the Double Murder of King Charles I'.

A Country Life

How sacred and how innocent
    A country life appears,
How free from tumult, discontent,
    From flattery or fears!
This was the first and happiest life,   5
    When man enjoyed himself;
Till pride exchanged peace for strife,
    And happiness for pelf.
'Twas here the poets were inspired,
    And sang their mysteries;   10
And while the listening world admired,
    Men's minds did civilise.
That golden age did entertain
    No passion but of love;
The thoughts of ruling and of gain   15
    Did ne'er their fancies move.
None then did envy neighbour's wealth,
    Nor plot to wrong his bed:
Happy in friendship and in health,
    On roots, not beasts, they fed,   20
They knew no law nor physic then,
    Nature was all their wit.
And if there yet remain to men
    Content, sure this is it.
What blessings doth this world afford   25
    To tempt or bribe desire?
For courtship is all fire and sword,
    Who would not then retire?
Then welcome dearest Solitude,
    My great felicity;   30
Though some are pleased to call thee rude,
    Thou art not so, but we.
Such as do covet only rest,
    A cottage will suffice:

8] *pelf*: riches.

13] *golden age*: in Greek mythology, the first age of mankind, one of purity, harmony, and stability.

Is it not brave to be possessed   35
    Of earth, but to despise.
Opinion is the rate of things,
    From hence our peace doth flow,
I have a better fate than kings,
    Because I think it so.   40
When all the stormy world doth roar,
    How unconcerned am I?
I cannot fear to tumble lower
    That never could be high.
Secure in these unenvied walls   45
    I think not on the state,
And pity no man's case that falls
    From his ambition's height.
Silence and innocence are safe;
    A heart that's nobly true   50
At all these little arts can laugh
    That do the world subdue.
While others revel it in state,
    Here I'll contented sit,
And think I have as good a fate   55
    As wealth and pomp admit.
Let some in courtship take delight,
    And to th'Exchange resort;
There revel out a winter's night,
    Not making love, but sport.   60
These never knew a noble flame,
    'Tis lust, scorn, or design:
While vanity plays all their game,
    Let peace and honour mine.
When the inviting spring appears,   65
    To Hyde Parke let them go,
And hasting thence be full of fears
    To lose Spring Garden show.

37] *rate*: value.
46] *I think not on the state*: see Philips, 'Upon the Double Murder of King Charles I',
    line 1.
51] *arts*: stratagems.
58] *th'Exchange*: the New Exchange, a fashionable market best known for its haberdashery
    and millinery shops.
66, 68] *Hyde Park*; *Spring Garden*: fashionable London pleasure gardens. See Pulter,
    Emblem 20, lines 25–26.

Let others (nobler) seek to gain
    In knowledge happy fate,   70
And others busy them in vain
    To study ways of state.
But I, resolved from within,
    Confirmed from without,
In privacy intend to spin   75
    My future minutes out.
And from this hermitage of mine
    I banish all wild toys,
And nothing that is not divine
    Shall dare to tempt my joys.   80
There are below but two things good,
    Friendship and honesty,
And only those alone I would
    Ask for felicity.
In this retired integrity,   85
    Free from both war and noise,
I live not by necessity,
    But wholly by my choice.

Note

'A Country Life' celebrates retreat from the tumult of contemporary state politics, into the peace and privacy of 'retired integrity' in the country (see also Philips, 'Invitation to the Country', and, for comparison, Pulter, 'The Invitation into the Country, to my Dear Daughters'). The trope of rural retirement is conventional, reaching back to Horace's Epode 2, *Beatus ille* ('The Happy Man'), but Philips's emphasis on 'dearest solitude' is an important development of the Horatian trope. Scott-Baumann argues for the influence of 'A Country Life' on Marvell's 'The Garden' and Cowley's retirement poetry (see *Forms of Engagement*).

78] *toys*: amusements.

Upon Mr Abraham Cowley's Retirement. Ode.

1.

No, no, unfaithful world, thou hast
      Too long my easy heart betrayed,
    And me too long thy football made;
    But I am wiser grown at last,
And will improve by all that I have past.   5
I know 'twas just I should be practised on,
      For I was told before,
    And told in sober and instructive lore,
How little all that trusted thee have won,
And yet I would make haste to be undone.   10
Now by my suff'ring I am better taught,
And shall no more commit that stupid fault.
    Go, get some other fool,
    Whom thou may'st next cajole:
On me thy frowns thou dost in vain bestow;   15
      For I know how
To be as coy and as reserved as thou.

2.

In my remote and humble seat
      Now I'm again possessed
    Of that late fugitive, my breast;   20
From all thy tumults and from all thy heat
I'll find a quiet and a cool retreat;
    And on the fetters I have worn
Look with experienced and revengeful scorn
    In this my sovereign privacy.   25
    'Tis true I cannot govern thee,
    But yet myself I may subdue,
And that's the nobler empire of the two.
    If ev'ry passion had got leave
    Its satisfaction to receive,   30
Yet I would it a higher pleasure call
To conquer one, than to indulge them all.

3.

For thy inconstant sea, no more
I'll leave that safe and solid shore;

No, though to prosper in the cheat,   35
   Thou should'st my destiny defeat,
And make me be beloved, or rich, or great,
   Nor from myself should'st me reclaim
With all the noise and all the pomp of fame.
   Judiciously I'll thee despise;   40
Too small the bargain, and too great the price,
     For them to cozen twice.
   At length this secret I have learned:
Who will be happy, will be unconcerned,
Must all their comfort in their bosom wear,   45
And seek their treasure and their power there.

   4.
   No other wealth will I aspire,
    But of nature to admire;
Nor envy on a laurel will bestow,
Whilst I have any in my garden grow.   50
     And when I would be great,
   'Tis but ascending to a seat
Which Nature in a lofty rock hath built;
A throne as free from trouble as from guilt,
    Where when my Soul her wings does raise   55
    Above what worldlings fear or praise,
With innocence and quiet pride I'll sit,
And see the humble waves pay tribute to my feet.
O life divine, when free from joys diseased,
Not always merry, but 'tis always pleased!   60

   5.
   A heart, which is too great a thing
To be a present for a Persian king,
Which God himself would have to be his court,
Where angels would officiously resort,
    From its own height should much decline,   65
    If this converse it should resign
     (Ill-natured world!) for thine.

42] *cozen*: cheat, deceive.

Thy unwise rigour hath thy empire lost;
    It hath not only set me free,
        But it hath made me see,   70
They only can of thy possession boast,
Who do enjoy thee least, and understand thee most.
For lo, the man whom all mankind admired,
(By ev'ry Grace adorned, and ev'ry Muse inspired)
    Is now triumphantly retired.   75
    The mighty Cowley this hath done,
And over thee a Parthian conquest won,
    Which future ages shall adore,
    And which in this subdues thee more
Than either Greek or Roman ever could before.   80

Note

The poet Abraham Cowley (1618–67) left London for a retired life in the country at Barn Elms in 1663. Philips wrote a poem on engraving her initials in a tree at Barn Elms, and Cowley wrote a Pindaric ode 'On Orinda's Poems' in 1663. Philips's poetry of rural retirement influenced Cowley (see her 'A Country Life'), and he in turn influenced her. This poem celebrating Cowley's retirement uses the loose and irregular Pindaric ode form, with lines of varying and arbitrary length, promulgated by Cowley in his *Pindarique Odes* (*Poems*, 1656).

77] *Parthian conquest*: It was proverbial that the Parthians fought while fleeing.

From *Poems* (1667)

Epitaph on her Son H.P. at St Sith's Church, where her Body also Lies Interred

What on earth deserves our trust?
You and beauty both are dust.
Long we gathering are with pain,
What one moment calls again.
Seven years' childless marriage past,   5
A son, a son is born at last:
So exactly limned and fair,
Full of good spirits, mien, and air,
As a long life promised,
Yet, in less than six weeks dead.   10
Too promising, too great a mind
In so small room to be confined:
Therefore, as fit in heav'n to dwell,
He quickly broke the prison shell.
So the subtle alchemist,   15
Can't with Hermes' seal resist
The powerful spirit's subtler flight,
But t'will bid him long good night.
And so the sun if it arise
Half so glorious as his eyes,   20
Like this infant, takes a shroud,
Buried in a morning cloud.

Note

Hector Philips, the poet's son, was born 23 April and died 2 May 1655, in Philips's seventh year of marriage. St Sith's church, London (otherwise known as St Benet Sherehog) burned down in the Great Fire in 1666.

Title] *H. P.*: Hector Philips.
5] Katherine married James Philips in 1648.
7] *limned*: drawn.
8] *mien*: expression.
15–18] a reference to alchemy and its attempt to find the secret of eternal life.
16] *Hermes' seal*: a hermetic seal, an airtight closure of a vessel, named after Hermes Trismegistus, the legendary founder of alchemy.

To my Antenor, March 16 1661/2

My dear Antenor now give o'er,
For my sake talk of graves no more,
Death is not in our power to gain,
And is both wished and feared in vain.
Let's be as angry as we will,   5
Grief sooner may distract than kill,
And the unhappy often prove
Death is as coy a thing as love.
Those whose own sword their death did give,
Afraid were, or ashamed to live;   10
And by an act so desperate,
Did poorly run away from fate;
'Tis braver much t'outride the storm,
Endure its rage and shun his harm;
Affliction nobly undergone,   15
More greatness shows than having none.
But yet the wheel in turning round,
At last may lift us from the ground,
And when our fortune's most severe,
The less we have, the less we fear.   20
And why should we that grief permit,
Which can nor mend nor shorten it?
Let's wait for a succeeding good,
Woes have their ebb as well as flood:
And since the parliament have rescued you,   25
Believe that providence will do so too.

Note

After the restoration of the monarchy in May 1660, the position of
parliamentarians such as Philips's husband James was perilous. Philips
wrote this poem to James a couple of weeks after the House of Commons
cleared him of signing the death warrant of the royalist Colonel John
Gerard as part of the (now illegal) High Court of Justice. Philips's friend
Sir Charles Cotterell had lobbied the Commons on her husband's behalf
(see her letters from 6 March and 18 March 1661/2 in Thomas (ed.),
Collected Works, vol. 2, pp. 19–20, 24).

Title] *Antenor*: Philips's coterie name for her husband, James Philips. Date: The date
    in the title of this poem would be 1662 in new-style dating.
17] *wheel*: the wheel of fortune.

Orinda upon Little Hector Philips

1.

Twice forty months in wedlock I did stay,
Then had my vows crowned with a lovely boy,
And yet in forty days he dropped away,
O swift vicissitude of human joy.

2.

I did but see him and he disappeared,   5
I did but touch the rosebud and it fell,
A sorrow unforeseen and scarcely feared,
So ill can mortals their afflictions spell.

3.

And now (sweet babe) what can my trembling heart
Suggest to right my doleful fate or thee,   10
Tears are my Muse and sorrow all my art,
So piercing groans must be thy elegy.

4.

Thus whilst no eye is witness of my moan,
I grieve thy loss (ah boy too dear to live)
And let the unconcerned world alone,   15
Who neither will, nor can refreshment give.

5.

An off'ring too for thy sad tomb I have,
Too just a tribute to thy early hearse,
Receive these gasping numbers to thy grave,
The last of thy unhappy mother's verse.   20

Note

Philips's son Hector was born on 23 April 1655 and died on 2 May of
the same year. This carefully-crafted poem on his death was set to music
by her friend and associate the court musician Henry Lawes. See Applegate,
'Katherine Philips's "Orinda upon Little Hector"' for the musical setting.

1] Katherine had married James Philips in 1648; Hector was their first child.
18] *hearse*: tomb, grave.

Margaret Cavendish (?1623–1673)

Margaret Cavendish was born around 1623 to the Lucas family of Essex. In her autobiography (*A True Relation of my Birth, Breeding and Life*), she remembers a happy childhood and an education focused on needlework and music. After a year living in Oxford with her sister, Margaret became a maid of honour to Queen Henrietta Maria, whose court was based in the city. She followed the court to Paris in 1644, and there she met and married William Cavendish, a royalist commander and widower thirty years her senior. William Cavendish was a minor Cavalier poet himself and a patron of poets such as Ben Jonson, some of whose works were performed at the Cavendish estate before the wars. William already fostered writing in the women of the family as his daughters from his first marriage, Jane Cavendish and Elizabeth Brackley, were also poets. Margaret's young married life was dominated, though, by the Civil War. She and her husband fled to continental Europe after his defeat at Marston Moor, and her brother Charles was executed in 1648 after the siege of Colchester (Cavendish wrote an elegy on her brother Lucas and his fellow commander Lisle, as did Hester Pulter).

The couple moved to Antwerp, living in Rubens's town house leased from his widow, and in Paris and Antwerp they mixed in richly varied intellectual circles, including the philosophers Constantin Huygens, René Descartes, Pierre Gassendi, and Marin Mersenne and fellow exiles Thomas Hobbes, Kenelm Digby, Edmund Waller, and William Davenant. Cavendish published from exile and continued to do so when she and her husband returned to England at the Restoration. Her early works were poetry and short essays, followed by plays, philosophical and fictional letters, and prose fiction in both romance and experimental modes. Cavendish's first two publications were collections of poetry which also included prefaces explaining her theories of authorship, publication, and poetics. These include some of the period's most explicit statements about the status of women writers, including modest yet defiant assertions of her originality and lack of learning, both of which should perhaps be taken as rhetorical strategies as much as ingenuous statements of her authorial practice. Cavendish's poetry ranges widely in subject-matter and tone, from an elegy on her brother's death to representations of an atomistic universe, elaborate similes, witty recipe poems, and sensitive accounts of the natural world.

Cavendish's poems, mostly published in the 1650s, do not often take explicitly political subjects but they do reflect the tensions, philosophical, and ethical questions raised by Civil War. While the Cavendishes were in exile in Paris, their friend Thomas Hobbes was there probably working on *Leviathan* (1651), in which he argued that man was compelled to form a social contract, ceding some individual authority by pledging obedience to a monarch in order to live in a more civilised fashion than the 'state of nature' which was inevitably one of conflict and disorder. In Cavendish's poetic dialogues between man and nature and between man and an oak, the natural world represents conscience and empathy while man represents Hobbesian self-interest. Her 'A Dialogue between a Bountiful Knight and a Castle Ruined in War' represents the ravages of the Civil War on the estates of the nobility (such as her husband, whose property was sequestered while he was abroad). The dialogue form provides an especially apt mode in which to represent the fractures and dislocations of Civil War, where neighbour fought against neighbour and where even individuals' consciences were often divided. Later she wrote antagonistically about the experimentalism of the New Science, but she was honoured by a visit to the Royal Society in 1667, the same year in which she published a biography of her husband. Like Lucy Hutchinson's life of her husband, Cavendish's biography is a history of the Civil War and a defence of her family's own involvement.

Figure 5 Frontispiece from Margaret Cavendish, *Poems and Fancies* (1653).

From *Philosophical Fancies* (1653)

Of Sense and Reason Exercised in their Different Shapes

If every thing hath sense and reason, then
There might be beasts, and birds, and fish, and men:
As vegetables and minerals, had they
The animal shape to express that way;
And vegetables and minerals may know,   5
As man, though like to trees and stones they grow.
Then coral trouts may through the water glide,
And pearled minnows swim on either side;
And mermaids, which in the sea delight,
Might all be made of watery lilies white;   10
Set on salt watery billows as they flow,
Which like green banks appear thereon to grow.
And mariners i'th'midst their ship might stand,
Instead of mast, hold sails in either hand.
On mountain tops the golden fleece might feed,   15
Some hundred years their ewes bring forth their breed.
Large deer of oak might through the forest run,
Leaves on their heads might keep them from the sun;
Instead of shedding horns, their leaves might fall,
And acorns to increase a wood of fawns withal.   20
Then might a squirrel for a nut be cracked,
If nature had that matter so compact:
And the small sprouts which on the husk do grow,
Might be the tail, and make a brushing show.
Then might the diamonds which on rocks oft lie,   25
Be all like to some little sparkling fly.
Then might a leaden hare, if swiftly run,
Melt from that shape, and so a pig become.
And dogs of copper-mouths sound like a bell;
So when they kill a hare, ring out his knell.   30
Hard iron men shall have no cause to fear
To catch a fall, when they a hunting were.
Nor in the wars should have no use of arms,

4] *animal*: as an adjective here 'animal' could mean voluntary and willed, i.e. a feature
   of humans but not vegetables or minerals.
28] *pig*: Cavendish note 'A Pig of lead'.

Nor feared to fight; they could receive no harms.
For if a bullet on their breasts should hit,   35
Fall on their back, but straight-ways up may get.
Or if a bullet on their head do light,
May make them totter, but not kill them quite.
And stars be like the birds with twinkling wing,
When in the air they fly, like larks might sing.   40
And as they fly, like wand'ring planets show,
Their tails may like to blazing comets grow.
When they on trees do rest themselves from flight,
Appear like fixed stars in clouds of night.
Thus may the sun be like a woman fair,   45
And the bright beams be as her flowing hair
And from her eyes may cast a silver light,
And when she sleeps, the world be as dark night.
Or women may of alabaster be,
And so as smooth as polished ivory   50
Or, as clear crystal, where hearts may be shown,
And all their falsehoods to the world be known.
Or else be made of rose, and lilies white,
Both fair, and sweet, to give the soul delight,
Or else be made like tulips fresh in May,   55
By nature dressed, clothed several colours gay.
Thus every year there may young virgins spring
But wither, and decay, as soon again.
While they are fresh, upon their breast might set
Great swarms of bees, from thence sweet honey get   60
Or, on their lips, for gilly-flowers, flies
Drawing delicious sweet that therein lies.
Thus every maid, like several flowers show,
Not in their shape, but like in substance grow.
Then tears which from oppressed hearts do rise,   65
May gather into clouds within the eyes:
From whence those tears, like showers of rain may flow
Upon the banks of cheeks, where roses grow.
After those showers of rain, so sweet may smell,
Perfuming all the air, that near them dwell,   70
But when the sun of joy, and mirth doth rise,
Darting forth pleasing beams from loving eyes.

61] *gilly-flowers*: clove-shaped flowers.

Then may the buds of modesty unfold,
With full-blown confidence the sun behold,
But grief as frost them nips, and withering die,   75
In their own pods entombèd lie.
Thus virgin cherry trees, where blossoms blow,
So red, ripe cherries on their lips may grow.
Or women, plum-trees, at each finger's end
May ripe plums hang, and make their joints to bend.   80
Men, sycamores, which on their breast may write
Their amorous verses, which their thoughts indite.
Men's stretched arms may be like spreading vines,
Where grapes may grow, so drink of their own wine.
To plant large orchards, need no pains nor care,   85
For every one their sweet fresh fruit may bear.
Then silver grass may in the meadows grow,
Which nothing but a scythe of fire can mow.
The wind, which from the north a journey takes,
May strike those silver strings, and music make.   90
Thus may another world, though matter still the same,
By changing shapes, change humours, properties, and name.
Thus Colossus, a statue wondrous great,
When it did fall, might straight get on his feet,
Where ships, which through his legs did swim, he might   95
Have blowed their sails, or else have drowned them quite.
The golden calf that Israel joyed to see,
Might run away from their idolatry.
The Basan bull of brass might be, when roar,
His metaled throat might make his voice sound more.   100
The hill, which Mahomet did call, might come
At the first word, or else away might run.
Thus Pompey's statue might rejoice to see,

76] *pods*: Cavendish note 'the huske'.
82] *indite*: say words which will be written down or repeated.
92] *humours*: the four fluids in the body thought to dictate a person's character (blood,
    phlegm, choler, and melancholy).
93] *Colossus*: the Colossus of Rhodes, a monumental statue and one of the seven
    wonders of the world.
97] *golden calf*: the object of the Israelites' idolatry; see Exodus 32:4.
99] *Basan bull*: a notoriously strong bull from the fertile region of Bashan (Psalm
    22:12). Cavendish puns on 'Basan' and 'brazen' (of brass).
101] *Mahomet*: Proverbially, Mahomet called the mountain to come to him.
103] *Pompey*: a Roman leader, defeated by Julius Caesar and then killed.

When killed was Caesar, his great enemy.
The wooden-horse that did great Troy betray,   105
Have told what's in him, and then run away;
Achilles' arms against Ulysses plead,
And not let wit against true valour speed.

Note

In this poem Cavendish takes vitalist views to a witty extreme: matter
not only is conscious and self-moving but possesses conscious will, so
minerals and vegetables develop human-like potential for reason and
action. The fantastical world of the poem blurs animate and inanimate;
human, animal, vegetable, and mineral. The poem is absurd and exuberant,
but it also intervenes in contemporary debates about the sentience of
creatures and the autonomy of matter. It also plays with lyric conventions.
While women were often imagined as having skin like ivory, here the
woman is made of ivory, just as the 'pearled minnows' are actually made
of pearl.

107] *Achilles' arms*: After Achilles' death, Ulysses (Odysseus) won his armour, fighting
against Ajax.

A Dialogue between the Body and the Mind

I write, and write, and't may be never read;
My books, and I, all in a grave lie dead.
No memory will build a monument,
Nor offer praise unto the soul's content.
But howsoever, Soul, lie still at rest,   5
To make thy fame to live, have done the best,
For all the wit that nature to me gave,
I set it forth, for to adorn thy grave.
But if the ruins of oblivion come,
'Tis not my fault, for what I can, is done,   10
For all the life that nature to me lends
About thy work, and in thy service spends.
But if thou think I take not pains, pray speak
Before we part, my body is but weak.
Soul:
Brain, thou hast done thy best, yet thou might go   15
To the grave learned, their subtle tricks to know:
And ask them, how such fame they do beget,
When they do write, but of another's wit.
For they have little of their own, but what
They have from others' brains, and fancies got.   20
Body:
O Soul! I shall not need to take such pains,
The labour will be more than all the gains:
For why! The world doth cozen and so cheat,
By railing at those authors' wits they get;
Muffling and hiding of their author's face,   25
By some strange language, or by some disgrace.
Their wit into an anagram they make,
That anagram for their own wit they take,
And here, and there they do a fancy steal,
And so of strangers make a commonweal.   30
Tell to the world they are true natives bred,
When they were borne all in another head
And with translating wit they march along,
With understanding praise they grow so strong,

17] *beget*: produce.
23] *cozen*: cheat or deceive.
30] *commonweal*: commonwealth.

That they do rule, by conquering Fame's great court: 35
From whence they send out all their false report.
This is the way, my Soul, that they do use,
By different language do the world abuse.
Therefore lie still thou troubled restless spirit,
Seek not for fame, unless thou hast a merit.   40
Soul:
Body, when thou art gone, then I die too,
Unless some great act in thy life thou do:
But prithee be not thou so wondrous nice,
To set my fame at a great merit's price.
Body:
Alas, what can I do to make thee live,   45
Unless some wise instructions thou canst give?
Can you direct me to some noble act,
Wherein vainglory makes no false compact?
Can you direct me which way I shall take,
Those that are in distress, happy to make?   50
Soul:
No, that's impossible, unless all hearts
Could be divided into equal parts.
Body:
Then prithee be content, seek thou no more;
'Tis Fortune makes the world to worship, and adore.

Note

With the puritan focus on conscience and interiority, and Descartes's
arguments about the division of body and mind, the medieval dialogue
genre acquired new dimensions in the seventeenth century. Cavendish's
poem has similarities to Andrew Marvell's 'A Dialogue between the Soul
and Body', in which the soul is trapped in the body and the body is
tortured by the morality and emotions of the 'tyrannic soul'. In Cavendish's
hands the dialogue is about how best to acquire fame: the body's actions
in life may be able to secure the afterlife of fame for the soul. The relation-
ship between soul and body is more collaborative, more strategic, and
less theological than in many such dialogues, and Cavendish ends by

---

43] *nice*: precise, particular.
48] *vainglory*: empty glory.
53] *prithee*: I pray you.

attributing power finally not to the body or the soul, but to 'Fortune'. For discussion and further examples, see Osmond, *Mutual Accusations*, and for the philosophical debate, see Sutton, 'Soul and Body in Seventeenth-Century British Philosophy'. See also Cavendish, 'A Dialogue betwixt Man and Nature'.

An Elegy

Her corpse was borne to church on grey goose wing,
Her sheet was paper white to lap her in.
And cotton dyed with ink, her covering black,
With letters for her scutcheons print in that.
Fancies bound up with verse, a garland made,   5
And at the head, upon her hearse was laid.
And numbers ten did bear her to the grave,
The Muses nine a monument her gave.

Note

In this poem Cavendish imagines the death of a female writer; her shroud is paper, her coat of arms is printed with letters rather than a crest, and the hearse is carried by the feet of a ten-syllable line of verse.

2] *sheet*: shroud, lap, wrap.
4] *scutcheons*: shields on which a coat of arms is painted.
7] *numbers ten*: the ten syllables or feet in a line of iambic pentameter.

From *Poems and Fancies* (1664)

The Poetress's Hasty Resolution

Reading my verses, I liked them so well,
Self-love did make my judgement to rebel
And thinking them so good, thought more to make,
Considering not how others would them take.
I wrote so fast, thought, lived I many a year,   5
A pyramid of fame thereon to rear.
Reason observing which way I was bent,
Did stay my hand, and asked me what I meant:
Will you, said he, thus waste your time in vain
On that which in the world small praise shall gain?   10
For shame, leave off, and do the printer spare,
He'll lose by your ill poetry, I fear:
Besides, the world already hath great store
Of useless books, wherefore do write no more.
But pity take, do the world a good turn,   15
And all you write cast into th'fire, and burn.
Angry I was, and Reason struck away,
When I did hear, what he to me did say.
Then all in haste I to the press it sent,
Fearing persuasion might my book prevent: 20
But now 'tis done, repent with grief do I,
Hang down my head with shame, blush, sigh, and cry.
Take pity, and my drooping spirits raise,
Wipe off my tears with handkerchiefs of praise.

Note

Cavendish was a 'print poet': she had all her works published, and she
also reflected on the medium of print and especially its values and dangers
for women. Here the poet debates with herself between the impulse for

---

Title] *Poetress*: poetess, female poet. 'Poetress' is a more unusual form of the word,
  perhaps deriving from the Latin *poetrix*.
9] *he*: Reason is described as 'she' in the first edition of *Poems, and Fancies* in 1653,
  and as 'he' in the revised edition of 1664. For another female Reason, see Hutchinson's
  Elegy 1, 'Leave off, you pitying friends, leave off'.

fame and the impulse to save herself from possible censure. Interestingly, Reason does not suggest that women should not publish, but that bad poets should not do so. This poem presents one of the contradictions characteristic of Cavendish: the unabashed desire for fame alongside the bashfulness implied by 'shame, blush, sigh, and cry'.

A World Made by Atoms

Small atoms of themselves a world may make,
For being subtle, every shape they take;
And as they dance about, they places find,
Of forms, that best agree, make every kind.
For when we build a house of brick, or stone,   5
We lay them even, every one by one:
And when we find a gap that's big, or small,
We seek out stones, to fit that place withal,
For when as they too big or little be,
They fall away, and cannot stay, we see.   10
So atoms, as they dance, find places fit,
And there remaining close and fast will knit.
Those which not fit, the rest that rove about,
Do never leave, until they thrust them out.
Thus by their forms, and motions they will be,   15
Like workmen, which amongst themselves agree;
And so by chance may a new world create,
Or else predestinate, may work by fate.

Note

In this poem Cavendish imagines a world made up of atoms which place
themselves in formations, like the various bricks used to build a house.
The atoms' movement is not random, but a 'dance', suggesting that the
atoms generate their own order and design. God is notably absent from
Cavendish's sceptical, atomistic vision. Writers such as Pierre Gassendi
and Walter Charleton had argued that God provided matter with motion,
thus making atomism endorse (rather than challenge) Christianity, but
Cavendish makes no such claim. Poems such as this one leave space for
both a Christian and a more Epicurean interpretation. See also the note
to Cavendish's 'Of Vacuum'.

Title] *Atoms*: In the seventeenth century 'atom' meant a particle of matter too small
to be seen or felt, not the more specific sense of 'atom' in the twenty-first century.
2] *subtle*: here can be both a physical description, meaning delicate, imperceptible, and
a figurative one, meaning ingenious, discerning.
8] *withal*: with the others; moreover. Used here probably for purposes of rhyme.

Of the Subtlety of Motion

Could we the several motions of life know,
The subtle windings, and the ways they go:
We should of unknown things dispute no more,
How they be done, but the great God adore.
But we with ignorance about do run,   5
To know the ends, and how they first begun.
Spending that life, which God in us did raise
To worship him, and in his works to praise,
With fruitless, vain, impossible pursuits,
In schools, lectures, and quarrelling disputes.   10
We never give him thanks that did us make,
But proud, as petty gods, our selves do take.

Note

Cavendish's stance in this poem is one of sceptical fideism. She does
not question God's existence, but she does assert firmly that he is unknow-
able to humankind and therefore not a suitable or productive subject for
her poetry. Some readers see this as a convenient way for her to avoid
religious writing and a sign of her near-atheism; others read it more at
face value as a statement of piety. This poem, like most, is revised in
1664, and in 1653 lines 3–4 read 'We should adore God more, and not
dispute / How they are done, but that great God can do't, the syntax of
which allows a potentially blasphemous reading: that we should question
whether God created the mysteries of the world.

Of Vacuum

Some think the world would fall, and not hang so,
If it had any empty place to go.
One cannot think that vacuum is so vast,
That the great world should in that gulf be cast.
But vacuum is like to a porous skin,   5
Where vapour doth go out, and air comes in;
And since that vapour fills those places small,
We cannot think, but they were empty all:
For were they all filled up, they could not make
Room, for succeeding atoms place to take.   10
Wherefore if atoms pass, and repass through,
They needs must empty places have to go.

Note

The existence and nature of vacuum was a lively topic of debate among natural philosophers in the seventeenth century. In her writings, Cavendish makes a case for the existence of vacuum and also for its non-existence: in *Philosophical and Physical Opinions* (1656) she includes chapters titled 'There is no Vacuity' and 'Of Vacuum'. As often in her philosophy, Cavendish takes a sceptical stance and seems interested in the debate rather than expressing a fundamental belief either way.

6] *vapour*: Cavendish note 'Atoms do so'.

Of Stars

We find that in th'East Indies stars there be,
Which we in our horizon ne'er did see;
Yet we do take great pains in glasses clear,
To see what stars do in the sky appear.
But yet the more we search, the less we know,   5
Because we find our work doth endless grow.
For who knows but those stars we see by night,
Are suns which to some other worlds give light?
But could our outward senses pace the sky,
As our imaginations thither fly;   10
If we were there, we might as little know,
As those which stay, and never up do go.
Then let no man, in fruitless pains life spend,
The most we know is, Nature death will send.

Note

'Of Stars' projects a telescopic vision, inspired by Cavendish's fascination with optical instruments (see *Observations upon Experimental Philosophy*, London, 1666, p. 86). She also argues, however, that reliance on observation should not replace experiments of the imagination. In *Observations upon Experimental Philosophy*, she wrote that 'Experimental Philosophy has but a brittle, inconstant and uncertain ground, and these artificial Instruments, as Microscopes, Telescopes, and the like, which are now so highly applauded, who knows, but may within a short time have the same fate, and upon a better and more rational enquiry, be found deluders rather than true Informers' (p. 86). In this poem she is sceptical about the idea that we can find out more by enhancing our 'outward senses' with telescopes. See also Cavendish's 'A World in an Earring', which presents a microscopic vision.

A World in an Earring

An earring may well a zodiac be,
Wherein a sun goes round, which we not see.
And planets seven about that sun may move,
And he stand still, as learnèd men would prove.
And fixed stars, like twinkling diamonds, placed   5
About this earring, which a world is, vast.
That same which doth the earring hold, the hole,
Is that we call the north and southern pole.
There nipping frosts may be, and winters cold,
Yet never on the lady's ear take hold,   10
And lightning, thunder, and great winds may blow
Within this earring, yet the ear not know.
Fish there may swim in seas, which ebb and flow,
And islands be, wherein do spices grow.
There crystal rocks hang dangling at each ear,   15
And golden mines as jewels may they wear
Earthquakes may be, which mountains vast down fling,
And yet ne'er stir the lady's ear, nor ring.
Meadows may be, and pastures fresh, and green,
And cattle feed, and yet be never seen: 20
And gardens fine, and birds which sweetly sing,
Although we hear them not, in an earring.
There may be night and day, and heat and cold
As also life and death, and young and old;
And youth may spring, and several ages die,   25
Great plagues may be, and no infection nigh.
Great cities there may be, and houses built,
Whose inside gay, and finely may be gilt.
Churches may they've, wherein priests teach and sing
And steeples too, yet hear the bells not ring.   30
From thence may pious tears to heaven up run,
And yet the ear not know which way they're gone.
Markets may be, where things are bought, and sold,
Though th'ear not knows the price their markets hold.
There governors may rule, and kings may reign,   35
And battles may be fought, and many slain.
And all within the compass of this ring,
Whence they no tidings to the wearer bring.
Within this ring wise counsellors may sit,
And yet the ear not one wise word may get.   40

There may be dancing all night at a ball,
And yet the ear be not disturbed at all.
Rivals may duels fight, where some are slain;
And lovers mourn, yet hear them not complain.
And death may dig a lover's grave, thus were   45
A lover dead, in a fair lady's ear.
But when the ring is broke, the world is done,
Then lovers are into Elysium gone.

Note

The fantastical vision of this poem engages critically with the findings of optical instruments such as the telescope and microscope. Galileo had published his telescopic findings half a century previously in *Starry Messenger* (*Sidereus Nuncius*, 1610), and in 1665 Robert Hooke would publish *Micrographia*, the first treatise of microscopy. Cavendish saw optical devices as providing an artificial view and one that was prone to error: in her *Observations upon Experimental Philosophy* (London, 1666) she asserted that 'the more the figure by art is magnified, the more it appears mis-shapen from the natural' (pp. 8–9). Here Cavendish finds the idea of microscopic worlds imaginatively stimulating; her vision is created by the imagination, not the telescope or microscope. See also her 'Of Stars'.

48] *Elysium*: paradise in Greek mythology.

The Purchase of Poets, or A Dialogue Betwixt the Poets, and Fame and Homer's Marriage

A company of poets strove to buy
Parnassus Hill, upon which Fame doth lie:
And Helicon, a well that runs below,
Of which all those that drink, straight poets grow.
But money they had none, for they're all poor,   5
And fancy, which is wit, is all their store.
Thinking which way this purchase they might make,
They all agreed they would some counsel take.
Knowing that Fame was owner to the well
And that she always on the hill did dwell,   10
They did conclude to tell her their desire,
That they might know what price she did require.
Then up the hill they got, a journey long,
Some nimbler feet had, and a breath more strong
Which made them get before, by going fast,   15
But all did meet upon the hill at last.
And when she heard them all, what they could say,
She asked them where their money was to pay?
They told her, money they had none to give,
But they had wit, by which they all did live;   20
And though they knew sometimes she bribes would take,
Yet wit, in Honour's court, did greatness make.
Said she, this hill I'll neither sell nor give,
But they that have most wit shall with me live.
Then go you down, and get what friends you can,   25
That will be bound, or plead for every man.
Then every poet was 'twixt hope, and doubt,
And envy strove to put each other out.
Homer, the first of poets, did begin;
For him was Greece and Troy bound; then came in   30
Virgil who brought Aeneas, he all Rome;

2] *Parnassus Hill*: a mountain in Greece thought of as the source of literary inspiration.

3] *Helicon*: a mountain in Greece and locations of fountains thought to be the source of poetic inspiration.

14] Cavendish note: 'Numbers'; Cavendish note: 'Fancy'.

29–31] Each classical poet brings the subjects of his epic poetry as his representatives, so Homer brings Greece and Troy (locations of *The Iliad*) and Virgil brings Aeneas and Rome (hero and location of *The Aeneid*).

For Horace all the country men did come:
For Juv'nal and Catullus all satyrs joined,
And in firm bonds they all themselves did bind.
Tibullus, Venus and her son did bring   35
For him, 'cause wanton verses he did sing.
Pythagoras his transmigration brings
For Ovid, sealing's bond with several things.
Lucan brought Pompey, th'senate all in arms,
And Caesar's army with his hot alarms: 40
Who mustered all i'th'Parthian fields, their hand
And seal did freely set to Lucan's band.
Poets, which epitaphs o'th'dead had made,
Their ghosts did rise, and would fair Fame persuade
To take their bonds, that they might live, though dead, 45
To after ages when their names were read.
The Muses nine came at the bar to plead,
But partial were, according as th'were fee'd.
At last all poets were cast out but three,
Who did dispute, which should Fame's husband be.   50
Pythagoras for Ovid thought it meet
To speak, whose numbers smooth, and words were sweet.
Ladies, said he, are for varieties,
And change as oft, as he makes beasts, birds, trees:
As many several shapes, and forms they take,   55
Some goddesses, and some do devils make.
Then let fair Fame sweet Ovid's lady be,
Since change doth please that sex, none's fit but he.
Then spoke Aeneas on brave Virgil's side,
Declared, he was the glory and the pride   60
Of all the Romans, who from him did spring,

32] *Horace*; *country men*: The Roman poet Horace wrote in praise of rural retreat.

33] *Juv'nal and Catullus*; *satyrs*: The Roman poets Juvenal and Catullus wrote satires and satirical love poetry, which were often connected (through a false etymology) with the mythical satyr, a half-man, half-horse creature, which Cavendish may be alluding to here.

35] *Tibullus, Venus and her son*: Tibullus wrote Latin love elegies; he brings as representatives Venus and Cupid, who was reputed to be the son of Venus and Mars.

37] *Pythagoras*; *transmigration*: Pythagoras believed in the transmigration, or reincarnation, of souls into other beings.

39] *Lucan*; *Pompey*: The Roman poet Lucan, in his *Pharsalia*, wrote of the conflict between Julius Caesar's army and Pompey leading the senate.

41] *Parthian fields*: Parthia is a region (in modern-day Iran), and Parthians were known proverbially for their fighting tactic of shooting as they retreated.

And whose high praise he in his verse did sing.
Then let him speed, even for Venus' sake,
Let him your husband be, none other take.
Then wise Ulysses in a rhet'ric style   65
Began his speech, his tongue was smooth as oil;
He bowed his head, and thus to Fame did speak:
I come to plead, although my wit is weak,
But since my cause is just, and truth my guide,
The way is plain, I shall not err aside.   70
Homer his lofty strain to heav'n flies high,
And brings the gods down from the airy sky:
And makes them side in factions, for mankind,
He's now for Troy, then Greece, as pleased his mind.
Then walks he down to the infernals deep,   75
And wakes the Furies out of their dead sleep:
With fancy's candles seeks about all hell,
Where every place, and corner he knows well.
Opening the gates where sleepy dreams do lie,
Walking into the Elysian fields hard by: 80
Tells you how lovers there their time employ,
And how pure souls in one another joy,
As painters shadows make by mixing colours,
So do the souls mix of platonic lovers;
Shows how heroic spirits there do play   85
Th'Olympic games, to pass the time away.
As how they run, leap, wrestle, swim and ride,
With many other exercises beside.
What poet ever did before him tell
The gods in heaven, and devils' names in hell?   90
Their mansions, and their pleasures he describes,
Their powers, and authorities divides,
Their chronologies, elder much than time,
And their adulteries he puts in rhyme:
Besides, great Fame, thy court he hath filled full   95
Of brave reports, which as an empty skull
Else would appear, and not like heaven's throne,

65] *Ulysses*: the Roman name for Odysseus, protagonist of Homer's *Odyssey. rhet'ric*:
    rhetorical, using arts of persuasion.
76] *Furies*: in classical mythology, three goddesses sent to avenge wrongs.
80] *Elysian fields*: paradise in Greek mythology, also known as Elysium.
86] *Olympic games*: games held in Olympia, southern Greece.

Nor like the firmament, with stars thick strewn:
Makes hell appear with a majestic face,
Because there are so many in that place. 100
Fame never could so great a queen have been,
If wit's invention had not arts brought in.
Your court by poets' fire is now made light,
Which quenched, you'd dwell as in perpetual night.
It heats men's spirits, and inflames their blood, 105
And makes them seek for actions great and good.
Then be you just, since you the balance hold,
Let not the leaden weights weigh down the gold.
It were injustice, Fame, for you to make
A servant low, his master's place to take, 110
Or you should thieves, that pick the purse, prefer
Before the owner, when condemned they were.
His are not servant lines; but what he leaves,
Each from him steals, and so the world deceives.
If so, great Fame, 'twill be a heinous fact 115
To worship you, if you from right detract.
Then let the best of poets find such grace
In your fair eyes, to choose him first in place.
Let all the rest come offer at your shrine,
And show yourself a goddess that's divine. 120
Then at your word, I'll Homer take, said Fame,
And if he prove not good, be you to blame.
Ulysses bowed, and Homer kissed her hands,
And they were joined in matrimonial bands;
And Mercury from all the gods was sent, 125
To give her joy, and wish her much content.
And all the poets were invited round,
All that were known, or in the world but found.
In measure and in time they danced about,
Each in their turn the Muses nine took out, 130
In numbers smooth did run their nimble feet,
Whilst music played, and songs were sung most sweet.
At last the bride, and bridegroom went to bed,
And there did Homer get Fame's maidenhead.

110] Cavendish note: 'Because all Poets imitate Homer'.
124] *matrimonial bands*: wedding rings (or binding agreements).
125] *Mercury*: Mercury was the messenger of the gods.
134] *maidenhead*: virginity.

Note

In this poem Cavendish stages a competition between great poets for possession of Parnassus and Helicon, mythical sources of inspiration. As Fame lives on Parnassus Hill, the poets must compete to win her hand in marriage. Each of the three major competitors brings his champions: Ovid brings Pythagoras; Virgil brings Aeneas; Homer brings Ulysses. Cavendish is playful, even subversive, in her treatment of these classical poets as competitive, self-promoting suitors.

Margaret Cavendish

A Dialogue betwixt Man and Nature

Man:
It is most strange,
How we do change.
First to live, and then to die,
Is the greatest misery;
To give us sense, for nought but pains to feel,   5
To make our lives only to be Death's wheel;
To give us reason, and yet not to know,
What we are made for, or what we must do.
Whether to atoms turn, or to heaven fly,
Or change into new forms, and never die,   10
Or else to the prime matter fall again,
Thence take new forms, and so always remain.
Nature gives no such knowledge to mankind,
But strong desires which do torment his mind:
And senses, which like hounds do run about,   15
Yet never can the perfect truth find out.
O Nature, Nature, cruel to mankind,
Gives knowledge none, but misery to find.
Nature:
Why doth mankind complain, and make such moan?
May not I work my will with what's my own?   20
But men among themselves contract, and make
A bargain for my tree; that tree they take:
Which cruelly they chop in pieces small,
And form it as they please, then build withal,
Although that tree by me, to stand, was graced,   25
Just as it grows, by none to be defaced.
Man:
O Nature, trees are dull, and have no sense,
And therefore feel no pain nor take offence.

6] *Death's wheel*: a motif, related to the Wheel of Fortune and the Wheel of Life, in
   which social hierarchies are shown to be insignificant in the face of death.
12] *prime matter*: a substance in its most basic essence, without any form, according
   to Aristotle.
21] *contract*: Cavendish suggests that men create a contract or bond between each
   other in which they agree to cut down the tree.

Nature:
But beasts have life and sense, and passions strong,
Yet cruel man doth kill, and doth them wrong;   30
To take that life before the time, which I
Ordained for them, 's to me an injury.
Man:
What ill man doth, Nature did make him do,
And he by Nature is prompt thereunto.
For it was in great Nature's power, and will,   35
To make him as she pleased, good, or ill.
Though beasts have sense, feel pain, yet whilst they live,
They reason want, for to dispute, or grieve.
Beasts have no pain, but what in sense doth lie,
Nor troubled thoughts, to think how they shall die.   40
Reason doth stretch man's mind upon the rack,
With hopes and joys pulled up, with fear pulled back.
Desire doth whip and makes him run amain,
Despair doth wound, and pulls him back again.
For Nature, thou mad'st man betwixt extremes,   45
Wants perfect knowledge, though thereof he dreams.
For had he been like to a stock, or stone,
Or like a beast, to live with sense alone.
Then might he eat and drink, and all be well,
Ne'er troubled be, neither for heav'n, nor hell.   50
Man knowledge hath enough for to inquire,
Ambition great enough for to aspire:
He hath this knowledge, that he knows not all,
And of himself his knowledge is but small:
Which makes him wonder, and think there are mixed   55
Two several qualities in nature fixed.
The one like love, the other like to hate,
And striving both they do shut out wise Fate.
And then sometimes, man thinks, as one they be,
Which makes that contraries so well agree;   60
That though the world was made by love and hate,
Yet all is ruled and governed by Fate.
These are man's fears; man's hopes run smooth and high,
Who thinks his mind is some great deity,
For though the body is of low degree,   65
In sense like beasts, their souls like gods shall be.

32] 's: a difficult elision of 'is' to retain metre.

Nature:
Says Nature, why doth man complain, and cry,
If he believes his soul shall never die?

Note

Here Cavendish uses the dialogue form to explore core questions about consciousness: what are we made for? How should we act? Should we understand ourselves through science or faith ('Whether to atoms turn, or to heaven fly')? Are our souls immortal? Cavendish is interested in the consciousness of animals and even plants, and mankind's rejection of and attacks on these are seen as a major failing in her poems such as 'The Hunting of the Hare' and 'A Dialogue between an Oak and a Man Cutting him Down'. This dialogue presents humans suffering from their unsatisfied desire for knowledge and understanding, 'the hunger of consciousness' (Watson, *Back to Nature*, p. 88). See also Cavendish's 'A Dialogue between the Body and the Mind'.

A Dialogue between an Oak and a Man Cutting him Down

Oak:
Why cut you off my boughs, which largely bend
And from the scorching sun you do defend,
Which did refresh your fainting limbs from sweat
And kept you free from thund'ring rains and wet?
When on my bark your weary head you'd lay,   5
Where quiet sleep did take all cares away.
The whilst my leaves a gentle noise did make,
And blew cool winds, that you fresh air might take.
Besides, I did invite the birds to sing,
That their sweet voice might you some pleasure bring.   10
Where every one did strive to do their best,
Oft changed their notes, and strained their tender breast.
In winter time, my shoulders broad did hold
Off blust'ring storms, that wounded with sharp cold,
And on my head the flakes of snow did fall,   15
Whilst you under my boughs sat free from all.
And shall thus be requited my good will,
That you will take my life, and body kill?
For all my care and service I have past,
Must I be cut, and laid on fire at last?   20
See how true love you cruelly have slain,
And tried all ways to torture me with pain:
First you do peel my bark, and flay my skin,
Chop off my limbs, and leave me nak'd and thin.
With wedges you do pierce my sides to wound,   25
And with your hatchet knock me to the ground.
I minced shall be in chips, and pieces small,
And this doth man reward good deeds withal.
Man:
Why grumble you, old Oak, when you have stood
This hundred years, as king of all the wood?   30
Would you forever live, and not resign
Your place to one that is of your own line?
Your acorns young, when you grow big and tall,
Long for your crown, and wish to see your fall;
Think every minute lost, whilst you do live,   35
And grumble at each office you do give.
Ambition doth fly high, and is above
All sorts of friendship and of natural love.

Besides, all subjects do in change delight,
When kings grow old, their government they flight: 40
Although in ease, and peace, and wealth they live,
Yet all those happy times for change they'll give,
Grow discontent, and factions still do make;
What good so e'er he doth, as evil take.
Were he as wise, as ever nature made,   45
As pious, good, as ever heav'n has saved:
Yet when he dies, such joy is in their face,
As if the devil had gone from that place.
With shouts of joy they run a new to crown,
Although next day they strive to pull him down.   50
Oak:
Why, said the Oak, because that they are mad,
Shall I rejoice, for my own death be glad?
Because my subjects all ungrateful are,
Shall I therefore my health, and life impair?
Good kings who govern justly at all times   55
Examine not men's humours, but their crimes,
For when their crimes appear, 'tis time to strike
Not to examine thoughts what they do like.
Though kings are never loved, till they do die,
Nor wished to live, till in the grave they lie: 60
Yet he that loves himself the less, because
He cannot get every man's high applause:
Shall by my judgement be condemned to wear
The asses' ears, and burdens for to bear.
But let me live the life that nature gave,   65
And not to please my subjects, dig my grave.
Man:
But here, poor Oak, you live in ignorance,
And never seek your knowledge to advance.
I'll cut you down, that knowledge you may gain,
Shalt be a ship, to traffic on the main: 70
There shall you swim, and cut the seas in two,
And trample down each wave, as you do go.
Though they do rise, and big are swelled with pride,
You on their shoulders broad, and back, shall ride:
And bow their lofty heads, their pride to check,   75
Shall set your steady foot upon their neck:
They on their breast your stately ship shall bear,
Till your sharp keel the wat'ry womb doth tear.

Thus shall you round the world, new land to find,
That from the rest is of another kind. 80
Oak:
O, said the Oak, I am contented well,
Without that knowledge, in my wood to dwell.
For I had rather live, and simple be,
Than run in danger, some strange sight to see.
Perchance my ship against a rock may hit; 85
Then am I straight in sundry pieces split.
Besides, no rest, nor quiet shall I have,
The winds will toss me on each troubled wave.
The billows rough will beat on every side,
My breast will ache to swim against the tide. 90
And greedy merchants may me over-freight,
Then should I drownèd be with my own weight.
With sails and ropes men will my body tie,
And I, a prisoner, have no liberty.
And being always wet, such colds shall take, 95
My ship may get a pose through holes, and leak,
Which they to mend, will put me to great pain,
Besides, all patched and pieced I shall remain.
I care not for that wealth, wherein the pains,
And troubles are far greater than the gains. 100
I am contented with what nature gave,
I'll not repine, but one poor wish I'd have,
Which is, that you my agèd life would save.
Man:
To build a stately house I'll cut you down,
Wherein shall princes live of great renown. 105
There shall you live with the best company,
All their delight, and pastime you shall see.
Where plays, and masques, and beauties bright will shine,
Your wood all oiled with smoke of meat, and wine,
There shall you hear both men and women sing 110
Far pleasanter than nightingales i'th'spring.
Like to a ball, there echoes shall rebound
Against the wall, and yet no voice be found.

96] *pose*: a cold in the head, or catarrh.
102] *repine*: express discontent.

Oak:
Alas, what music shall I care to hear,
When on my shoulders I such burdens bear?   115
Both brick and tiles upon my head are laid,
Of this preferment I am sore afraid.
With nails and hammers they will often wound
And pierce my sides, to hang their pictures round.
My face is smudged with smoke of candle lights,   120
In danger to be burnt in winter nights.
No, let me here a poor old oak still grow;
Such vain delights I matter not to know,
For fruitless promises I do not care,
More honour 'tis, my own green leaves to bear,   125
More honour 'tis, to be in nature's dress
Than any shape, that men by art express.
I am not like to men, would praises have,
And for opinion make myself a slave.
Man:
Why do you wish to live, and not to die,   130
Since you no pleasure have, but misery?
Here you the sun with scorching heat doth burn
And all your leaves so green to dryness turn,
Also with winter's cold you quake, and shake,
And in no time, or season, rest can take.   135
Oak:
I'm happier far, said th'Oak, than you mankind;
For I content in my condition find.
Man nothing loves, but what he cannot get,
And soon doth surfeit of one dish of meat,
Dislikes all company, displeased alone,   140
Makes grief himself, if fortune gives him none,
And as his mind is restless, never pleased;
So is his body sick, and oft diseased.
His gouts and pains do make him sigh, and cry,
Yet in the midst of them would live, not die.   145
Man:
Alas, poor Oak, you do not know, nor can
Imagine, half the misery of man.
All other creatures only in sense join,
But man has something more, which is divine.
He hath a mind, and doth to heav'n aspire,   150
For curiosities he doth inquire:

A wit that nimble is, and runs about
In every corner, to seek Nature out
For she doth hide herself, afraid to show
Man all her works, lest he too powerful grow.   155
Like as a king, his favourite waxing great,
May well suspect, that he his pow'r will get;
And what creates desire in a man's breast
That nature is divine, which seeks the best:
For no perfection he at all doth prize   160
Till he therein the gods doth equalise:
If you, as man, desire like gods to be,
I'll spare your life, and not cut down your tree.

Note

This is one of several dialogues in which Cavendish articulates the perspective of the natural world (here an oak, elsewhere a stag) in debate with the threatening human. Man represents his actions as glorifying the tree by association. His promises are clearly void as the tree does not care about prestige in the human world. Cavendish renders the Oak's perspective more rational and sympathetic than the man's, and the tree becomes king-like, even Christ-like ('With nails and hammers they will often wound, / And pierce my sides'). Her sympathy for the natural world has been seen as a very modern form of ecological consciousness. See Rees, *Gender, Genre, Exile*; McColley, *Poetry and Ecology*; and Watson, *Back to Nature*; and see Cavendish, 'The Hunting of the Hare'.

156] *waxing*: growing, becoming.

A Dialogue between a Bountiful Knight and a Castle Ruined in War

Knight:
Alas, poor Castle, how great is thy change
From thy first form! To me thou dost seem strange:
I left thee comely, and in perfect health,
Now thou art withered, and decayed in wealth.
Castle:
O noble Sir, I from your stock was raised,   5
Flourished in plenty, and by all men praised:
For your most valiant father did me build,
Your brother furnished me, my neck did gild:
Towers upon my head like crowns were placed,
Walls, like a girdle, went about my waist.   10
And on this pleasant hill he set me high,
To view the vales below, as they do lie,
Where like a garden is each field and close,
Where fresh green grass, and yellow cowslip grows.
There did I see fat sheep in pastures go,   15
And hear the cows, whose bags were full, to low.
By wars I'm now destroyed, all right's o'erpowered,
Beauty and innocency are devoured.
Before these wars I was in my full prime,
And held the greatest beauty in my time,   20
But noble Sir, since I did see you last,
Within me has a garrison been placed.
Their guns, and pistols all about me hung,
And in despite their bullets at me flung
Which through my sides those passages you see,   25
Made, and destroyed the walls that circled me.
And left my rubbish on huge heaps to lie,
With dust I'm choked, for want of water, dry.
For those small leaden pipes, which winding lay,
Under the ground, the water to convey,   30
Were all cut off, the water murmuring,
Run back with grief to tell it to the spring.

Title] Cavendish note: 'Bolsover Castle'.
3] *comely*: beautiful, handsome.
9] Cavendish note: 'The crest in the wainscot gilt'.
16] *bags*: udders.

My windows broke, the winds blow in, and make
That I with cold like shivering agues shake.
O pity me, dear Sir, release my band,   35
Or let me die by your most noble hand.
Knight:
Alas, poor castle, I small help can bring,
Yet shall my heart supply the former spring:
From whence the water of fresh tears shall rise,
To quench thy drought, I'll spout them from mine eyes.   40
That wealth have I for to release thy woe,
I'll offer for a ransom to thy foe,
But to restore thy health, and build thy wall,
I have not means enough to do't withal.
Had I the art, no pains then I would spare,   45
But all what's broken down, I would repair.
Castle:
Most noble Sir, you that me freedom give,
May your great name in after-ages live.
This your great bounty may the gods requite,
And keep you from such enemies and spite   50
And may great fame your praises sound aloud:
Gods give me life to show my gratitude.

Note

Here the Castle represents the Cavendish estate in Derbyshire, Bolsover
Castle (as Cavendish notes), and the Knight presumably William Cav-
endish, Margaret Cavendish's husband. The Knight returning after civil
war finds his castle ravaged by conflict, having been captured by parlia-
mentarian troops. William Cavendish was a royalist commander loyal to
Charles I and II. He fled England after the defeat of his troops at Marston
Moor in 1644 and lived on the continent with Margaret Cavendish. On
his return to England at the Restoration, Cavendish was not rewarded
by Charles II, and this poem marks the sadness of the returning family
at the condition of their estates and the ravages suffered by the country
as a whole through the Civil War period.

34] *agues*: fevers or diseases.

The Clasp

Give me a free and noble style, that goes
In an uncurbèd strain, though wild it shows,
For though it runs about it cares not where,
It shows more courage, than it doth of fear.
Give me a style that nature frames, not art: 5
For art doth seem to take the pedant's part.
And that seems noble, which is easy, free,
And not bound up with o'er-nice pedantry.

Note

In *Poems and Fancies*, Cavendish includes several 'clasp' poems which seem to connect sections of the book. Like many of Cavendish's poems, this one was revised between its first and second publications, and this poem is formally much more regular in 1664 than in 1653. Cavendish may or may not have intended to be somewhat ironic in carefully regularising a poem that rejects pedantry and rules.

Title] *Clasp*: a fastening, such as a buckle or clip for clothing, and also for the covers of a book.

6] *pedant*: an overly learned person, often one who pays excessive attention to unimportant matters.

The Hunting of the Hare

Betwixt two ridges of ploughed land sat Wat,
Whose body pressed to th'earth, lay close and squat.
His nose upon his two forefeet did lie,
With his grey eyes he glared obliquely.
His head he always set against the wind;   5
His tail when turned, his hair blew up behind
And made him to get cold; but he being wise,
Doth keep his coat still down, so warm he lies.
Thus rests he all the day, till th'sun doth set,
Then up he riseth his relief to get   10
And walks about until the sun doth rise,
Then coming back in's former posture lies.
At last, poor Wat was found, as he there lay,
By huntsmen, which came with their dogs that way,
Whom seeing, he got up, and fast did run,   15
Hoping some ways the cruel dogs to shun.
But they by nature had so quick a scent,
That by their nose they traced what way he went
And with their deep, wide mouths set forth a cry,
Which answered was by echo in the sky.   20
Then Wat was struck with terror, and with fear,
Seeing each shadow thought the dogs were there
And running out some distance from their cry,
To hide himself, his thoughts he did employ.
Under a clod of earth in sand-pit wide,   25
Poor Wat sat close, hoping himself to hide.
There long he had not been, but straight in's ears
The winding horns, and crying dogs he hears:
Then starting up with fear, he leaped, and such
Swift speed he made, the ground he scarce did touch.   30
Into a great thick wood straightways he got,
And underneath a broken bough he sat
Where every leaf that with the wind did shake,
Brought him such terror, that his heart did ache.
That place he left, to champaign plains he went,   35
Winding about, for to deceive their scent
And while they snuffling were, to find his track,

1] *Wat*: traditionally the name for a hare.
35] *champaign*: flat land.

Poor Wat, being weary, his swift pace did slack.
On his two hinder legs for ease he sat,
His forefeet rubbed his face from dust and sweat,   40
Licking his feet, he wiped his ears so clean,
That none could tell that Wat had hunted been.
But casting round about his fair grey eyes,
The hounds in full career he near him spies:
To Wat it was so terrible a sight,   45
Fear gave him wings, and made his body light,
Though he was tired before, by running long
Yet now his breath he never felt more strong.
Like those that dying are, think health returns,
When 'tis but a faint blast, which life out burns.   50
For spirits seek to guard the heart about,
Striving with death, but death doth quench them out.
The hounds so fast came on, and with such cry,
That he no hopes had left, nor help could spy.
With that the winds did pity poor Wat's case,   55
And with their breath the scent blew from that place.
Then every nose was busily employed,
And every nostril was set open wide:
And every head did seek a several way,
To find the grass or track where the scent lay.   60
For witty industry is never slack,
'Tis like to witchcraft, and brings lost things back.
But though the wind had tied the scent up close,
A busy dog thrust in his snuffling nose:
And drew it out, with that did foremost run,   65
Then horns blew loud, the rest to follow on.
The great slow hounds, their throats did set a bass,
The fleet swift hounds, as tenors next in place;
The little beagles did a treble sing,
And through the air their voices round did ring   70
Which made such consort as they ran along;
That, had they spoken words, 't had been a song,
The horns kept time, the men did shout for joy,
And seemed most valiant, poor Wat to destroy:
Spurring their horses to a full career,   75
Swam rivers deep, leaped ditches without fear:

44] *career*: gallop.
61–62] These lines are italicised, suggesting that they are proverbial.

Endangered life, and limbs, so fast they'd ride,
Only to see how patiently Wat died.
At last, the dogs so near his heels did get,
That their sharp teeth in his breech did set,   80
Then tumbling down, he fell with weeping eyes,
Gave up his ghost, and thus poor Wat he dies.
Men whooping loud, such acclamations made,
As if the devil they imprisoned had,
When they but did a shiftless creature kill;   85
To hunt, there needs no valiant soldier's skill.
But men do think that exercise, and toil,
To keep their health, is best, which makes most spoil.
Thinking that food, and nourishment so good,
Which doth proceed from others' flesh and blood,   90
When they do lions, wolves, bears, tigers see,
Kill silly sheep, they say, they cruel be.
But for themselves all creatures think too few,
For luxury, wish God would make more new.
As if God did make creatures for man's meat,   95
And gave them life, and sense, for man to eat;
Or else for sport, or recreation's sake,
For to destroy those lives that God did make:
Making their stomachs graves, which full they fill
With murdered bodies, which in sport they kill.   100
Yet man doth think himself so gentle and mild,
When of all creatures he's most cruel, wild,
Nay, so proud, that he only thinks to live,
That God a God-like nature did him give.
And that all creatures for his sake alone   105
Were made, for him to tyrannise upon.

Note

George Gascoigne's *The Noble Art of Venery or Hunting* (1575), largely a
practical guide on hunting techniques, includes a poem, 'The Hare, to
the Hunter', in which the hare indicts men's bloodlust and comments
on how all animals show each other compassion except for man. In

---

80] *breech*: rump.
85] *shiftless*: helpless, without cunning.
92] *silly*: defenceless; often used of sheep.

Shakespeare's *Venus and Adonis* (1593), the goddess also imagines the hunting of 'poor Wat' (line 697). It was a fairly common rhetorical exercise to write from different perspectives but Cavendish's poems on the relationship between man and the natural world are unusual in the level of their sympathetic imagining of the perspective of animals and even plants (see Watson, *Back to Nature*).

A Description of an Island

There was an island rich by nature's grace,
In all the world it was the sweetest place:
Surrounded with the seas, whose waves not missed
To do her homage, and her feet they kissed.
Each wave did seem by turn to bow down low,   5
And proud to touch her, when as they did flow.
Armies of waves in troops high tides brought on,
Whose wat'ry arms did glister as the sun:
And on their backs burdens of ships did bear,
Placing them in her havens with great care;   10
Not mercenary, for no pay they'd have,
But as her guard did watch to keep her safe;
And in a ring they circled her about,
Strong as a wall, to keep her foes without.
The winds did serve her, and on clouds did ride,   15
Blowing their trumpets loud on every side;
Serving as scouts, they searched in every lane,
And galloped in the forests, fields, and plain.
While she did please the gods, she did live safe,
And they all kind of pleasures to her gave   20
For all this place was fertile, rich, and fair.
Both woods, and hills, and dales, in prospects were.
Birds pleasure took, and with delight did sing,
In praises of this isle the woods did ring;
Trees thrived with joy, for she their roots well fed,   25
And tall with pride, their tops did over-spread;
Danced with the winds, when they did sing and blow,
Played like a wanton kid, or a swift roe.
Their several branches several birds did bear
Which hopped, and skipped, and always merry were,   30
Their leaves did wave, and rushing make a noise:
And many ways strived to express their joys.
All flowers there looked fresh, and gay with mirth,
Whilst they were danced upon the lap of earth:

3–4] *whose waves not missed / To do her homage*: the waves did not forget to pay homage
to the island.
8] *glister*: sparkle, glitter.
22] *prospects*: views.
28] *roe*: a kind of deer.

Th'isle was their mother, they her children sweet,   35
Born from her loins, got by Apollo great,
Who dressed and pruned them often with great care,
And washed their leaves with dew to make them fair.
Which being done, he wiped those drops away,
With webs of heat, which he weaves every day,   40
Paint them with several colours intermixed,
Veiled them with shadows every leaf betwixt;
Their heads he dressed, their hairy leaves spread out,
Wreathed round their crowns his golden beams about.
For he this isle esteemed above the rest;   45
Of all his wives, he had loved her best.
Daily he did present her with some gift:
Twelve ells of light, to make her smocks for shift
Which every time he came, he put on fair,
That lovely she and handsome might appear.   50
And when he from her went, the world to see,
He left his sister her for company:
Whose name is Cynthia, though pale, yet clear,
Which makes her always in dark clouds appear.
Besides, he left his stars to wait on her   55
Lest she should grieve too much, when he's not there.
And from his bounty clothed them all with light,
Which makes them twinkle in a frosty night.
He never brought hot beams, to do her harm,
Nor let her take a cold, but lapped her warm;   60
He mantles rich of equal heat o'erspread,
And covered her with colour crimson red.
He gave another o'er her head to lie,
The colour is a pure bright azure sky,
And with soft air did line them all within,   65
Like furs in winter, in summer satin thin,

36] *Apollo*: major Greek and Roman god associated with poetry, music, and also the
    sun, to which Cavendish alludes here.
40] Cavendish note: 'Sun beams'.
41] Cavendish note: 'There would be no colours if no light'.
48] Cavendish note: 'These smocks are the days'.
48] *ells*: an ell is a measure of length. *smocks*; *shift*: undergarments.
52] Cavendish note: 'The moon'.
53] *Cynthia*: the moon.
56] *Lest*: in case.
60] *lapped*: wrapped.

With silver clouds he fringed them about,
And spangled meteors glist'ring hung without.
Thus gave he change, least she should weary grow,
Or think them old, and so away them throw.   70
Nature adorned this island all throughout,
With landscapes, riv'lets, prospects round about.
Hills over-topped the dales, which level were,
And covered all with cattle, feeding there.
Grass grew up even to the belly high,   75
Where beasts, that chew their cud, lay pleasantly.
Whisking their tails about, the flies to beat,
Or else to cool them from the sultry heat.
Nature, her love to th'gods willing to show,
Sent plenty in, like Nile's great overflow;   80
And temperate seasons gave, and equal lights,
Warm sunshine days, and dewy moonshine nights.
And in this pleasant island, peace did dwell,
No noise of war, or sad tale could it tell.

Note

Cavendish extols the virtues of the British Isles (she probably means these to represent England, Scotland, and Wales, which were not officially brought together as Great Britain until 1707). The island is an idealised, feminised figure whose fecundity is combined with a natural order. John of Gaunt's 'this sceptred isle' speech in Shakespeare's *Richard II* (2.1.31–68), probably known to Cavendish, is a more famous poetic praise of the British Isles using similar tropes of the chosen land and land of plenty. In this poem's partner piece, 'The Ruin of this Island', Cavendish views the country after civil war.

78] *sultry*: oppressively hot.
80] *Sent plenty in, like Nile's great overflow*: The river Nile runs through northern Africa and when it floods leaves a rich, fertile silt on the land.

The Ruin of this Island

This island lived in peace full many a day
So long as she unto the gods did pray,
But she grew proud with plenty, and with ease,
Adored her self, and did the gods displease.
She flung their altars down, and in their stead,   5
Set up her own, and would be worshippèd:
The gods grew angry, and commanded Fate
To alter, and to ruin quite the state.
For they had changed their mind of late, they said,
And did repent unthankful man th'had made: 10
Fates wondered much, to hear what said the gods,
That they and mortal men were at great odds;
And found them apt to change, thought it did show,
As if the gods did not poor men foreknow.
For why, said they, if men do evil grow,   15
The gods foreseeing all, men's hearts did know,
Long, long, before they did man first create;
If so, what need they change, or alter fate?
'Twas in their power to make them good or ill:
Wherefore men cannot do just what they will.   20
Then why do gods complain against them so,
Since men are made by them such ways to go?
If evil power hath gods to oppose,
Two equal deities it plainly shows;
The one pow'r cannot keep obedience long   25
If disobedient power be as strong
And being ignorant how men will prove,
Know not how strong, or long will last their love.
But may't not be the course of God's decree,
To love obedience wheresoe'er it be?   30
They from the first a changing power create,
And for that work make destiny and fate.
It is the mind of man, that's apt to range,
The minds of gods are not subject to change.
Then did the Fates unto the planets go   35
And told them they malignity must throw
Into this island, for the gods would take
Revenge on them, who did their laws forsake.
With that the planets drew, like with a screw,
Bad vapours from the earth, and then did view   40

241

What place, to squeeze that poison on, which all
The venom had got from the world's great ball.
Then through men's veins, like molten lead it came,
And did like oil their spirit all inflame,
Where malice boiled with rancour, spleen, and spite,   45
In war, and fraud, injustice took delight;
Thinking which way their lusts they might fulfil,
Committed thefts, rapes, murders at their will.
Parents and children did unnatural grow,
And every friend was turned a cruel foe.   50
Nay, innocency no protection had,
Religious men were thought to be stark mad,
In witches, wizards they did put their trust,
Extortions, bribes, were thought to be most just.
Like Titan's race, all did in tumults rise   55
And 'gainst the heavens utter blasphemies;
The gods in rage unbound the winds to blow
In a strange nation, formerly their foe,
Where they themselves did plant, the natives all
Were by them killed, for th'gods had sworn their fall.   60
Compassion wept, and Virtue wrung her hands,
To see that right was banished from their lands.
Thus winds, and seas, the planets, fates, and all,
Conspired to work her ruin, and her fall.
But those that keep the laws of God on high,   65
Shall live in peace, i'th'grave rest quietly
And ever after like the gods shall be,
Enjoy all pleasure, know no misery.

Note

In this poem, counterpart to 'A Description of an Island', Cavendish imagines Civil War wracking the island. Here the English Civil War is seen as a punishment for rebellion and lack of faith, with an allusion to the myth of the rebellious Titans, and perhaps also the rebel angels expelled from heaven. Many writers saw Civil War as God's retribution, either for Charles's wickedness or for the parliamentarians' wickedness in challenging Charles, but Cavendish makes less of a partisan political point and instead creates a mythologising portrait of the disordered isles.

55] *Titan's race*: race of deities in Greek mythology who rebelled against Zeus.

In the original printed versions both plural 'gods' and singular 'God' are capitalised, so that the distinction between pagan and Christian is not emphasised as it is in this modernised version. The final lines of the poem do, though, seem to show Cavendish distinguishing the two. See also her 'A Description of an Island'.

Wherein Poetry Chiefly Consists

Most of our modern writers nowadays,
Consider not the fancy but the phrase,
As if fine words were wit; or, one should say,
A woman's handsome, if her clothes be gay,
Regarding not what beauty's in the face,   5
Nor what proportion doth the body grace.
As when her shoes be high, to say she's tall,
And when she is strait-laced, to say she's small;
When painted, or her hair is curled with art,
Though of itself but plain, and her skin swart.   10
We cannot say, that from her thanks are due
To nature, nor those arts in her we view.
Unless she them invented, and so taught
The world to set forth that which is stark naught.
But fancy is the eye, gives life to all;   15
Words, the complexion, as a whited wall;
Fancy the form is, flesh, blood, skin and bone;
Words are but shadows, substance they have none.
But number is the motion, gives the grace,
And is the count'nance of a well-formed face.   20

Note

In her poems and prefaces, Cavendish propounds a theory of literature
that promotes originality, naturalness, and wit over learning, allusion,
and form. In this poem, her rejection of 'dress' is an interesting coun-
terpoint to the way in which her poems were carefully revised, put in
new dress, for their second publication in 1664. See also her 'The Clasp'
('Give me a free and noble style').

8] *strait-laced*: wearing a tight bodice or corset.
10] *swart*: swarthy, dark.
14] *stark naught*: absolutely nothing.

A Description of a Shepherd's and Shepherdess's Life

The shepherdesses which great flocks do keep
Are dabbled high with dew, following their sheep,
Milking their ewes, their hands doth dirty make;
For they being wet, dirt from their dugs do take.
Through the sun's heat their skin doth yellow grow,   5
Their eyes are red, lips dry with winds that blow.
Their shepherds sit on tops of mountains high,
And on their feeding sheep do cast an eye,
Which to the mount's steep sides they hanging feed
On short moss grass, not suffered to bear seed.   10
Their feet are small, but strong each sinew's string,
Which makes them fast to rocks and mountains cling;
The while the shepherd's legs hang dangling down,
He sets his breech upon the hill's high crown.
Like as a tanned hide, so is his skin,   15
No melting heat, or numbing cold gets in,
And with a voice that's harsh against his throat,
He strains to sing, yet knows not any note:
He, lazy, yawning lies upon his side,
Or on his back, and hath his arms spread wide;   20
Or snorting sleeps, and dreams of Joan his maid,
Or of hobgoblins, wakes, as being afraid.
Motion in his dull brains doth plough and sow,
Not plant, and set, as skilful gardeners do.
Then takes his knife half broke, but ground again;   25
And whittles sticks his sheep-coat up to pin:
Or cuts some holes in straw to pipe thereon
Some amorous tunes, which pleases his love Joan.
Thus rustic clowns are pleased to spend their times,
And not as poets feign, in verse and rhymes,   30
Making great kings and princes pastures keep,
And beauteous ladies follow flocks of sheep:
And dance 'bout maypoles in a rustic sort,
When ladies scorn to dance without a court.

2] *dabbled*: made wet.
4] *dugs*: teats.
13] *dangling*: moving lightly, swinging.
22] *hobgoblins*: imps or sprites.
28] *Joan*: generic woman's name.

They would their lovers hate, if they should come   35
With leather jerkins, breeches made of thrum,
And buskins made of frieze that's coarse and strong,
And clouted shoes, tied with a leather thong.
Those that are nicely bred, fine clothes still love,
A fair white hand doth hate a dirty glove.   40

Note

In this poem Cavendish subverts the pastoral tradition of idealising descriptions of shepherds and shepherdesses with her own decidedly more grubby and realistic view. While the conventional shepherdess is naturally beautiful, Cavendish points out that she is more likely to be dirty and have yellow skin, dry lips, and red eyes from the outdoors, rather than the white skin, red lips, and blue or dark eyes of convention. Instead of playing beautiful music and composing poetry, the shepherd 'strains to sing, yet knows not any note'.

36] *thrum*: a weaving term for a fringe of threads.
37] *buskins*: boots. *frieze*: cloth made from coarse wool.
38] *clouted*: patched.

Margaret Cavendish

The Clasp: Of Fairies in the Brain

Who knows, but that in every brain may dwell
Those creatures we call fairies, who can tell?
And by their several actions they may frame
Those forms and figures, which we fancies name.
And when we sleep, those visions, dreams we call,   5
May by their industry be raised all;
And all the objects, which through senses get,
Within the brain they may in order set.
And some pack up, as merchants do each thing,
Which they sometimes may to the memory bring.   10
And thus, besides our own imaginations,
May fairies in our brain beget inventions.
If so, then th'eye's the sea, where by the gale
Of passions, on salt tears their ship doth sail,
And when a tear doth break, as it doth fall,   15
Or wiped away, they may a shipwreck call.
There from the stomach vapours do arise,
And fly up to the head, as to the skies
And as great storms, their houses down may blow,
Where, by their fall, the head may dizzy grow.   20
And when those houses they build up again,
With knocking they may put the head to pain;
When they dig deep, perchance a tooth may ache,
And from a tooth a quarry-bone may take;
Which they, like stone, may build their house withal: 25
If much took out, the tooth may rotten fall.
Those that dwell near the ears, are very cool,
For they are both the south, and northern pole.
The eyes are sun and moon, which give them light,
When open, day, when shut, it is dark night.   30

Note

In this poem, Cavendish conjectures playfully that tiny fairies in the
brain could be the cause of imagination, dreams, and memories, functions
of the mind which seventeenth-century natural philosophy was exploring.
See also her 'A World in an Earring'.

9] Cavendish note: 'All objects which the senses bring in, are like merchandises brought
   from foreign parts'.
25] *withal*: along with the rest; as well.

Upon the Funeral of my Dear Brother, Killed in these Unhappy Wars

Alas! Who shall my funeral mourner be,
Since none is near that is allied to me?
Or who shall drop a sacrificing tear,
If none but enemies my hearse shall bear?

For here's no mourner to lament my fall,   5
But in my fate, though sad, rejoicèd all,
And think my heavy ruin far too light,
So cruel is their malice, spleen and spite!

For men no pity nor compassion know,
But like fierce beasts in savage wildness go,   10
To wash and bathe themselves in my poor blood,
As if they health received from that red flood.

Yet will the winds my doleful knell ring out,
And showering rain fall on my hearse about;
The birds, as mourners, on my tomb shall sit,   15
And grass, like as a covering, grow on it.

Then let no spade, nor pickaxe come near me,
But let my bones in peace rest quietly;
He, who the dead dislodges from their grave,
Shall neither blessedness, nor honour have.   20

Note

In 1653 this poem was entitled simply 'Of a Funeral' but in 1664 it became 'Upon the Funeral of my Dear Brother, Killed in these Unhappy Wars'. Cavendish probably felt able to be more specific in her political comment after the Restoration, as the poem now commemorates the death of her royalist brother Charles Lucas, who was executed by parliamentarian forces in 1648. The poem's form is also changed, from stanzas in which only the last two lines rhyme to stanzas of two couplets, a stanza is omitted (see 'Textual notes'). On elegies for Charles Lucas (and George Lisle, who died with him) see Brady, 'Dying with Honour'; and see Pulter, 'On those Two Unparalleled Friends, Sir George Lisle and Sir Charles Lucas'.

14] *hearse*: tomb, grave.

Lucy Hutchinson (1620–1681)

Lucy Hutchinson was an educated republican and religious Independent (believing that church congregations should govern themselves rather than be subject to ecclesiastical or state governance). She was born in 1620 to enlightened parents, Sir Allen Apsley and Lucy St John, who furnished the young Lucy Apsley with an education rivalling that of most boys of the period. While Lucy Apsley's later identity as a puritan and parliamentarian was influenced by her mother's religion, her father's strong royalist connections also influenced the writer. Both her brothers fought for the king, and her cousin Anne St John married Henry Wilmot, Earl of Rochester, and was the mother of John Wilmot, the Restoration's most notorious courtly debauché. Hutchinson's royalist associations are played out in her reading matter, and the poems included in this anthology reveal diverse literary influences. Lucy Apsley married John Hutchinson in 1638 and several years later moved to Nottinghamshire, where John Hutchinson took up the post of governor of Nottingham Castle. Hutchinson's *Memoirs of the Life of Colonel Hutchinson* recounts in detail her husband's actions through civil war and her version of its causes. John Hutchinson spent much time and thought over his decision to sign Charles I's death warrant.

The couple spent the 1650s mostly at the Owthorpe estate, managing the land and property, and it was probably at this time that Hutchinson wrote much of her poetry, including her version of Lucretius' Epicurean poem *De rerum natura*, which was one of the first translations into English of this radical and influential work. This was not a time of retreat from politics, however, as shown by 'To Mr Waller upon his Panegyric to the Lord Protector', her vicious parody of Edmund Waller's 'Panegyric to my Lord Protector'. This poem shows the couple's increasing frustration and disillusionment at what had happened to the godly republic for which they had hoped and worked. This was only intensified at the

Restoration. Though John Hutchinson was not executed with many other regicides, he was certainly at risk, and it was probably the support of his wife's family (through both St John and Apsley sides) which saved him. Hutchinson also tells in *Memoirs* of how she intervened even more actively, forging his signature on a letter recanting his republican views. Whether Hutchinson did indeed forge her husband's letter, or whether he wrote it and wished to whitewash his reputation after his death by claiming he remained true to his principles, is still a matter of considerable scholarly debate.

John Hutchinson was, however, arrested in 1663 on suspicion of participation in a Fifth Monarchist plot and died in prison in 1664. Much less is known about Hutchinson's life in the decade after her husband's death. She managed the Owthorpe estate and continued to write, producing among other things a manuscript collection of poignant and political elegies on her husband's death and probably also working on her biblical poem *Order and Disorder*. Lucy Hutchinson's full literary corpus has only recently come to light, and several manuscripts discovered or rediscovered in the past two decades have shown that she was a major poet as well as the author of *Memoirs*, long a crucial resource for Civil War historians. Across poetry and prose, print and manuscript, Hutchinson's writing bears the marks of her fervent hostility to corrupt rulers and her remarkably broad education, adventurous reading habits, and energetic intellect.

Lucy Hutchinson

From, *De rerum natura*

Book 1, lines 1–152

Fair Venus, mother of Aeneas' race,
Delight of gods and men, thou that dost grace
The starry firmament, the sea, the earth;
To whom all living creatures owe their birth,
By thee conceived, and brought forth to the day;   5
When thou (o goddess) come, storms fly away
And heaven is no more obscured with showers.
For thee the fragrant earth spreads various flowers,
The calmed ocean smiles, and at thy sight
The serene sky shines with augmented light,   10
Then doth the spring her glorious days disclose
And the released, life-giving west wind blows.
Thy power possessing, first, birds of the air
They thy approach with amorous notes declare,
Next when desires the savage herd incite   15
They swim through streams, and their fat pastures slight
To follow thee, who in seas, rivers, hills,
In the birds' leafy bowers, and in green fields,
Instilling wanton love into each mind,
Mak'st creatures strive to propagate their kind.   20
Since all things thus are brought to light by thee,
By whom alone their natures governed be,
From whom both loveliness and pleasure springs,
Assist me while the nature of these things
I sing to Memmius whom thou (goddess) hast   25
With all excelling gifts and virtues graced;
Wherefore sweet language in my thoughts infuse
And let not wars' harsh sounds disturb my Muse;

1] *Venus*: the Roman goddess of love, spring, and (partly through association with the Greek Aphrodite) fertility. She is also the lover of Mars. *Aeneas' race*: In the *Aeneid*, Virgil's hero Aeneas is the son of Venus and Anchises (a mortal man).

3] *firmament*: the sky or heaven.

12] *west wind*: The wind coming from the west was thought to be mild and to bring spring, as personified by Roman Favonius and Greek Zephyrus.

25] *Memmius*: Lucretius' patron, and also that of Catullus, Memmius was an orator, a praetor (Roman magistrate), and possibly a tribune, banished for political dishonesty, perhaps electoral malpractice, in 52 BC.

251

Make sea and land a quiet calm possess
For only thou with peace can mortals bless,   30
Since Mars, the mighty God that rules in arms,
Lies in thy lap, bound with love's powerful charms,
And resting there his head in full delight,
On thy rich beauty feeds his greedy sight;
Hanging with amorous kisses on thy face,   35
While thou (o goddess) dost this god embrace,
While he doth in thy sacred lap remain,
Sweet peace for Rome by gentle prayers obtain,
For neither can we with a quiet mind
In time of war, pursue the work designed,   40
Nor can brave Memmius, full of pious cares
For public good, neglect those great affairs.

    And thou (o Memmius) from all business freed,
Give my true reasonings an attentive heed,
Lest what my faithful love presents thee, should   45
As worthless be cast by, not understood.
For of the gods, of their celestial seat,
And the first rise of things, my labours treat:
Whence nature doth form, growth, and food impart
To all, whither their dissolved frames revert,   50
What we in reasoning the first matter call
Generative bodies, and the seeds of all,
How these first bodies include everything,
How out of them all other bodies spring.

    The divine nature doth itself possess   55
In immortality, and everlasting peace,
Removed far off from mortal men's affairs,
Neither our sorrows, nor our dangers shares,
Rich in itself, of us no want it hath,
Not moved with merits, nor disturbed with wrath.   60
    When human life on earth was much distressed,
With burdensome superstition sore oppressed,

31–32] *Mars ... Lies in thy lap*: In Roman myth Venus and Mars, the god of war, were lovers.

41, 43] See note on line 25.

47] Hutchinson note: 'The argument of the poem'.

55] Hutchinson note: 'A description of the divine nature'.

61] Hutchinson note: 'A Mention of Epicurus whose philosophy our poet translates'.

Who from the starry regions showed her head,
And with fierce looks poor mortals menaced,
A Greek it was that first durst lift his eyes   65
Against her, and oppose her tyrannies;
Whose courage neither heaven's loud threat'nings quelled,
Nor tales of gods, nor thunderbolts repelled,
But rather did his valour animate,
To force his way through nature's close-barred gate;   70
Wherefore his vigorous soul prevailed, and far
He went beyond those flaming walls which are
Bounds to the universe, his conquering thought
Searched into every depth, from whence he brought
The knowledge of all things to light, and taught   75
What could admit beginnings, what could not,
What powers are limited, and what are free,
And why the bounds of things still fixed be.
Thus in her turn now superstition lies
Trod down, while victory heaves us to the skies.   80
        But here I fear these principles to thee
May wicked seem, leading t'impiety:
Yet often superstition in old times
Hath been an author of foul impious crimes.
The Grecian chiefs, the world's choice men, constrained   85
By a too cruel zeal, at Aulis stained
The goddess's knives in Iphianassa's blood,
While she poor victim in the temple stood,
With sacred fillets flowing on each side
Of her sad cheeks, and all at once espied   90
Her much grieved father, the sad officers,
The sheathèd steel, and the spectators' tears.
Struck mute with fear, she bent her knees on earth,
Yet neither this, nor that her royal birth
First gave a father's title to a king,   95
Could to the wretch relief at that time bring,

81] Hutchinson note: 'An apology for his doctrine showing the mischief superstition
   hath brought forth'.
86] *Aulis*: town where the Greek army, led by Agamemnon, prepared to attack Troy
   in Homer's account.
87] *Iphianassa*: the original name for Iphigeneia, daughter of Agamemnon, sacrificed
   by her father in attempt to assuage the goddess Artemis, whom he had offended.
89] *sacred fillets*: a ribbon or fabric headdress worn by sacrificial victims.

Whom trembling to the altar men's rude hands
With violence haled, not to complete the bands
Of glorious nuptials, with th'accustomed rite,
But that the virgin, ripe for marriage, might   100
A woeful victim, by her father slain,
A prosperous voyage for his fleet obtain.
Such mischiefs superstition could persuade.
Even you yourself attempts have sometimes made,
Vanquished with terror, when the priests did tell   105
Their frightful tales, from our truths to rebel.
For I could easily many dreams invent,
Which would quite overthrow and change th'intent
Of all your life, perplexing with just fear
Your whole estate; for if men saw there were   110
A certain bound to their calamity,
Then superstitious forms and threats would be
Withstood by all, which none dares now oppose,
Since after death they dread eternal woes.
For the soul's nature is mysterious,   115
Whether at our birth infused, or born with us,
Whether in death it with the body ends,
Or after death to hell's vast caves descends,
Or into other beasts itself conveys,
As our great Ennius mentions in his lays,   120
Who Helicon, first of th'Italians, found,
Whence he with never-fading laurel crowned,
In his immortal verse these secrets brought;
Who singing of th'Acherusian temples, taught
That not our souls nor bodies there remain,   125
But pale ghosts which our images retain.

98] *haled*: dragged or pulled.
102] *voyage for his fleet*: Agamemnon sacrificed his daughter to appease Artemis, who
was keeping his battle ships becalmed.
119] *into other beasts itself conveys*: the idea that souls moved from one body to another
at death, called metempsychosis or transmigration, and often associated with
Pythagoras.
120] *Ennius*: a Roman philosopher who propounded metempsychosis in his history
of Rome, the *Annals*. *lays*: lyrics or songs.
121] *Helicon*: a mountain in Greece and locations of fountains thought to be the source
of poetic inspiration.
124] *th'Acherusian temples*: The river Acheron, which passed through the lake Acherus,
was one of the rivers of the underworld in ancient Greek and Latin mythology.

Hence, said he, Homer's weeping shadow came,
Homer, who still survives in lasting fame,
And nature's mysteries with salt tears told.
Since then our thoughts do labour to behold 130
Superior things, the motion of the sun
And moon, the power by which all things are done,
On earth, let subtle reason search to find
The cause of souls, the nature of the mind,
And what's that obvious thing which doth affright 135
Our thoughts, sick, sleeping, waking to our sight
And ears presenting shapes, and sounds of those
Whose dry bones, long since dead, dark graves enclose.
How hard a task I've taken to rehearse
The Greek obscurities in Latin verse, 140
The scantness of the tongue, and novelty
Of things whereof I treat, makes me well see,
Yet doth your virtue, and the hope t'obtain
Your pleasing friendship, lessen all the pain,
Inducing me to spend my wakeful nights 145
In searching words, which may convey clear light
Into your mind, that so you may discern
All hidden things, and nature's mysteries learn;
For not the sun, nor the bright beams of day,
Can the mind's mists and terrors drive away, 150
But nature's contemplation, wherein
Our disquisitions we from hence begin.

Note

Lucretius' project was to provide a rational and materialist account 'of the nature of things' (as in the poem's title, *De rerum natura*) without gods at its centre. Drawing on Epicurus, he developed a model of the universe composed of atoms (although Lucretius does not use the term 'atom', Hutchinson does). In this opening passage, Lucretius invokes a goddess, Venus, but uses her to represent not supernatural power but the vital power of nature; Venus personifies springtime and the ineluctable natural impulse to reproduce. The passage moves on to a rejection of superstition because it causes irrational cruelty such as Agamemnon's

127] *Homer's weeping shadow*: Ennius was reputed to have claimed that he was the reincarnation of Homer.

sacrifice of his daughter Iphianassa (Iphigeneia). Lucretius argues that humans seek supernatural frameworks of belief because of their fears of death, and that debunking these fears will liberate humans from such senseless cruelty.

See Chaucer's *Troilus and Criseyde* for another opening invocation to Venus, and Spenser's *The Faerie Queene*, IV.10. See Cavendish, 'The Purchase of Poets, or A Dialogue Betwixt the Poets, and Fame and Homer's Marriage' for a more playful and irreverent treatment of classical poets and her 'A World Made by Atoms' and 'Nature Calls a Council' for different, but equally materialist, accounts of the world's origins.

Book 2, lines 1048–1180

Attend then my discourse, wherein a new
True face of things, presents itself to you.
There's nothing plain, of which belief is not   1050
With difficulty at the first begot,
And all, that man at first with wonder sees,
Loses its admiration by degrees.
What greater miracle can mortals frame
Than the pure azure sky, the glorious flame   1055
Of every star which wanders there, the bright
Orb of the moon, the sun's refulgent light,
Which were they yet unknown, how would men gaze
On such strange objects, how would they amaze
The sense of vulgar men, who scarce would dare   1060
To credit that such things in nature were,
Who now cloyed with the frequent sight despise
The glorious view of the bright arched skies.
No longer then, with strangeness terrified
Let reason be your thoughts' access denied;   1065
But with strict judgement weigh the whole dispute
And if't be true, assent, if not, confute.
        Here then the mind enquires, by reason's light,
Since space beyond the world is infinite,
What those vast regions are, what they can show,   1070
Where the free mind desires so much to go?
First know, that space is unconfined and wide,
Neither above, beneath, nor on each side,
As its own nature, and our doctrine shows,
Do any bounds th'unfathomed deep enclose.   1075
Thus can it no way probable appear,
Since boundless space lies open everywhere,
And seeds innumerable exercise
Perpetually in these profundities,
Their varied motions, that one small world can   1080
In this created heaven and earth contain,

1048] Hutchinson note: 'The difficulty of penetrating strange things'.
1057] *refulgent*: radiant, glorious.
1065] i.e. do not deny reason access to your thoughts.
1068] Hutchinson note: 'The reason of this world may persuade us there are more
    worlds springing from the same causes'.

Such infinite operations, when as all
This universe had its original
From free encounters of the seeds, who met
Oft with vain strokes, did at the length beget,   1085
By casual occursions, this great frame,
And from one right conjunction came
Both heaven, earth, sea and every animal;
We must confess, the matter then may fall
Elsewhere into the like conjunctures, and frame there   1090
Such worlds as this, enclosed with ambient air.
Again much matter fitted, large room made
When neither things nor causes are delayed,
Productions must ensue, where seeds amount
To such vast numbers, as no age can count;   1095
Where the same force and natures they enjoy,
Which they in other places may employ,
To congregate more worlds than this of ours;
We must acknowledge that those powers
In diverse places several worlds do build,   1100
With other men and various creatures filled.
Besides, as in the sum of things, no one
Is singly born, no creature grows alone,
But wheresoe'er we turn our thoughts, we find
In each race multitudes of the same kind,   1105
As, first amongst the animals, we trace
The mountains' wild inhabitants, the race
Of mortal men, mute herds, that bright scales wear,
And every fowl which cleaves the liquid air.
By the same reason, it must be confessed,   1110
The heaven, earth, seas, sun, moon, and all the rest,
Are not alone in single beings found
But all, in numbers numberless, abound,
Whose lives so long preserve their fixèd term
And so long last their native bodies firm,   1115
As all those generations they contain

1086] *occursions*: collisions.
1090] *conjunctures*: joinings, conjunctions.
1091] *ambient*: surrounding.
1109] *liquid*: clear, bright.

Do undissolved in their kinds remain.
    Nature, if this you rightly understand,
Will thus appear free from the proud command
Of sovereign power, who of her own accord   1120
Doth all things act, subjected to no lord.
The gods do in eternal calmness rest
Their holy lives with quiet pleasures blessed;
What power almighty, sitting at the helm
Can guide the reins of such a boundless realm?   1125
What god can turn heaven's orbs, and feed those fires
With the thick vapours fruitful earth expires?
Whose presence can at once fill every place?
Who can with black mists darken heaven's face,
And shake the clouds with thunder's loud report,   1130
With dreadful lightnings trouble his own court,
Whence the disturbèd god in rage retires,
And darts at mortals his consuming fires,
Which, oft ill-aimed, the innocent destroy
While wicked men their guilty lives enjoy?   1135
Now after every world's nativity,
That time wherein earth, sea, and heaven be
At first disclosed, new seeds from th'outward space,
Whose vast circumference doth that world embrace,
Arrive, and, by their new access, beget   1140
Motions, which make the universe complete,
Which do enlarge the sea and th'earth's extent,
And which display the glorious firmament,
Advancing the celestial courts above
And, far from earth, the purer air remove.   1145
Yet all these bodies, wheresoe'er the force
Of others hurry them, still have recourse
To their own kind, so waters still retire
To waters, air to air, and fire to fire,
As earth to earth resolves, till nature bring   1150
By these renewed supplies, to every thing
That perfect growth, that can no more receive
An augmentation, which doth then arrive

1118] Hutchinson note: 'Of the undisturbed quiet of the gods and the free actings of
    nature – horribly impious –'.
1136–38] Hutchinson note: 'The progress of the seed after every world's nativity'.

When vital conduits no more food convey
Then what elsewhere doth flow, and pass away.   1155
Nature the ages of all things ordains
And to a certain pitch their growths restrains;
For all who joyfully climb to that ascent
Which doth their lives to mature age augment,
Take in more bodies than again they lose,   1160
While all their food through narrow conduits flows,
Till the full age enlarge the veins so wide
That more food passes out, than is supplied.
Bodies to things come and return again
By several ways, but still more enter in   1165
Till things unto their full-ripe ages climb,
And then their force and vigour from that time
Doth lessen by degrees, and still decay,
Till age at length convey it quite away.
Now every thing, as't grows more vast and great,   1170
So doth it from all parts evacuate
More bodies, neither can the veins admit
Through their conduits food enough for it;
Nor can the large dilated arteries
Carry so much as will that bulk suffice,   1175
Or feed so vast a nature with supplies;
Which weakened by th'efflux, at length must fail
And quite fall down, when outward blows assail,
When food decays and vigorous motions cease,
Which should that outward violence suppress.   1180

Note

Lucretius continues his project of presenting 'a new / True face of things'
by stripping away superstition, foregrounding the understanding of nature,
and relegating supernatural powers to their rightful, lower place. He
describes mankind's changing perceptions of the world and the distorting
effect of novelty and familiarity. Our perception of phenomena which
are miraculous – the sky, seas, stars, and moon – is 'cloyed with the

---

1154] *When vital conduits no more food convey*: This line has been added in to the
    manuscript in Lucy Hutchinson's hand, the scribe presumably having missed it out
    accidentally.
1177] *efflux*: a flowing-out of water or gas.

260

frequent sight'. This passage combines a sense of wonder at the natural world ('the pure azure sky, the glorious flame / Of every star which wanders there') with a desire for the understanding gained by a 'free mind' through 'reason's light'. As in the first book, Lucretius does not deny the existence of deities, but firmly dethrones them; nature, he argues, is 'subjected to no lord'. Moreover, he suggests that it is likely that there are 'more worlds than this of ours' in the universe. Hutchinson finds the passage 'horribly impious' in her marginal note, though notably she does not omit it from this presentation copy of her translation. See Cavendish, 'A World in an Earring' and 'Of Stars'.

Book 4, lines 1019–1321

Now to whatever thoughts men's minds are tied,
Those businesses in which they're most employed,   1020
Those studies upon which they're most intent,
Their dreams unto their fancies represent.
So lawyers manage causes, statutes write;
Commanders wars pursue, and battles fight;
Sailors with the opposing winds contend;   1025
So we our search in nature's mysteries spend,
Translating them into our native speech.
So every other art, and study which
Employs men's busy minds, their dreams repeat.
Those who upon excessive pleasures set   1030
Their daily thought, when now sleep hath bereft
Their sense of real enjoyments, yet hath left
Open way for images t'approach the mind,
In them a review of their pleasures find.
Their dreams restoring all those sportful days   1035
Wherein they, as awake, believe they gaze
Upon the chorus dancing in just time,
They think they hear soft lutes and well-tuned rhyme,
On crowded theatres, see those glorious sights
With which the oft-changed scene men's eyes delights.   1040
Thus from the works they daily exercise
Their will and inclinations, men's dreams rise.
Not only theirs but every beast's, so we
Oft in their sleeps may generous horses see
Panting and bathed in sweat, as if they did,   1045
Loosed from the post, contend with eager speed
To gain the victor's palm; so the swift hound,
As having the fresh scent of wild beasts found,
Oft in his dreams sets up his fiercest cry,
Thrusts forth his legs, and casts his nose on high,   1050
And in the air oft winds the flying harts,
Pursuing whose vain images, he starts
Amazèdly from sleep, with swift speed runs,
Till quitting these vain apprehensions,

1019] Hutchinson note: 'The reason of dreams'.
1022] *fancies*: imaginations.

They to themselves return; and then again   1055
Those gentler whelps which in the house remain,
Oft shake off their soft sleeps, and start upright
As if some unknown face came in their sight.
But as each creature springs of fiercer kind
So are they to more turbulent dreams inclined   1060
And many sorts of birds, and fearful doves,
Fly to the shelter of the hallowed groves,
Dreaming they are by greedy kites pursued
Who strive to seize their carcasses for food.
Man's noble thought, designing mighty deeds,   1065
Dreams of such brave heroic actions breeds.
Kings dream they conquer towns, great battles gain,
Or that they're captived, ready to be slain,
At which they shriek out with amazed cries;
Some fight, some mourn oppressed with miseries,   1070
Some in the panthers or the lion's jaws,
Roar with the terror those vain fancies cause.
Sleeping, some matters of great moment tell,
And oft-times their most secret deeds reveal.
Some dream of death, some of steep mountains whence   1075
Their o'erwhelmed bodies fall with violence,
Frighted with which, they waken in amaze
And cannot suddenly their terrors chase.
Some dream of thirst, and sitting on the brink
Of pleasant springs or floods, the whole stream drink;   1080
Young boys who dream of puddles wet
The shining Babylonian coverlet.
And youths who first attain their manly age
The images of beauty into lusts engage

[...]

So to consume in sloth their best of time   1200
Or when by a mistress left in doubt, desire
Rages within their breasts like unquenched fire,
Or if they see her eyes on others glance
Or laughter in her scornful countenance.

1084, 1200] Hutchinson note: 'The cause and effects of love which he makes a kind
  of dream but much here was left out for a midwife to translate whose obscene art
  it would better become then a nicer pen'. Hutchinson does indeed omit lines here;
  see the note to this extract on p. 267.

These ills molest love's best and happiest state,   1205
Those which attend a cross and adverse fate
Exceed all number, and are daily seen.
Wherefore 'tis best for men not to let in
This enemy of quiet, but with care
To shun the foe; for love's entangling snare   1210
With heed may be avoided, but to get
Freedom again, catched in that snaring net,
To break of love's strong cords, is harder far;
And yet even those who in his fetters are,
If they resist not their own liberty   1215
Themselves again may from that thraldom free.
Pass by the errors, first of thine own thoughts
Nor yet take notice of thy mistress' faults,
For men, whom love blinds, oft extol that grace
Which is not real in their idol's face.   1220
Thus many who are foul, and ugly prove
Objects of adoration and of love.
So several beauties, several fancies please
When men are poisoned with love's foul disease,
For they who languish in that torturing pain   1225
Perceive not what sad ill they entertain:
A foul ungraceful slut black Melichra,
Dorcas dry kex, Palladion's eyes are grey,
Pumilio a dwarf, Charita tart and small,
And full of jeers, another large and tall   1230
Cataplexis proud and majestical,
Balba wants utterance, stammers when she speaks,
Lisping Trauliza holds her tongue and sneaks,
Malicious, hot Lampadian is a scold,
Withered Ischnos, dying, lean and old.   1235

1216] Hutchinson note: 'The remedy of love's inconveniences'.
1226–39] Continuing his theme that lust causes us to delude ourselves, Lucretius here
    imagines a series of euphemistic terms which men use to disguise women's faults.
    So the name Melichra suggests 'honey-coloured' while the woman is dark; Dorcas
    associates the dried-up woman with the lively 'gazelle'; a fiery-tempered woman is
    a 'little lamp' (Lampadian). Early modern translators took a variety of approaches
    to this passage, with Thomas Creech and John Dryden anglicising the euphemisms.
    This already complex passage is further complicated as Hutchinson does not
    straightforwardly translate Lucretius, sometimes because of problems with the Latin
    text she was using (see Hutchinson, *The Translation of Lucretius*, ed. Barbour and
    Norbrook, vol. 1, pp. 674–76, for a full discussion of this passage).
1228] *kex*: a sapless, dry person.

A wasting rotten cough consumes Rhadine,
Big-breasted Ceres, foggy with the wine.
Simula false, Silena lecherous,
Big-lipped Philema, Satura gluttonous,
And many more, nor can I here declare   1240
All the defects which in these creatures are.
But grant a loveliness in every face,
Let Venus' beauty all their fair limbs grace,
Yet since many share like perfection,
What need you tie yourself to any one?   1245
Without her you have lived, and you may spy,
Even in the best, concealed deformity.
All with perfumes their nasty savours hide,
Which their own waiting maids, loathe and deride.
But the excluded lover at her doors   1250
Stands weeping, kisses the proud posts, strews flowers,
Sprinkles sweet essences, hangs up fresh wreaths,
But being let in, offended when she breathes,
He seeks out fair pretences to be gone,
Forgets the speech he did before so con,   1255
Condemns his folly, which ascribed to her
What none on mortals justly can confer;
This to our wantons is so known, that they
Most of their parts behind the arras play,
Wisely concealing their defects from those   1260
Whose loved addresses they are loath to lose;
But vain's their subtlety, for wise thought may
All their concealment and their arts survey;
Nor will ingenious women, free from pride
Human defects from honest lovers hide.   1265
Nor do the female sex their sighs still feign
Sometimes their breasts a real love contain.
One fire, them and their lovers doth inflame,
Their joys are equal, their desires the same.
Nor could all birds, beasts, herds and flocks increase, 1270
Unless desires the females did possess.
Both sexes must all generations make,
In which some offsprings more the sire partake,
Some more the dam, and so we find

1255] *con*: learn (in order to recite).

Even in the generations of menkind,   1275
Their father's images some children bear,
Some like their mothers, and their grandsires are.
For in their parents' bodies are mixed seeds
Which this variety of figures breeds;
Wherein the little offspring do arise   1280
With their forefathers' countenance, shape, hair, voice.
Sometimes in girls the father's face we see,
The mother's in the boy's, sometimes they be
Made up of both, and so we in one face
Lines both of father and of mother trace;   1285
And whom the children do most represent
That parent's nature is most prevalent.
Nor must we to the high powers attribute
That they, cursing our age, deny us fruit,
Sweet children which might cheer the pensive heart,   1290
When they a father's happy name impart,
Yet thinking thus, men to the altars bring
With mournful tears, their bloody offering,
Burn incense, and devout hands heave
Praying the gods to make their wives conceive;   1295
When barrenness not from those powers proceeds,
But too much drying heat or moisture breeds
Its causes in the parents, when they be
Of constitutions which do ill agree.
For natures must in their conjunctions suit   1300
Or else they never can conceive their fruit.
Thus some are barren in their first wife's days
And many children by a second raise.
Some, who unmarried take their liberty
And in their wand'ring lusts unfruitful be,   1305
When they their wild desires with wedlock bound
Have their chaste joys with plenteous issue crowned.
'Tis here observable what food men use,
For as some more to fruitfulness conduce,
So barrenness is caused by other meat.   1310
Wives also should take heed that they be neat
Nor need our husband's care to be in love,

1288] Hutchinson note: 'The cause of barrenness'.
1311] *neat*: tidy, but also elegant, comely, refined.

Sometimes unhandsome women good wives prove;
Her modest carriage, and her cleanly dress,
Her wise behaviour, and her gentleness   1315
Will yield her husband a contented life,
And custom will incline him to his wife.
The least attempts in long time will prevail,
And make the strongest oppositions fail,
So on hard rocks, still-dropping water wears   1320
The solid stone, by its continued tears.

Note

In Lucretius' rational explanation of the world, dreams are not symbolic nor visitations by gods, but are explained as reflections of our daily activities and preoccupations. This passage shows Lucretius' complex attitude to women and gender, ranging from stereotypes of grotesque female corporeality to startling assertions of gender equality. Both these extremes are shaped by Lucretius' materialist view of identity, which stresses biological imperatives: women must have the same desires as men or we would not reproduce ourselves. He also portrays the fickleness of men's views of women. Hutchinson's omission of Lucretius' account of sex (lines 1085–1199) has drawn much attention, partly because it is one of the rare moments where we see the translator commenting on the radical and bold poem she translates, but this should not be read as a rejection of the poem in its entirety, nor as exclusively motivated by gender. John Evelyn was also troubled by this passage of the poem (see Hutchinson, *The Translation of Lucretius*, ed. Barbour and Norbrook). The materialist image of love with which the passage ends may seem unromantic, even anti-romantic, though the process of familiarisation and custom does seem largely positive here and perhaps also reflects the humanistic value placed on friendship (see Nussbaum, *The Therapy of Desire*). Compare 'The Recovery', where the couple are reunited after John Hutchinson's death in a rock symbolic of Godlike durability and stability but perhaps also a Lucretian materiality (see Goldberg, 'Lucy Hutchinson Writing Matter').

From British Library, Additional MS 17018

To Mr Waller upon his Panegyric to the Lord Protector

1

Whilst with a smooth but yet a servile tongue
You court all factions, and have sweetly sung
The triumphs of your country's overthrow,
Raising the glory of her treacherous foe.

2

Let partial spirits praise aloud the verse   5
And with like flattery your soft lines rehearse;
Let those who still with present powers comply
Join to insult o'er vanquished liberty.

3

Yet you who would his highness' praise express
Even in your eulogies his crimes confess,   10
Exalting his vast pride which hath suppressed
Less unconfined ambition in the rest.

4

Before the first great wound of civil hate
Was healed, he made new rents in the weak state;
To his usurpèd throne the neighbours come   15
Instead of cure to fetch a sadder doom.

5

The sea's our own, and yet all nations meet
The English exiles in the English fleet;
The tyrant's uncontrolled breath wafts o'er
The British natives to the Indian shore.   20

5] *partial*: prejudiced (in favour of Waller).

13] *great wound of civil hate*: the Civil War, though Hutchinson is keen to argue that this wound could be healed by a better ruler (rather than by a return to monarchy, as royalist opponents of course demanded).

14] *new rents in the weak state*: Hutchinson sees Cromwell compromising the achievements of the Civil War and republic.

20] *Indian shore*: Cromwell was committed to the controversial military expedition to the Spanish West Indies, the 'western design'.

6

All Europe's states who this isle's glory saw
With envious eyes whilst she their pride did awe,
In this conjunction do on Britain smile
The basest ruler and the noblest isle.

7

Whether this portion of the world were rent   25
By Heaven's just hand from kings of high descent
Or by this smooth-tongued traitor undermined,
'Twas for our heavy punishment designed.

8

Hither the oppressed may henceforth resort
Justice to crave but find no help at court   30
Until the false dissembler not alone
Be unto us, but unto the whole world known.

9

Fame swifter than the wingèd navy flies
And tells th'Iberians his deep policies,
Whose armèd guards whilst namely he assails;   35
Th'attempt fills all shores with ridiculous tales.

10

With such a chief the noblest nation blessed
Could never hope t'advance his plumèd crest
In honour's field, we then whom war doth hire
Can only think in bondage to expire.   40

11

He being made in his usurpèd reign
Lord of the world's great waste the ocean;
The enclosed isle with sad exactions grieves,
And foreign lands more troubles than relieves.

26] *By Heaven's just hand from kings of high descent*: Hutchinson suggests that the regicide might be divinely ordained (the opposite argument to Waller's royalist critics) but that this new state has been jeopardised by Cromwell's own tyranny.

30] *at court*: as in Waller's original (though in his hands this was a positive), Cromwell's 'court' refers to his legal role overseeing a court of law, but also implies monarchical ambitions.

34] *tells th'Iberians his deep policies*: See note to line 20. Cromwell had tried to keep his military plans secret.

12

Angels and we have one prerogative: 45
That none can at our happy seats arrive,
Yet hence the quiet nations he invades
And bars the oppressed natives, strangers' aid.

13

Our little world with blessings doth abound,
A pleasant heaviness a fruitful ground   50
Of her own growth hath all that nature craves
And all that's rare as tribute from the waves.

14

Whence the usurper doth his treasures raise
And grievous imposts upon all things lays.
Yet none what the ocean or the earth supplies   55
Can his ambitious greedy thoughts suffice.

15

Not choicest aromatics, nor rich wine,
Nor bright silks which our scornèd fetters line,
Can comfort the unwilling slaves that be
Cheated of their more precious liberty.   60

16

Whilst freeborn English sent to other soils
Are there killed up with sickness and vain toils
To augment His Highness' treasure and his name
Not satisfied with any wealth or fame.

17

What of the noblest kind our own land breeds?   65
All our courageous men and warlike steeds
Are yielded up or grasped by his vast power,
Yet his ambitious thoughts would more devour.

48] *And bars the oppressed natives, strangers' aid*: and forbids the oppressed native people
of England from being assisted by foreigners.
54] *imposts*: taxes, duties (imposition).

18

What the third Richard, the eighth Henry too,
The false-tongued Bolingbroke forbore to do,   70
What never conqueror practised on this state
Was kept till your prince came to urge our fate.

19

When for more worlds the Macedonian cried
We wished not Thetis in her lap to hide
Another yet; a world reserved to be   75
Enslaved under a greater tyranny.

20

He did his honour-thirsting army lead
Against the wealthy Persian and the Mede,
And when his pride with victory was cloyed
The vanquished law and liberty enjoyed.   80

21

But we are spoiled of ours and with the bold
Intruding Scot whom poverty and cold
Encouraged to provoke our English state
Till it subdued them, share one slavish fate.

22

'Tis not our arms alone keeps them at home   85
For they are wealthy with our spoils become,

69–72] *third Richard; eighth Henry; Bolingbroke*: Hutchinson invokes three of the country's
most vilified monarchs, Richard III, Henry VIII, and Bolingbroke (Henry IV), as
more reserved in their rule than Cromwell.

73–76] *Macedonian; Thetis*: Britain was a world beyond the sea (Thetis, a sea nymph)
unknown to Alexander the Great (the Macedonian). Waller imagines the British
Isles as saved for Cromwell's glorious possession ('a world reserved for you / To
make more great'), which Hutchinson reverses to see it as reserved for Cromwell's
'greater tyranny'.

78] w*ealthy Persian and the Mede*: Alexander the Great conquered the Persian and
Median armies. While Waller had presented Cromwell's enemies as 'unwarlike',
Hutchinson describes them as 'wealthy', thus imputing to Cromwell more mercenary
motives in his foreign policy.

82] *Intruding Scot*: Cromwell having played a major part in suppressing Scottish forces
during the Civil War, in 1654 parliament passed the Act of Union granting parlia-
mentary representation to the Scottish. Instead of seeing the Act with Scotland as
bringing a glorious union, Hutchinson says that now England and Scotland 'share
one slavish fate' (line 84), ruled by Cromwell.

Our gold to his garrisons is sent
And there among the blue-capped rebels spent.

23

Only to injure us, as he did them grace,
Whilst in our senate he allowed them place,   90
Who else with soldiers curbed must henceforth know
No warm relief from their cold hills of snow.

24

The Irish and the Scots indeed may be
Pleased with their conqueror's calamity,
And glad their envious hate when they shall find   95
Themselves and their late lords in one yoke joined.

25

The barbarous provinces rejoiced so
When Caesar did the senate overthrow,
And made the freeborn citizens at home
Endure like bondage with the slaves of Rome.   100

26

Holland courted his friendship to prevent
Their dreaded, just, impending punishment,
Which while the commonwealth entirely stood
Threatened their falsehood and ingratitude.

27

His exaltation only gave delight   105
To such as the state's anger did affright;
The Belgian lords into distresses brought
Obtained a league who would have pardon sought.

28

Our soft remorse made civil wars to cease
And we are healed now with the axe of peace,   110

98, 149] *Caesar*: Waller's poem, and much pro-Protectorate writing, presented Cromwell
  as Caesar-like. Hutchinson uses this association for her own, republican ends.

101–04] the First Anglo-Dutch War, commercial as much as political, ended in 1654.
  Waller presented this as Cromwell's triumph, though Hutchinson sees it as a
  capitulation.

Which doth our quiet spirits disengage,
Turns our affections and revives our rage.

29

Tigers have courage and the rugged bear,
Man whom he conquers ought to spare,
But he alone takes pride in battles won,   115
Restoring none of those that are undone.

30

To punish willing, but to pardon loathe;
He strikes with one hand, and he grips with both.
Treading on all that prostrate lie he grieves
For the death only which the wretch relieves.   120

31

When fate or error had our kings misled
And the unhealed wounds of our long war bled,
The only plague heaven's anger could send down
Was such a sword to follow such a crown.

32

A chief who, issuing from an obscure line,   125
Makes us despair that wellborn men may shine,
In whose wild nature mean ones hope no good
And noble are not safe in his mean blood.

33

He whose debaucheries in times of peace
Make us suspect his riot will not cease,   130
Who never could over private passions reign,
Licensed by power, his rage will scarce restrain.

34

Who lavished out his wife's inheritance,
Ruined the children that he should advance
And gamed away his little thriftless stock;   135
Slept not like David for he kept his flock.

136] *Slept not like David for he kept his flock*: Waller had compared Cromwell to David,
whose 'princely virtues slept … while the flock he kept', stressing his humility in
working as a shepherd before being anointed king by God. Hutchinson retorts that
David, unlike Cromwell, kept his flock safe.

35

Then when his country's cruel flames burst forth
With a fierce courage and a feignèd worth,
He in her cause did eager zeal pretend
And by close fraud to his proud height ascend.   140

36

Still as he was he trampled down the state,
Who by his charms then senseless of his weight
Felt no distemper till Death closed her sight
And darkness covered the whole sphere of light.

37

Had he some ages past this throne of glory   145
Thus profaned; at mention of his story
Horror would seize us, but while tyrants live
Their foul deeds still a flattering gloss receive.

38

This Caesar found in our dissembling age
Which made him desperately himself engage   150
When the mistaken senators who broke
His fetters feared no other galling yoke.

39

And in the dark night like the radiant stars
Shined forth after the tempest of our wars
Till this new mist did from this earth arise,   155
Blacking again the lustre of our skies.

40

If Rome's great senate parting with that sword
Which of the conquered world had made them lord
Were enslaved by it in their servant's hands,
Could ours hope less whilst he shared those commands?   160

157] *Rome's great senate parting with that sword*: Waller's poem suggests that the Roman
  Senate *could* not wield its power, and thus had to give it to Caesar, just as the new
  republic needed to transfer its power to Cromwell (who could wield it effectively);
  Hutchinson instead suggests that by handing over its power, the republic would be
  'enslaved' by Cromwell, who should be serving the state.

41

Who with such zeal pursued the prince's fall
Falsely supplanted both the generals,
Contrived the self-denying ordinance
To suppress theirs and his own power advance.

42

Whilst kept in dens wild beasts gently obey   165
Who tame and feed them, but if ever they
Find an occasion to enlarge their power,
Their masters are the first whom they devour.

43

As by severe Augustus's Rome at last
Into Tiberius's grinding jaws was cast;   170
So England now oppressed with the like curse
Groans under him, fears his successor's worse.

44

Let the unbridled muses, then painting the shame
Of such unworthy bondage reinflame
True English hearts, and make their country see   175
How glorious 'tis to rescue liberty.

45

Let's storm his towns, his armies overcome,
And when the flatterer hears our thundering drum,
Then shame and dread your warbling voice will choke
And you will all your undue praise revoke.   180

161–64] *prince's fall*; *generals*; *self-denying ordinance*: Hutchinson here blames Cromwell
for having pursued his own personal power after the fall of Charles I by taking
control of the army from the generals and through the self-denying ordinance,
which had as its explicit agenda the limiting of personal power.

169–70] *Augustus*; *Tiberius*: Waller's poem had presented Cromwell as like Augustus
in bringing peace to England, while Hutchinson draws attention to another possible
implication; if Cromwell is like Augustus, surely a tyrant will succeed him as Tiberius
did his stepfather Augustus? The latter part of Tiberius' reign was marked by terror
and persecution.

46

Changed acts and powers changed raptures will infuse
Till men at length detest so base a muse,
As unto all heads bays and olives brings
Those who uphold and those who pull down kings.

47

No generous hearts will envy his renown   185
That rides triumphant in the paper crown.
A modest scorn perhaps may bend those eyes
Which you and him do equally despise.

Note

This poem is a verse-by-verse, at times line-by-line, riposte to Edmund
Waller's 'A Panegyric to my Lord Protector'. Waller had been a royalist
but, like many of his peers, reconciled himself to Cromwell's government,
and went further than most of his peers in writing an effusive panegyric
on the Lord Protector. Waller's poem appeared in May 1655 amid calls
for Cromwell to accept the crown, and Waller uses monarchical images
to praise Cromwell. While this was rhetorically effective, it also provoked
hostile responses from both royalists (who saw Cromwell as usurping
the rightful king) and republicans (who saw Cromwell as an absolutist
monarch by another name). Lucy Hutchinson belonged to the latter
camp, and in her skilful and vehement attack on the panegyric she attacks
Waller's praise as well as its object, Cromwell. She attacks his 'servile
tongue' which smooths over political wrongs and differences, and transfers
Augustan language to Cromwell. Using Waller's own images and rhymes,
Hutchinson incisively recasts his praise as blame, revealing as arbitrary
and facile Waller's praise of Cromwell. Cromwell is no protector but
instead a 'dissembler' (line 31), and this slur extends to Waller. Waller
would fulfil the suspicions of critics like Hutchinson in 'court[ing] all
factions' when, five years later, he wrote an effusive panegyric celebrating
the return of the monarchy. For Hutchinson's poem printed facing Waller's
and analysis of the poem, see Norbrook, 'Lucy Hutchinson versus Edmund
Waller'.

183] *bays and olives*: These leaves were awarded to winners of the Olympic and Pythian
   Games, and more broadly seen as symbolic of public glory.
186] *paper crown*: Hutchinson scorns the paper crown represented by Waller's panegyric,
   referring to the crown of bay and olive leaves with which Waller crowns Cromwell
   at the end of his poem, and perhaps also to the contemporary campaign to crown
   Cromwell as king.

Lucy Hutchinson

From *Elegies*

1. 'Leave off, you pitying friends, leave off'

Leave off, you pitying friends, leave off; in vain
Do you persuade the dead to live again.
In vain to me your comforts are applied,
For 'twas not he, 'twas only I that died.
In that cold grave which his dear relics keeps,   5
My light is quite extinct where he but sleeps;
My substance into the dark vault was laid
And now I am my own pale empty shade.
If this your mirth or admiration move
Know 'tis but the least miracle of love,   10
The effect of human passion such as mine
Which ends in woe and death. But love divine,
Whose sacred flame did his pure bosom fire
With more stupendous working, doth aspire
Until it life and victory completes,   15
Fixing transformèd men in blessèd seats.
This holy fire refined his happy soul
And first did nature's strong impulse control
Brought the wild passions under servitude
The haughty flesh and rebel sense subdued,   20
Made carnal reason freely to lay down
At the lord's feet her sceptre and her crown.
When this pure flame had burnt away the dross
It made him rich by universal loss;
Out of the pile a phoenix did arise   25
Enlightened with quick penetrating eyes,
Which distant heaven into the mind did draw
And the disguised world in its own form saw.
At the emission of their powerful ray
Th'old sorcerer's strong enchants fled away: 30
The groves, the palaces, the pleasant pools,
Arbours, sweets, music – beauty's feast that fools,

23] *dross*: scum or waste produced when melting metals.
30] *enchants*: an unusual word for enchantments, probably used here for metrical
    reasons.

Charmed by the mighty witch, real esteem,
Appeared a loathsome dunghill unto him
Who through their deformed vizards too   35
And the dark mantle sin about them threw.
In prison's exile, solitude, disgrace
And death itself beheld a lovely face;
On God alone he fixed his steadfast look
Till God into himself his creature took   40
Who all things else with God-like eyes now viewed
And, seeing them in God, saw they were good.
Thus was delighted in the creature streams
While they were gilt with the creator's beams,
But when that heavenly sun withdrew no more   45
Did he the unreflecting glass adore;
Nor in the shadow stayed but wheresoe'er
The glorious substance pleased next to appear
Thither did his attending heart remove
And solaced there his chaste, his constant love.   50
Love which alone best relishes its sweets
Where it least of the world's disturbance meets,
By whose great power he free in prison remained
And in the Bloody Tower with triumph reigned,
Despising his oppressors' rage, while they   55
By lusts enslaved in sadder thralldom lay
This conquered the assaults of wrath, grief, fear;
This did his head above the wild waves rear;
This painted dismal rocks and barren sands
With beauties equal to the fruitful lands;   60
This gave calamity a lovely face
And put on honour's crown upon disgrace;
This did the fever's force and fire abate;
His soul in her last conflicts recreate;
His perfect sense from feeling pain did keep   65
And gave him rest without the aid of sleep;
This sweetly carried off expiring breath

33] *real esteem*: deem to be real (rather than ephemeral); alternatively, 'real' could also
   be a spelling of 'royal', so there may be a political subtext through the pun.
35] *vizards*: masks.
54] *Bloody Tower*: one of the many towers making up the Tower of London, and associated
   with the mysterious disappearance of the young princes said to have been murdered
   by their uncle Richard III.

And brought him new life in approaching death,
Which could not fix its horrors in his face
That pale and cold retained a smiling grace.   70

Note

This poem opens the collection of elegies with allusions to a characteristi-
cally wide range of lyric modes, from Cavalier drinking song to Christian
platonic elegy. The colloquial 'Leave off' with which Hutchinson opens
the manuscript suggests the casual intimacy of poems such as the royalist
Alexander Brome's 'To his Friend that had Vowed Small Beer': 'Leave
off, fond hermit, leave thy vow, / And fall again to drinking'. Hutchinson
immediately rejects such royalist excess and even solicitous friendship,
however, isolating herself in her grief and creating a rapturous meditation
on John Hutchinson's triumph over both political enemies and death.
See Longfellow, *Women and Religious Writing*.

2. To the Sun Shining into her Chamber

Bright day star look not in at me;
Thou canst not in thy circuit see
A spectacle of greater woe,
And those wrongs that have made me so
Were in thy guilty presence done. 5
Thou sawest, o thou all-seeing sun,
The blood of noble patriots shed
By those ingrates for whom they bled.
Thou were their torch bearer when they
To prison and exile were led away 10
The glory of the unthankful land
And bound the nation's conquering hand.
Thou sawest my desolation made
And comest thou now my ruin to upbraid?
Let me and my just griefs alone; 15
Go guild the tyrant's bloody throne,
Cast lustre on the strumpet's face,
Reveal their glories in full grace
And let the great ones by thy light
Act crimes, which used to black the night. 20
But keep away thy prying beams
From looking on those silent streams
Which from our eyes in secret fall,
Wailing a public funeral.

Note

Like the first elegy, this poem opens by alluding to a happier context before moving into sorrow and rage. Hutchinson evokes John Donne's lyric of erotic fulfilment 'The Sun Rising', where the self-assured lover tries to banish the sun: 'Busy old fool, unruly sun, / Why dost thou thus, / Through windows, and through curtains call on us?' (and see also *Romeo and Juliet*, 'It was the nightingale and not the lark'). It is with grief, though, rather than her lover, that the speaker of this poem wants to be left alone, and she moves then through the agony of grief to a potent anger at the Restoration regime which led to her husband's death as she challenges the sun to go and illuminate political and moral crimes: 'Go guild the tyrant's bloody throne … And let the great ones by thy light / Act crimes which used to black the night'.

2(a). 'Ah! Why doth death its latest stroke delay'

Ah! Why doth death its latest stroke delay
If we must leave the light, why do we stay,
By slow degrees, more painfully to die,
And languish in a long calamity?
Have we not lost by one false cheating sin,   5
All peace without, all sweet repose within?
Is there a pleasure yet that life can show,
Doth not each moment multiply our woe?
And while we live thus in perpetual dread,
Our hopes and comforts long before us dead,   10
Why should we not our angry Maker pray,
To take at once our wretched lives away?
Hath not our sin all nature's pure bands rent
And armed against us every element?
Have not our subjects your allegiance broke?   15
Doth not each fly scorn our unworthy yoke,
Are we not half with hunger pined?
Before we bread amongst the brambles find:
All pale diseases in our members reign,
Anguish and grief no less our sick souls pain.   20
Wherever I, my eyes or thoughts convert,
Each object adds new torture to my heart.
If I look up, I dread heaven's threat'ning frown;
Thorns prick my eyes when shame hath cast them down.
Dangers I see, looking on either hand,   25
Before me all in fighting posture stand.
If I cast back my sorrow-drownèd eyes
I see our ne'er to be re-entered paradise;
The flaming sword, which doth us thence exclude,
By sad remorse and ugly guilt pursued.   30
If on my sin-defilèd self I gaze,
My nakedness and spots do me amaze;
If I on thee a private glance reflect
Confusion does my shameful eyes deject.
Seeing the man I love by me betrayed,   35
By me, who for his mutual help was made;
Who to preserve thy life ought to have died,
And I have killed thee by my foolish pride.
Defiled thy glory and pulled down thy throne

O! That I had but sinned and died alone,   40
Then had my torture, and my woe been less
I yet had flourished in thy happiness.

Note

This poem has been subject to several interpretations from the seventeenth century to the present. A note by Julius Hutchinson (a relative of Lucy and John Hutchinson, grandfather of the Julius Hutchinson who would later edit Hutchinson's *Memoirs*) in the manuscript explains that this poem was 'transcribed out of my other Book', which is now lost. It also comments: 'these verses were written by Mrs Hutchinson on the occasion of the Colonel her Husband's being then a prisoner in the Tower, 1664'. This precise historical context is complicated, though, by the presence of these same lines in Hutchinson's Genesis poem, *Order and Disorder*, where they are a complaint spoken by Eve in her grief at having succumbed to Satan's temptation (5.401–42). A further context that connects guilt and grief is the claimed involvement of Lucy Hutchinson in forging a recantation of her husband's republicanism at the Restoration in order to save his life – an act which caused him grief at the disappointment of fellow radicals, and which Hutchinson herself came to see as a betrayal of his principles. The poem can, then, be read in three quite distinct contexts, biographical and biblical: Lucy Hutchinson's grief at her husband's death; her guilt at her part in John Hutchinson's recantation; Eve's betrayal of Adam by eating the forbidden fruit. See Longfellow, *Women and Religious Writing*; Norbrook, 'Memoirs and Oblivion'; Lobo, 'Lucy Hutchinson's Revisions of Conscience'.

3. Another on the Sunshine

Heaven's glorious eye, which all the world surveys,
This morning through my window shot his rays,
Where with his hateful and unwelcome beams
He gilt the surface of afflictions' streams.
In anger at their bold intrusion I   5
Did yet into a darker covert fly,
But they like impudent suitors, brisk and rude,
Me even to my thickest shade pursued.
Whom when I saw that I could nowhere shun
I thus began to chide th'immodest sun: 10
How gaudy masquer dare thou look on me
Whose sable coverings thy reproaches be?
Thou to our murderers thy taper bear'st
Th'oppressive race of men thou warm'st and cheer'st;
The blood which thou hast seen pollutes thy light   15
And renders it more hateful than the night;
All good men loathe you, grown a common bawd,
The brave that lead'st impieties abroad
Who smiling dost on lust and rapine shine
Nor shrink'st thy head in at disgorged wine.   20
Which sinners durst not let thee see before
Now thy conniving looks they dread no more
Because thou makest their pleasant gardens grow
And cherishest the fruitful seeds they sow.
In fields which unto them descended not   25
By violence, bribery and oppression got;
Thou saw'st the league of God himself dissolved
Which a whole nation in one curse involved;
Thou saw'st a thankless people slaught'ring those
Whose noble blood redeemed them from their foes;   30
Thy stained beams into the prison came
But lost their boasts, outshined with virtue's flame;
Thou saw'st the innocent to exile led
And for all this veildest not thy radiant head,

6] *covert*: covering, shelter.
11] *masquer:* performer in a masque, a lavish musical and theatrical performance usually
associated with the court.
19] *rapine*: plunder, pillage, robbery.
21] *Which*: That which.
34] *veildest*: veiled.

But comest as a gay courtier to deride   35
Ruins we would in silent shadows hide.
Since then thou wilt thrust into this dark room
By thine own light read thy most certain doom.
Darkness shall shortly quench thy impure light
And thou shalt set in everlasting night;   40
Those whom thou flatt'rest shall see you expire
And have no light but their own funeral fire.
There shall they in a dreadful wild amaze
At once see all their glorious idols blaze.
Thy sister, the pale empress of the night,   45
Shall never more reflect thy borrowed light;
Into black blood shall her dark body turn,
While your polluted spheres about you burn
And the elemental heaven like melting lead
Drops down upon the impious rebels head.   50
Then shall our king his shining host display
At whose approach our mists shall fly away
And we illuminated by his sight
No more shall need thy ever quenched light.

Note

As its title indicates, this poem continues the theme of earlier elegies in
the manuscript, the speaker's rejection of the sun's intrusion into her
secluded grief. See the note to Hutchinson's Elegy 2, 'To the Sun Shining
into her Chamber', for the genre of aubade (welcome to the dawn) which
Hutchinson plays with, and especially John Donne's anti-aubade 'The
Sun Rising'. Like Hutchinson, Donne defies the sun's intrusion, but
while his poem does so with glee at the lovers' happiness, the speaker
here speaks in grief and also political protest. She threatens the sun with
apocalyptic destruction: 'By thine own light read thy most certain doom'.

41] *flatt'rest*: flattered.
45] *Thy sister*: the moon.
50] *impious rebels*: While it was those opposing the king who were most often referred
   to as rebels, Hutchinson here seems to cast the supporters of Charles II as rebels,
   more particularly rebels to God (hence 'impious').
51] *our king*: Christ. *shining host*: God of hosts, an Old Testament term for God indicating
   his omnipotence; also, an army.

7. To the Garden at Owthorpe

Poor desolate garden, smile no more on me
To whom glad looks rude entertainments be.
While thou and I for thy dear master mourn
That's best becoming that doth least adorn.
Shall we for any meaner eyes be dressed   5
Who had the glory once to please the best?
Or shall we prostitute those joys again
Which once did his noble soul entertain?
Forbid it, honour and just gratitude,
'Tis now our best grace to be wild and rude.   10
He that impaled you from the common ground,
Who all thy walls with shining fruit trees crowned,
Me also above vulgar girls did raise
And planted in me all that yielded praise;
He that with various beauties decked thy face,   15
Gave my youth lustre and becoming grace;
But he is gone and these gone with him too.
Let now thy flowers rise, charged with weeping dew
And, missing him, shrink back into their beds;
So my poor virgins hang their drooping heads   20
And, missing the dear object of their sight,
Close up their eyes in sorrow's gloomy night.
Let thy young trees which, sad and fading, stand
Dried up since they lost his refreshing hand,
Tell me too sadly how your noblest plant   25
Degenerates if it usual culture want.
There spreading weeds which, while his watchful eyes
Checked their pernicious growth, durst never rise;
Let them o'errun all the sweet fragrant banks,
And hide what grows in better ordered ranks.   30
Too much, alas, this parallel I find

4] *That's best becoming that doth least adorn*: that which is least ornamental is the most appropriate.

7] *prostitute*: debase or offer for sale; offer one's body for sex.

10] *rude*: humble, unrefined.

13] *vulgar*: ordinary, common.

20] *virgins*: flowers (many common flower names incorporate the Virgin Mary; e.g. virgin-bower or Virgin Mary's honeysuckle).

26] *culture*: cultivated land; cultivation of plants; cultivation or development of human mind or body.

In the disordered passions of my mind
But thy late loveliness is only hid,
Mine like the shadow with its substance fled.
Another gardener and another spring   35
May into you new grace and new lustre bring,
While beauty's seeds do yet remain alive.
But ah, my glories never can revive
No more than new leaves or new smiling fruit
Can reinvest that tree that's dead at root.   40
When to his worthy memory thou then
Hast offered one year's fruit, thou may'st again
In gaudy dresses to thy next lord shine
And show weak semblance of his grace in thine.
For all that's generous, healthful, sweet and fair,   45
Imperfect emblems of his virtue are.
But could I call back hasty flying time
The vanished glories that decked once my prime,
To me that resurrection would be vain
And like ungathered flowers would die again.   50
In vain would doting time, which can no more
Give such a lover, loveliness restore.

Note

Here Hutchinson writes about the garden at Owthorpe, the Hutchinson family estate in Nottinghamshire where she had lived with her husband. Directly addressing the garden, the speaker develops the 'parallel' of bereaved wife and estate: both languish without the tender cultivation and care of the master of the estate. Here, though, Hutchinson suggests the analogy ends, as the garden may be restored and renewed by a future master while the beauty and passion of the estate's lady can never 'revive' again. The poem draws on the country house poem tradition most famously exemplified in Ben Jonson's 'To Penshurst', where the estate emblematises the owners' virtues. Hutchinson's poem diverges through being elegiac (the estate owner is absent), and through placing the female figure at the centre (compare Aemilia Lanyer's 'The Description of Cookham'), evoking the tradition of female complaint. See Lewalski, 'The Lady of the Country-House Poem'.

Lucy Hutchinson

10. The Recovery

My love, life, crown, peace, treasure, joys were lost
And, seeking them, long was my frail bark tossed
On sorrow's raging flood where storms prevailed,
And the poor leaking vessel every way assailed.
The cordage cracked, the shrouds and main mast tore,   5
Vain skill and industry could help no more.
Then helpless in these extremes, at last
Love's rock appeared and there we anchor cast.
But thrice-blessed storm thus was I brought
Where I could only find the things I sought;   10
This rock is both world's centre, all that's sweet,
Great, beauteous, pleasant in this fixed point meet.
Here heaven's bright glory to frail earth descends;
Here earth advanced to heaven, its frailty ends,
For the pure nature taking in the cross   15
By its powerful touch to gold converts the dross.
And as it through the fleshly medium shines
That body transubstantiates and refines.
In this rock is truth's crystal healing spring,
Which shows the perfect form of every thing,   20
Strengthens the weak and doth the sick eyes cure
That they the radiant mirror may endure.
Here saw I the dear object of my love
Wearing the martyr's crown, enthroned above
In such glory that I could no more   25
His exaltation as my loss deplore.
But here I ceased t'admire one single ray
Where the unclosed sun did all display;
My love, his love and loveliness were all
Recovered here in their original.   30
Here they concentred and refined were
At once both lost and found in the first fair
Whose powerful attractions charm us so

2] *bark*: small boat.
5] *cordage*; *shrouds*: ropes in the ship's rigging.
16] *dross*: scum or waste produced when melting metals.
28] *unclosed*: an unusual adjective meaning simply not closed, open, here with a sense of entirely visible, not concealed (*all* the sun's rays are visible).
31] *concentred*: brought together at a centre; creating a centre.

We can no more consider things below,
And as they draw and fix our greedy sight   35
So draw we from them life and full delight.
The bright reflections made me a new crown
While death and sorrow could no more cast down;
Sweet peace from thence into my soul distilled,
And joys that left not one desire unfilled.   40
Now my late ignorant wishes I disdain,
Discerned the cheat of joys that after pained;
Here viewed, the lustre mortals so admire
Are gloomy slime and night's misleading fire;
Created beauties, which blind souls adore,   45
Here cease to be their idols any more;
For here they're seen but dark declining streams
Gilt as they pass with light's reflected beams.
The celebrated works of vain men's hands
Are paper frames erected on the sands   50
Which, loosened and dispersed with every wind,
No memory, no impression leave behind.
That fixed world where I sought to fix before
Here looked on was a cheating flying shore,
Which while with strong contest we strive to gain   55
Engages more in the tempestuous main.
But sullen fogs and thick mists vanished here
The tumult of the waves, which did appear
So horrid late unto the now-cleared sense,
Seemed the well-measured dance of providence.   60
Th'awaking thunders, whose loud dreadful sound
No less men's trembling hearts than rent clouds wound,
Heard in this rock are the harmonious noise
Of love and wisdom's sweet according voice.
O rock of life, o quick'ning power of love   65
Here let me fix, nor hence again remove,
My wand'ring eyes to gaze on transient things,
That glitter borne along on time's swift wings;
But still in motion are lest we should see
What lies and cozenage in their fair shows be.   70

41] *late*: recent.
43] *Here viewed*: viewed from here.
54] *flying*: fleeting, transient.
62] *rent*: ripped.
70] *cozenage*: cheating.

Let my recovered soul for ever more
Rejoice in what I lately did deplore
That wreck which cast me upon you, I who
Till I did things in thy clear mirror view,
Mistook th'appearances of ill and good   75
And nothing in its true form understood.

Note

This poem imagines the experience of religious doubt as like being a
boat on a rough sea (compare Thomas Wyatt, 'My gallery charged with
forgetfulness' and other poems inspired by Petrarch's 'Rime 189'). Here
the speaker's grief for her dead husband has provoked doubt of God's
providential plan, a doubt which is restored or recovered to faith in the
course of the poem as she comes to see her loss as her husband's exaltation
through union with God (line 26). Drawing perhaps on Psalm 18:2 ('The
Lord is my rock'), she imagines the storm-tossed boat finally secured by
love's rock. This biblical image of stability is combined with imagery of
reflections, copies, and originals which draw on both Christian Platonism
and also the process of writing itself (compare her *Memoirs*, where she
says of her husband, 'What I shall write of him is but a copy of [him]
... The original of all excellence is God him[self]'.) This poem about
centres and concentring acts also as the centre of the collection of poems
(tenth of twenty-two poems). See Longfellow, *Women and Religious Writing*,
and Keeble, '"But the Colonel's Shadow"'.

12. Musings in my Evening Walks at Owthorpe

With unseen tears and unheard groans
O'er those cold ashes and dried bones
I weep my wretched life away.
No joy comes with the cheerful day,
No rest comes with the silent night;   5
What terrors my dark soul affright,
Whatever doth itself present
Brings food unto my discontent.
The trees about the garden stand
Drooping for want of that kind hand   10
That set and cherished them before
And praised the grateful fruits they bore.
The flowers hang down their drooping heads
And languish on their undressed beds,
Which now no more retain that grace   15
His presence brought to every place.
The murmuring springs rise and complain
Then shrink into the earth again
Lest they foul mixtures should endure
Since he who kept their channels pure   20
No more on their green banks appears.
The clouds offer to lend me tears
While they sail o'er the empty pile
Which his loved presence did erewhile
So gloriously adorn and fill.   25
Where'er I go affliction still
Takes up my walks and still I find
Something that calls my loss to mind.
His dispersed image which I see
Amongst his children joys not me   30
Who pine with an unfilled desire,
Which seeks him in each one entire.
It grieves me that a generous plant
Should his one skilful culture want

23] *pile*: here in the sense either of a heap (of soil, in the uncultivated flowerbeds) or
    of a stronghold (the estate).
24] *erewhile*: formerly, a while ago.
31] *unfilled*: unfulfilled; unsatisfied.
33] *generous*: abundant; vigorous; fertile; of good stock.
34] *want*: lack.

And grow in an infectious air   35
Which the best natures will impair.
Even my books that used to be
The solace of my life while he
Was my instructor and approved
The pleasant lines I chose and loved,   40
No more my sick thoughts recreate
Who all my old delights now hate,
And all the new ones I have found
Do but unrip my heart's deep wound.
While with his memory I converse   45
His glories to myself rehearse
Hoping they should my grief abate
I add to my own sorrow's weight;
What though those glories were my crown
His death hath thrown my empire down   50
And better never to have been
Raised high than live a fallen queen.
Ill grieves not him who good ne'er knows
But past joys heighten present woes,
Ah me, where shall I seek relief   55
If even my pleasures feed my grief,
Where'er I look, above, below,
In every side beset with woe,
All men from my misfortune run
The prosperous still the wretched shun.   60
No friends to comfort me abide
They flowed out with my ebbing tide,
The proud my humble state despise
My sorrow glads my enemies,
They who with envy lately burned,   65
To scorn have all their envy turned.
Yet do my ills exceed their curse
Who most hate cannot wish me worse.
My flatterers who did adore
My happier state know me no more.   70
You servile slaves where are you all

36] *Which the best natures will impair*: which will hinder the growth of even the strongest
plants.
39] *approved*: sanctioned; and perhaps also, demonstrated the truth of.
40] *pleasant*: giving pleasure or satisfaction.
44] *unrip*: to cut, tear open; to disclose (with possible pun in manuscript spelling 'unreap').

Who once did me your princess call?
Even then I loathed your flatteries
And now your sick souls despise.

Note

This poem, which again meditates on the estate which has lost its master, moves away from the genre of country house poem towards an extended pathetic fallacy in which the natural world grieves with the speaker. Again, Hutchinson uses some quite specific terms from agriculture to imagine the plants deprived of the gardener's 'skilful culture'. The term 'culture' expands to the literary environment, as the speaker herself pines for the man with whom she read books. In this passionately grieving complaint, Hutchinson rejects the usual solaces of children (they represent only a 'dispersed image' of their father). She characteristically combines personal and politically-charged anger, as the fickleness of her friends might suggest those who rejected the Hutchinsons at the Restoration (lines 61–74).

14. On the Spring, 1668

As the triumphant sounds and shows
Of conquerors to their captives be,
Such is the glory that now grows
On the restored world to me.

The shining rays that gild the skies   5
And glad all other mortals' sight
Add but more pain to my bleared eyes
And drive me from the torturing light.

The lately-buried corn is seen
Smiling again in its new birth,   10
All mantled in its gaudy green
But my joys lie still hid in earth.

I hear the chastely amorous dove
Answered again by her kind mate,
But what I say to my dead love   15
Only the rocks reverberate.

As mourners who their blacks cast by,
New flowers the banks and trees adorn,
But still grief's sable livery
In my sad heart and eyes is worn.   20

You comely daughters of the spring
Raise not your heads with so much pride;
For time that changes everything
Forbids your triumphs to abide.

That sun that now so flatters you   25
And in your virgins' bosoms plays,
Will shortly change your pleasant hue
And scorch you with his burning rays.

6] *glad*: make glad, cause to rejoice.
7] *bleared*: dimmed with tears.
9] *lately-buried*: recently planted.
11] *mantled*: cloaked, clothed.
17] *blacks*: black mourning clothes.
19] *sable*: black.
21] *comely*: handsome, fair, beautiful. *daughters of the spring*: flowers.
26] *virgins*: flowers (many common flower names incorporate the Virgin Mary, e.g. 'virgin-bower' or 'Virgin Mary's honeysuckle').

That air whose wanton breath doth now
Respire your sweets in every place,   30
Like false men soon will stormy grow
And scatter you in your disgrace.

Blessed mates whom love and life unites
Death also must your joys conclude;
You must like me lose your delights   35
And waste your age in solitude.

And you fair skies grown calm and bright
Again your cloudy veils must wear,
And weep black showers for your lost light
When battles in your bowels are.   40

If natural glories have no stay
Less steady are mens' tottering states,
Either by slow time stolen away
Or rudely thrown from their proud heights

Why should it pain me then to see   45
Others the precipices climb?
Mine's past; their ruins future be:
Who lies low falls no second time.

Note

This poem represents the renewal of the natural world rejected in the
elegies, addressed in the form of the Hutchinson estate in 'To the Garden
at Owthorpe' and 'Musings in my Evening Walks at Owthorpe'. The
speaker ironically contrasts the season of rebirth and growth to her own
mood of grief and anger. The world is 'restored' by the spring, which
may also suggest the Restoration regime of Charles II which saw Hutch-
inson's husband's imprisonment and death. She ends with the rather
bleak consolation that she has fallen so low that she can experience no
further pain or defeat, while her enemies who are now in favour (presum-
ably politically) have far to fall.

30] *Respire your sweets*: breathe out or give off the sweet smell of spring.
40] *bowels*: gut, often thought of as the seat of compassion and pity (as we use 'heart');
    interior, centre.
41] *stay*: support (either nautical, a rope; or architectural, a buttress or supporting
    structure).
42] *Less*: even less.
48] *Who lies low*: He or she who lies low.

20. 'You sons of England whose unquenched flame'

You sons of England whose unquenched flame
Of pious love may yet that title claim,
Let not your rash feet on that marble tread
Before you have its sad inscription read.
Behold, it weeps; do not these tears presage   5
Descending showers on this prodigious age,
Where only rocks for innocent bloodshed mourn
While human hearts to flinty quarries turn?
Now read, this stone doth close up the dark cave
Where liberty sleeps in her champion's grave.   10

Note

This poem is one in a series of some eight draft epitaphs and is followed
in the manuscript by the poem actually used on John Hutchinson's grave,
'This monument doth not commemorate'. It connects John Hutchinson's
death explicitly with his political career and principles, imagining him
as the champion of liberty. Presumably drafted for possible use on the
gravestone, this poem further alludes to images of rocks, durability, and
erosion used elsewhere in the elegies and in the extract here from Lucretius,
book 4.

From *Order and Disorder*

Preface

These meditations were not at first designed for public view, but
fixed upon to reclaim a busy roving thought from wandering in the
pernicious and perplexed maze of human inventions; whereinto
the vain curiosity of youth had drawn me to consider and translate
the account some old poets and philosophers give of the original   5
of things: which though I found it blasphemously against God, and
brutishly below the reason of a man, set forth by some erroneously,
imperfectly and uncertainly by the best; yet had it filled my brain
with such foolish fancies, that I found it necessary to have recourse
to the fountain of truth, to wash out all ugly wild impressions, and   10
fortify my mind with a strong antidote against all the poison of
human wit and wisdom that I had been dabbling withal. And this
effect I found; for comparing that revelation God gives of himself
and his operations in his Word with what the wisest of mankind,
who only walked in the dim light of corrupted nature and defective   15
traditions, could with all their industry trace out or invent; I found
it so transcendently excelling all that was human, so much above
our narrow reason, and yet so agreeable to it being rectified, that
I disdained the wisdom fools so much admire themselves for; and
as I found I could know nothing but what God taught me, so I   20
resolved never to search after any knowledge of him and his produc-
tions, but what he himself hath given forth. Those that will be wise
above what is written may hug their philosophical clouds, but let
them take heed they find not themselves without God in the world,
adoring figments of their own brains, instead of the living and true   25
God.

    Lest that arrive by misadventure, which never shall by my consent,
that any of the puddled water my wanton youth drew from the
profane Helicon of ancient poets should be sprinkled about the
world, I have for prevention sent forth this essay; with a profession   30
that I disclaim all doctrines of God and his works but what I learnt
out of his own word, and have experienced it to be a very unsafe
and unprofitable thing for those that are young, before their faith
be fixed, to exercise themselves in the study of vain, foolish atheistical
poesy. It is a miracle of grace and mercy, if such be not deprived   35
of the light of truth, who having shut their eyes against that sun,
have, instead of looking up to it, hunted glow-worms in the ditch

bottoms. It is a misery I cannot but bewail, that when we are young, whereas the lovely characters of truth should be impressed upon the tender mind and memory, they are so filled up with ridiculous 40 lies, that 'tis the greatest business of our lives, as soon as ever we come to be serious, to cleanse out all the rubbish our grave tutors laid in when they taught us to study and admire their inspired poets and divine philosophers.

But when I have thus taken occasion to vindicate myself from 45 those heathenish authors I have been conversant in, I cannot expect my work should find acceptance in the world, declaring the more full and various delight I have found in following truth by its own conduct; nor am I much concerned how it be entertained, seeking no glory by it but what is rendered to him to whom it is only due. 50 If any one of no higher a pitch than myself be as much affected and stirred up in the reading as I have been in the writing, to admire the glories and excellencies of our great creator, to fall low before him, in the sense of our own vileness, and to adore his power, his wisdom, and his grace, in all his dealings with the children of men, 55 it will be a success above my hopes; though my charity makes me wish everyone that hath need of it the same mercy I have found.

I know I am obnoxious to the censures of two sorts of people: first, those that understand and love the elegancies of poems: they will find nothing of fancy in it; no elevations of style, no charms 60 of language, which I confess are gifts I have not, nor desire not on this occasion; for I would rather breath forth grace cordially than words artificially. I have not studied to utter anything that I have not really taken in. And I acknowledge all the language I have, is much too narrow to express the least of those wonders my soul 65 hath been ravished with in the contemplation of God and his works. Had I had a fancy, I durst not have exercised it here; for I tremble to think of turning Scripture into a romance; and shall not be troubled at their dislike who dislike on that account, and profess they think no poem can be good that shuts out drunkenness, and 70 lasciviousness, and libelling satire, the themes of all their celebrated songs. These (though I will not much defend my own weakness) dislike not the poem so much as the subject of it.

But there are a second sort of people, whose genius not lying that way, and seeing the common and vile abuse of poesy, think 75 Scripture profaned by being descanted on in numbers; but such will pardon me when they remember a great part of the Scripture was originally written in verse; and we are commanded to exercise our spiritual mirth in psalms and hymns and spiritual songs; which

if I have weakly composed, yet 'tis a consenting testimony with the   80
whole church, to the mighty and glorious truths of God which are
not altogether impertinent, in this atheistical age; and how imperfect
soever the hand be that copies it out, truth loses not its perfection,
and the plainest as well as the elegant, the elegant as well as the
plain, make up a harmony in confession and celebration of that   85
all-creating, all-sustaining God, to whom be all honour and glory
for ever and ever.

Note

This preface appears in *Order and Disorder*, printed anonymously in 1679.
It does not appear in the longer manuscript version of the poem. In this
preface, Lucy Hutchinson compares *Order and Disorder* to *De rerum natura*
by the Roman poet Lucretius, which she had translated some two decades
earlier. Hutchinson presents *Order and Disorder* as an 'antidote' to *De
rerum natura*, championing the Christian scriptural account of the world's
origins in Genesis over the materialist, anti-divine account given by
Lucretius. Hutchinson also justifies her decision to write a biblical poem
with a scriptural precedent, arguing that much of the Bible was originally
written in verse. Compare Cowley, *Davideis*.

Canto 1, lines 1–150

My ravished soul a pious ardour fires
To sing those mystic wonders it admires,
Contemplating the rise of everything
That, with Time's birth, flowed from th'eternal spring:
And the no less stupendous providence   5
By which discording natures ever since
Have kept up universal harmony;
While in one joint obedience all agree,
Performing that to which they were designed
With ready inclination; but mankind   10
Alone rebels against his maker's will,
Which, though opposing, he must yet fulfil.
And so that wise Power, who each crooked stream
Most rightly guides, becomes the glorious theme
Of endless admiration; while we see,   15
Whatever mortals' vain endeavours be,
They must be broken who with power contend,
And cannot frustrate their creator's end,
Whose wisdom, goodness, might and glory shines
In guiding men's unto his own designs.   20
    In these outgoings would I sing his praise,
But my weak sense with the too glorious rays
Is struck with such confusion that I find
Only the world's first chaos in my mind,
Where light and beauty lie wrapped up in seed   25
And cannot be from the dark prison freed
Except that Power, by whom the world was made,
My soul in her imperfect strugglings aid,
Her rude conceptions into forms dispose,

2] *mystic*: mystical.
5] *stupendous*: astounding, marvellous.
11] Hutchinson note: 'Isaiah 10:5–7 etc'.
17] Hutchinson note: 'Ecclesiastes 6:10'.
18] Hutchinson note: 'Isaiah 27:4'.
19] Hutchinson note: 'Genesis 45:4–5'.
20] Hutchinson note: 'Acts 2:23'.
21] Hutchinson note: 'Genesis 50:20'.
21] *outgoings*: emanations.
27] *Except*: unless.

And words impart which may those forms disclose.   30
        O thou eternal spring of glory, whence
All other streams derive their excellence,
From whose love issues every good desire,
Quicken my dull earth with celestial fire
And let the sacred theme that is my choice   35
Give utterance and music to my voice,
Singing the works by which thou art revealed.
What dark eternity hath kept concealed
From mortals' apprehensions, what hath been
Before the race of time did first begin,   40
It were presumptuous folly to inquire.
Let not my thoughts beyond their bound aspire;
Time limits mortals, and time had its birth,
In whose *Beginning God made Heaven and Earth*.
        God, the great *Elohim*, to say no more,   45
Whose sacred name we rather must adore
Than venture to explain; for he alone
Dwells in himself, and to himself is known,
And so even that by which we have our sight
His covering is: *He clothes himself with light*.   50
Easier we may the winds in prison shut,
The whole vast ocean in a nutshell put,
The mountains in a little balance weigh,
And with a bulrush plumb the deepest sea,
Than stretch frail human thought unto the height   55
Of the great God, immense and infinite,
Containing all things in himself alone,
Being at once in all, contained in none.
        Yet as a hidden spring appears in streams,
The sun is seen in its reflected beams,   60
Whose high, embodied glory is too bright,
Too strong an object for weak mortal sight.

32] Hutchinson note: 'James 1:17'.
37] Hutchinson note: 'Romans 1:15'.
41] Hutchinson note: 'Deuteronomy 29:29'.
44] Hutchinson note: 'Genesis 1:1'.
47] Hutchinson note: 'Job 11:7'.
48] Hutchinson note: '1 Timothy 6:16, 1:17'.
50] Hutchinson note: 'Psalms 104:2'.
53] Hutchinson note: 'Isaiah 40:12'.
57] Hutchinson note: 'Job 38'.

So in God's visible productions we
What is invisible in some sort see;
While we, considering each created thing,   65
Are led up to an uncreated spring,
And by gradations of successive time
At last unto eternity do climb;
As we in tracks of second causes tread
Unto the first uncausèd cause are led.   70
And know, while we perpetual motion see,
There must a first, self-moving power be,
To whom all the inferior motions tend,
In whom they are begun, and where they end.
This first eternal cause, th'original   75
Of being, life, and motion, God we call;
In whom all wisdom, goodness, glory, might,
Whatever can himself or us delight,
Unite, centring in his perfection,
Whose nature can admit but only one;   80
Divided sovereignty makes neither great,
Wanting what's shared to make the sum complete.
And yet, this sovereign sacred unity
Is not alone, for in this one are three,
Distinguished, not divided, so that what   85
One person is, the other is not that;
Yet all the three are but one God most high,
One uncompounded, pure divinity,
Wherein subsist so the mysterious three
That they in power and glory equal be;   90
Each doth himself and all the rest possess

63] Hutchinson note: 'Romans 1:20'.
64] Hutchinson note: 'Hebrews 11:27'.
69–70] *second causes ... the first uncausèd cause*: God is the cause or origin of all, so
through examining the created world we can understand him who created it.
68] Hutchinson note: 'Isaiah 44:6'.
73] Hutchinson note: 'Romans 11:36'.
74] Hutchinson note: 'Acts 17:24, 26, 28'.
80] Hutchinson note: 'Ephesians 4:5'.
83] Hutchinson note: 'The Trinity'.
84] Hutchinson note: '1 John 5:7'.
85] Hutchinson note: 'Matthew 28:19'.
86] Hutchinson note: 'Matthew 3:16, 17'.
91] Hutchinson note: 'John 14:10'.

In undisturbèd joy and blessedness.
There's no inferior, nor no later there,
All coeternal, all coequal, are.
And yet this parity order admits: 95
The Father first eternally begets
Within himself, his Son, substantial word
And wisdom as his second, and their third
The ever-blessèd Spirit is, which doth
Alike eternally proceed from both.   100
These three, distinctly thus, in one divine,
Pure, perfect, self-supplying essence shine;
And all cooperate in all works done
Exteriorly, yet so as every one
In a peculiar manner suited to   105
His person doth the common action do.
Herein the Father is the principal,
Whose sacred counsels are th'original
Of every act; producèd by the Son,
By the Spirit wrought up to perfection.   110
I'the creation thus, by the Father's wise decree
Such things should in such time, and order be,
The first foundation of the world was laid.
The fabric by th'eternal word was made
Not as th'instrument, but joint actor, who   115
Joyed to fulfil the counsels which he knew.
By the concurrent Spirit all parts were

92] Hutchinson note: 'Proverbs 8:22, 30'.
93] Hutchinson note: 'John 1:1'.
94] Hutchinson note: 'Philippians 2:6'; 'John 5:18'.
97] Hutchinson note: 'John 1:14'.
98] Hutchinson note: '1 Corinthians 1:14'.
99] Hutchinson note: 'John 16:13, 14'.
100] Hutchinson note: 'John 15:16'.
103] Hutchinson note: 'John 5:17'.
107] Hutchinson note: 'Hebrews 12:19'.
108] Hutchinson note: 'Isaiah 42:4'.
109] Hutchinson note: 'John 5:26'.
110] Hutchinson notes: '1 Corinthians 8:6'; 'John 5:19'.
111] Hutchinson note: 'Ephesians 1:11'.
112] Hutchinson note: '2 Timothy 1:9'.
113] Hutchinson note: 'John 1:3'.
114] Hutchinson note: 'Hebrews 1:2'.
115] Hutchinson note: 'John 5:19, etc.'.
117] Hutchinson note: 'Genesis 1:2'.

Fitly disposed, distinguished, rendered fair,
In such harmonious and wise order set
As universal beauty did complete. 120
This most mysterious triple unity,
In essence one, and in subsistence three,
Was that great *Elohim* who first designed,
Then made, the worlds, that angels and mankind
Him in his rich outgoings might adore, 125
And celebrate his praise for ever more;
Who from eternity himself supplied,
And had no need of anything beside,
Nor any other cause that did him move
To make a world but his extensive love, 130
Itself delighting to communicate;
Its glory in the creatures to dilate,
While they are led by their own excellence
T'admire the first, pure, high intelligence;
By all the powers and virtues which they have, 135
To that omnipotence who those powers gave;
By all their glories and their joys to his
Who is the fountain of all joy and bliss;
By all their wants and imbecilities
To the full magazine of rich supplies, 140
Where power, love, justice, and mercy shine
In their still-fixèd heights, and ne'er decline.
No streams can shrink the self-supplying spring,
No retributions can more fullness bring
To the eternal fountain which doth run 145
In sacred circles, ends where it begun,

118] Hutchinson note: 'Job 26:13'.
123] *Elohim*: Hebrew name for God.
125] Hutchinson note: 'Revelation 4:11'.
126] Hutchinson note: 'Psalms 147, 148'.
127] Hutchinson note: 'Acts 17:24'.
132] *dilate*: amplify, diffuse.
134] Hutchinson note: 'Job 33:12'.
135] Hutchinson note: 'Psalms 95:31'.
136] Hutchinson note: 'Revelations 19:6'.
138] Hutchinson note: 'Psalms 16:11'.
139] Hutchinson note: 'Genesis 17:10'.
144] Hutchinson note: 'Job 35:7'.
145] Hutchinson note: 'Psalms 16:2'.
146] Hutchinson note: 'Revelations 1:8'.

And thence with unexhausted life and force
Begins again a new, yet the same, course;
It instituted in time's infant birth,
When the creator first made *Heaven and Earth.*   150

Note

Hutchinson opens her biblical poem with an invocation, though not to
a classical muse. While Milton in *Paradise Lost* called on Urania, Hutch-
inson invokes both her own faith ('pious ardour') and God or the Holy
Spirit ('that power, by whom the world was made'). Hutchinson's poem
blends epic form (here evoked through the invocation) and meditation
(as in the practice here of using biblical marginalia to contemplate her
own faith). Her description of the poem exploring 'the rise of everything'
echoes the letter prefacing her translation of Lucretius' *De rerum natura*,
suggesting parallels between this Christian account and the pagan, atomist
account of the world given in Lucretius. She also emphasises the status
of the physical world as a reflection of the divine (lines 65–66), as in
others of her poems. See Hutchinson, 'The Recovery', and Philips, '2
Corinthians 5:19'. See also John Milton, *Paradise Lost*, the invocation in
1.1–25, and for a different representation of the Trinity, God's account
of his creation of the Son, 5.603–15. See Norbrook, 'Milton, Lucy
Hutchinson and the Lucretian Sublime'.

147] Hutchinson note: 'Isaiah 41:4'.
150] Hutchinson note: 'Genesis 1:1'.

Canto 3, lines 91–188

There is an arch i'the middle of the face
Of equal necessary use and grace,
For there men suck up the life-feeding air
And panting bosoms are dischargèd there.
Beneath it is the chief and beauteous gate   95
About which various pleasant graces wait;
When smiles the ruby doors a little way
Unfold, or laughter doth them quite display
And, opening the vermilion curtains, shows
The ivory piles set in two even rows   100
Before the portal, as a double guard
By which the busy tongue is helped and barred;
Whose sweet sounds charm, when love doth it inspire,
And when hate moves it, set the world on fire.
Within this portal's inner vault is placed   105
The palate, where sense meets its joys in taste.
On rising cheeks, beauty in white and red
Strives with itself, white on the forehead spread;
Its undisputed glory there maintains,
And is illustrated with azure veins.   110
The brows, love's bow and beauty's shadow are;
A thick-set grove of soft and shining hair
Adorns the head, and shows like crowning rays,
While th'air's soft breath among the loose curls plays.
Besides the colours and the features, we   115
Admire their just and perfect symmetry,
Whose ravishing resultance is that air
That graces all, and is not anywhere;
Whereof we cannot well say what it is,
Yet beauty's chiefest excellence lies in this,   120
Which mocks the painters in their best designs,

92] *equal necessary*: equally necessary.
102] Hutchinson note: 'Proverbs 25:11'.
103] Hutchinson note: 'Ecclesiastes 12:11'.
104] Hutchinson note: 'James 3:6'.
111–14] while many poets (including Milton in *Paradise Lost*) use hair to explore
  gender difference, Hutchinson here gives a lavish description of hair as a feature
  of mankind, and even perhaps associates it more with male beauty as when she
  describes her husband in *Memoirs*.
117] *resultance*: result.

And is not held by their exactest lines.
     But while we gaze upon our own fair frame,
Let us remember too from whence it came
And that, by sin corrupted now, it must   125
Return to its originary dust.
How indecently doth pride then lift that head
On which the meanest feet must shortly tread?
Yet at the first it was with glory crowned,
Till Satan's fraud gave it the mortal wound.   130
This excellent creature God did Adam call
To mind him of his low original,
Whom he had formed out of the common ground
Which then with various pleasures did abound.
     The whole earth was one large delightful field   135
That, till man sinned, no hurtful briars did yield.
But God, enclosing one part from the rest,
A paradise in the rich spicy east
Had stored with nature's wealthy magazine,
Where every plant did in its lustre shine,   140
But did not grow promiscuously there:
They all disposed in such rich order were
As did augment their single native grace
And perfected the pleasure of the place
To such a height that th'ape-like art of man,   145
Licentious pens or pencils, never can
With all th'essays of all-presuming wit,
Or form or feign aught that approaches it.
Whether it were a fruitful hill or vale,
Whether high rocks or trees did it impale,   150

126] Hutchinson note: 'Job 4:19'.
129] Hutchinson note: 'Ecclesiastes 7:29'.
131–32] Adam is both a proper name and a common word in the Hebrew language, meaning 'man' or (as a collective noun) 'mankind'. Commentators at the time also noted the etymological connection between 'Adam' and 'red earth', hence Hutchinson's suggestion that Adam was named to remind him of his origin (or 'original') in the ground.
135–36] According to Genesis, there were no weeds in Eden until after the fall.
137] Hutchinson note: 'Genesis 2:8'.
139] *magazine*: store.
141] *promiscuously*: indiscriminately.
145] *ape-like*: imitative.
147] *essays*: attempts, experiments.
148] *Or*: either.

Or rivers with their clear and kind embrace
Into a pleasant island formed the place,
Whether its noble situation were
On earth, in the bright moon, or in the air,
In what forms stood the various trees and flowers,   155
The disposition of the walks and bowers,
Whereof no certain word, nor sign, remains,
We dare not take from men's inventive brains.
    We know there was pleasant and noble shade
Which the tall-growing pines and cedars made,   160
And thicker coverts, which the light and heat
Even at noonday could scarcely penetrate.
A crystal river, on whose verdant banks
The crownèd fruit-trees stood in lovely ranks,
His gentle wave through the garden led,   165
And all the spreading roots with moisture fed.
But past th'enclosure, thence the single stream,
Parted in four, four noble floods became:
Pison, whose large arms Havilah enfold,
A wealthy land enriched with finest gold,   170
Where also many precious stones are found;
The second river, Gihon, doth surround
All that fair land where Cush inhabited,
Where tyranny first raised up her proud head
And led her bloodhounds all along the shore,   175
Polluting the pure stream with crimson gore.
Eden's third river Hiddekel they call,
Whose waters eastward in Assyria fall.
The fourth, Euphrates, whose swift stream did run
About the stately walls of Babylon   180

161] Hutchinson note: 'Genesis 3:8'.
162] Hutchinson note: 'Genesis 2:10'.
165] *through*: originally spelt 'thorough' and so disyllabic.
169–79] *Pison*; *Gihon*; *Hiddekel*; *Euphrates*: according to Genesis 2:10–14 these are the
    four rivers in Eden (Hiddekel is also called the Tigris).
169] Hutchinson note: 'Genesis 2:11'.
172] Hutchinson note: 'Genesis 2:13'.
173] *Cush*: a son of Ham, and the father of Nimrod.
175] *bloodhounds*: in Genesis 10:9, Nimrod is described as 'a mighty hunter before the
    Lord'.
178] *Assyria*: ancient nation on the Tigris, now part of modern Iraq.
179] Hutchinson note: 'Genesis 2:14'.
180] *Babylon*: an ancient city on the Euphrates, in Mesopotamia.

And in the revolution of some years
Swelled high, fed with the captived Hebrew's tears.
God in the midst of paradise did place
Two trees that stood up dressed in all the grace,
The verdure, beauty, sweetness, excellence,   185
With which all else could tempt or feast the sense.
On one, apples of knowledge did abound,
And life-confirming fruit the other crowned.

Note

This extract from Canto 3 of *Order and Disorder* moves from a blazon of
Adam to a description of Eden and its geography. Hutchinson's blazon
deploys architectural terms (rather than other common blazon vocabularies
such as fruit and flowers: see for instance Spenser, *Amoretti*, 64), as she
does also when blazoning her husband in Elegy 5 'On the Picture in
Armour'. Hutchinson engages with a lively topic of debate when she
describes biblical geography, and her description of the rivers introduces
the political danger of tyranny, as Cush was the father of Nimrod, the
world's first tyrant. As at several other points in the poem, Hutchinson
claims to reject conjecture (line 158). Yet the passage itself shows her
moving beyond this injunction. See Cavendish's different reworkings of
the blazon 'A Hodge-Podge for Nature's Table' and 'Of Sense and Reason
Exercised in their Different Shapes'. See also Milton, *Paradise Lost*,
3.218–318.

184] Hutchinson note: 'Genesis 2:9'.

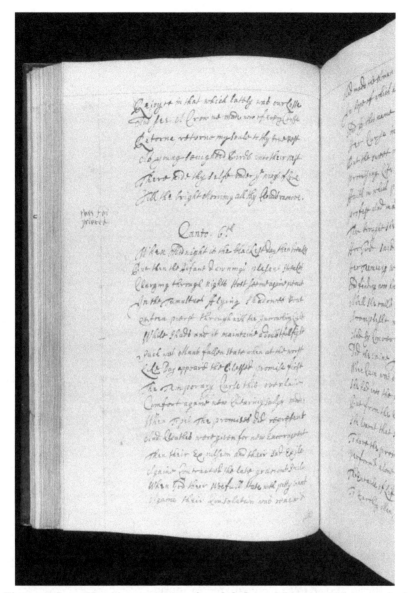

Figure 6 Lucy Hutchinson, manuscript of *Order and Disorder*, with a marginal note at the end of Canto 5 that the poem is 'this far printed'.

Canto 9, lines 1–122

Noah and his sons gladly God's promise heard
And, in the hopes of their successors cheered,
Those dreadful horrors from their thoughts expelled
Which seized their frighted souls when they beheld
The old world's ruin; that sad sight forgot,   5
The dead they now vainly lamented not,
Applying all their thoughts and busy cares
To plant and build for their succeeding heirs.
Now were the sunny hills covered with vines
And from the swelling grapes they pressed forth wines;   10
Then Noah of the sparkling juice drunk deep
And stupefied with liquor fell asleep,
Whom Ham his scoffing son in lewd plight found,
Immodestly uncovered on the ground.
     Of all the generous and useful plants   15
Earth nourisheth for her inhabitants
None more abounds with blessings than the vine,
In whose fair arms numberless bottles shine,
All filled with precious noble powerful juice
Which doth a thousand miracles produce.   20
It reinflames sick nature's dying fires,
New vigour adds to those whom labour tires,
Revives sad hearts oppressed with loads of grief,
To low dejected spirits gives relief,
It valour animates, dispels cold fears,   25
Vigour of youth recalls to wasted years,
Conquers that dull, that poor unmanly shame
That in faint breasts smothers a glorious flame,
Raises dull fancy to its noblest flights,
Quickens the dead and languid appetites,   30
The baths of it cold palsied limbs restore.
For these, and many sovereign virtues more,
The after-ages held those men divine
Who taught the nations the first use of wine;
Wine which they did to sacred altars bring   35
As the most rich and precious offering
They could elect among those various fruits
Heaven's bounty by the kind earth contributes.
But what e'er most excels in its right use
Is most pernicious in its vile abuse;   40

Wine which drunk moderately doth mortals bless
So many various ways, by its excess
As many various mischiefs doth produce
And turns a poisonous and bewitching juice,
Whose operation by the effects is shown   45
When it doth sovereign Reason disenthrone;
Reason that ruled as monarch in the breast
The great distinction between man and beast
Which, charmed by it, hath no force to control
The transportation of the feeble soul   50
Whose lustful and whose raging appetite
The too enflaming liquor doth excite.
According to the rate that it prevails,
The understanding and the memory fails
Forgotten are friendship's and nature's ties,   55
All obligation and all injuries.
There rivals bury for a while their hate
And wretches drown the sense of their sad state,
Princes forget their ranks and great affairs
Cast off their kingdom's necessary cares   60
And revel in their drunken jollities
Till unwatched foes the silly beasts surprise.
So was Belshazzar cut off in his sin
When the besieging Persians suddenly broke in;
So have great conquerors oft met sudden falls,   65
And drunk themselves into their funerals
While the Lethean cups sealed up their eyes,
Forgetting all the dangers of surprise.
Oft so, forgetful of eternity,
The vulgar drunkards in their surfeits die   70
Who wine adore, because it will not let them think
A serious thought of heaven till into hell they sink.
To it they sacrifice their glorious days

63–64] *Belshazzar … besieging Persians*: Belshazzar, also spelt Balthasar (the son of
Nebuchadnezzar according to Daniel 5:2), was King of Babylon when it was
overthrown by the Persians. The biblical account of his court has him drinking wine
from sacred goblets, entertaining concubines, and worshipping idols until he is
chastised for this behaviour by the mysterious (and now proverbial) 'writing on the
wall', interpreted by Daniel.

67] *Lethean cups*: In Greek mythology Lethe is a river in Hades. Its water, once drunk,
allows the souls of the dead to forget their former life, so it is broadly associated
with forgetfulness.

Racking their wits to celebrate its praise,
Nor give tired nature the relief of sleep   75
Till they their brains in their crowned goblets steep.
When the wine, working with wild fancy, makes
False dreams of pleasure, horrid sad mistakes
Which, waking, too unhappily they find
Yet the infection rooted in the mind.   80
They violently court their plague again
Run into brutishness and thirst for pain,
For where the force of conquering drink prevails,
The sight grows dim, the active vigour fails,
The weak legs cannot bear the member's weight   85
But march with an uncertain staggering gait.
The eyes deeper sunk no liveliness retain,
Black misty vapours fume up to the brain;
Trembling the hands, numbness the joints invades,
Sickness the stomach, the fresh colour fades;   90
All o'er cold sweats and ghastly paleness creep
Till the faint spirits yield to a deathlike sleep
Which lays all down in their transformèd shapes:
Some wanton and ridiculous like apes;
Some roaring with more senseless furious wrath   95
Than the fierce mastiff or the lion hath;
Some acting goats whose bloods hot lust doth fire;
Some nasty swine that wallow in foul mire;
Some filthy dogs by loathsome vomits made;
The stupid ass the sottish drunkard played.   100
Nor from the form of man alone estranged,
But in their proper inclinations changed;
The powerful charm makes cowards brave and bold,
Makes misers cast away their hoarded gold;
The silent talk, the talkative sit dumb   105
The froward kind, the patient quarrelsome,
Base minds to high and haughty thoughts erecting,
And to mean actions noble souls dejecting.
It makes the cold and chaste burn with wild fires,

82] *brutishness*: like a brute or lower animal, lacking reason and understanding. The
    scribal spelling in the manuscript is 'bruitishness' with a possible pun on 'bruit'
    meaning noise, clamour, or rumour.
100] *sottish*: foolish, stupid.
106] *froward*: perverse, ungovernable.

In the hot lover drowns all fierce desires,   110
Th'effeminate to manly acts excites,
The bold and brave inclines to soft delights
Makes sly dissemblers hidden truth reveal
And th'open-hearted everything conceal.
Nor doth it always work by contraries   115
By horrid transformation and disguise
As oft it doth men's inclinations draw
Without regard of any bound or awe
To the extremest acting of their powers
Which all their merit and their praise devours   120
Rend'ring them monstrous who exceed all rules,
Exposing wise men to the scorn of fools.

Note

This passage from the start of Canto 9 explores events narrated in Genesis 9 in which Noah, having survived the flood, falls into sinful behaviour and in particular drunkenness. Hutchinson's critique of drinking is both religious and political. She sees it as a sin that erodes the ties of friendship and those of nature and corrupts man's reason. Hutchinson elaborates upon the biblical passage to stress the danger and unseemliness of drunkenness in court, drawing out parallels to the Restoration court of Charles II, which was notoriously libertine. She also brings in to her narrative the analogous case of Belshazzar, King of Babylon (Daniel 5), in order to draw out the political and specifically anti-courtly resonance of this episode.

From *Memoirs of the Life of Colonel Hutchinson*

'All sorts of men through various labours press'

All sorts of men through various labours press
To the same end: contented quietness.
Great princes vex their labouring thoughts to be
Possessed of an unbounded sovereignty;
The hardy soldier doth all toils sustain   5
That he may conquer first, and after reign;
Th'industrious merchant ploughs the angry seas
That he may bring home wealth, and live at ease,
Which none of them attain; for sweet repose
But seldom to the splendid palace goes;   10
A troop of restless passions wander there,
And only private lives are free from care.
Sleep to the cottage bringeth happy nights,
But to the court, hung round with flaring lights,
Which th'office of the vanished day supply,   15
His image only comes to close the eye,
But gives the troubled mind no ease of care.
While country slumbers undisturbed are,
Where, if the active fancy dreams present,
They bring no horrors to the innocent.   20
Ambition doth incessantly aspire
And each advance leads on to new desire;
Nor yet can riches av'rice satisfy,
For want and wealth together multiply:
Nor can voluptuous men more fullness find,   25
For enjoyed pleasures leave their stings behind.
He's only rich who knows no want; he reigns
Whose will no severe tyranny constrains;
And he alone possesseth true delight
Whose spotless soul no guilty fears affright.   30
This freedom in the country life is found,
Where innocence and safe delights abound:

15] *Which th'office of the vanished day supply*: light which the sun had provided before it set.

Here man's a prince; his subjects ne'er repine
When on his back their wealthy fleeces shine.
If for his appetite the fattest die,   35
Those who survive will raise no mutiny:
His table is with home-got dainties crowned,
With friends, not flatterers, encompassed round;
No spies nor traitors on his trencher wait,
Nor is his mirth confined to rules of state;   40
An armed guard he neither hath nor needs,
Nor fears a poisoned morsel when he feeds;
Bright constellations hang above his head,
Beneath his feet are flowery carpets spread;
The merry birds delight him with their songs,   45
And healthful air his happy life prolongs.
At harvest merrily his flocks he shears,
And in cold weather their warm fleeces wears;
Unto his ease he fashions all his clothes;
His cup with uninfected liquor flows: 50
The vulgar breath doth not his thoughts elate
Nor can he be o'erwhelmed by their hate;
Yet, if ambitiously he seeks for fame,
One village feast shall gain a greater name
Than his who wears th'imperial diadem,   55
Whom the rude multitude doe still condemn.
Sweet peace and joy his blessed companions are;
Fear, sorrow, envy, lust, revenge, and care,
And all that troop which breeds the world's offence,
With pomp and majesty, are banished thence.   60
What court then can such liberty afford?
Or where is man so uncontrolled a lord?

Note

The dating of this poem remains uncertain, and the manuscript from
which it was copied in the nineteenth century is now lost. It is likely to
have been written when the Hutchinsons were at Owthorpe, their

---

33] *repine*: express discontent.
34] *When on his back their wealthy fleeces shine*: In the country, man's only subjects are
    his sheep.
39] *trencher*: dish.
55] *diadem*: crown.

Nottinghamshire estate, either in the 1640s or in the early 1660s before John Hutchinson was arrested. The poem draws on Horatian images and rhetoric to represent rural retreat as superior to courtly business, its relative quietism in striking contrast to the disillusioned rage of the elegies. See Wiseman, *Conspiracy and Virtue*.

Textual introduction

Our aim in this anthology is to present the work of our selected poets in clear, modernised texts for use by students at undergraduate level and above. Much editorial ink has been spilled on the politics and technicalities of how to present early modern texts for student and scholarly readers, and editors of early modern women's texts in particular have often been heavily invested in producing faithful or diplomatic editions of women's works. Such editions, with old spelling, and often replicating deletions and insertions to texts that were written in manuscript, provide a rich insight into processes of composition and the idiosyncrasies of manuscript presentation; however, they do not result in the most accessible or user-friendly texts for reading and studying poems in a classroom context. It has often been pointed out that for the big-name canonical poets – Shakespeare, Donne, Marvell, Milton – any number of modernised editions are available, while for women authors of the same period, modernised editions have been hard to come by. And there can be little question that this affects how we have read poems by early modern women. Modernised editions are not only easier for students and beginning scholars to use, encouraging close reading and comparisons with other well-known examples of early modern poetry; they also undoubtedly carry with them the whiff of canonicity, of 'great literary authorship', and engender more serious approaches to the work.[1]

We have, therefore, aimed in this anthology to treat the selected women's poems according to the broad editorial principles behind anthologies such as *The Norton Anthology of English Literature*. Our texts are modernised in their spelling and punctuation, including capitalisation and the use of i/j and u/v. The layout of lines and stanzas has been regularised. Annotations on the page are explanatory, being designed to facilitate an informed understanding of the poems. More specialised textual notes are found here at the back of the volume.

While the texts in this anthology are modernised, we have not abandoned an interest in the poems' conditions of production and in the contexts in which they originally occurred. Each set of poems is arranged according to their groupings in the copy-texts that we have chosen, in order to reflect something of the poems' complex textual histories. Anne Bradstreet's poems first appeared in *The Tenth Muse Lately Sprung up in America* (1650), and the later volume of *Several Poems* (Boston, 1678) included revised texts of those poems, as well as a number of new ones. We have used *The Tenth Muse* as our copy-text in this edition for all poems that occurred in it, and *Several Poems* for poems printed only there. We have made this choice in part because the versions of the poems that occur in *The Tenth Muse* speak more directly to the context of the English Civil War, into which that volume was brought from New England and in which it was published. It is most clearly in those texts that Bradstreet is a poet *of the English Civil War*. Most of Bradstreet's poems were revised between the two volumes of her verse (whether by her or not is impossible to tell), but one was revised so comprehensively that we have chosen to present it here in two full versions. 'An Elegy upon that Honourable and Renowned Knight, Sir Philip Sidney' thus occurs twice, enabling full comparison of the different versions that were printed in 1650 and 1678.

Hester Pulter's poems occur only in University of Leeds Library, Brotherton Collection, MS Lt q 32, which is therefore our copy-text. Katherine Philips sits at the other end of the spectrum to Pulter in terms of textual complexity: there are two printed editions of *Poems* (1664 and 1667), of contested degrees of authorial sanction, an early autograph manuscript (known as 'Tutin'), and several other manuscript volumes, including the important Rosania manuscript compiled after her death. We have chosen here to use the autograph Tutin manuscript, National Library of Wales MS 775B, as our copy-text for poems that occur in it; we have used *Poems* (1664) for those that are not in Tutin; and we have used *Poems* (1667) for those that occur in neither of the earlier two copy-texts. Poems are arranged in our anthology according to the groupings in which they were presented in those copy-texts, because we think that offers some insight into the ways in which Philips was presented and read. It seems significant, for example, that when Philips's poetry was first printed in 1664, her state-political poems, on members of the royal family and events of the Civil War, Interregnum, and Restoration, were all placed at the beginning of the volume – suggesting that Philips should be read as a poet writing on matters of political significance.[2]

For Margaret Cavendish, the two major editions of *Poems and Fancies* in 1653 and 1664 each have strongly competing claims both to textual authority and to the more resonant political moment. While 1653 is usually prioritised as the first iteration of Cavendish's distinctive poetry in print, there is a strong case to be made that she corrected, or arranged correction of, the second edition of 1664, which does indeed represent a more skilful and fluid verse style. We have, therefore, opted to use *Poems and Fancies* of 1664 as our copy-text, collated against the earlier printing in 1653. For Lucy Hutchinson, decisions about copy-text have for the most part been more straightforward because many of her poems, like Pulter's, are extant only in single manuscript witnesses. The exception is *Order and Disorder*, of which a five-canto version was printed anonymously in 1679, and a longer version exists in manuscript only, in Beinecke Rare Book and Manuscript Library, MS Osborn fb 100. In this case, we have taken the print version as our copy-text where the poem existed in print, collated it with the manuscript, and used the manuscript as copy-text for the passage from a later canto which was not published.

While these selections of copy-text are complex, we hope that they go some way towards indicating the ways in which these five poets were produced and published – in manuscript, print, or both – as poets of their social and political moments. All texts have been edited afresh from a single instance of the chosen copy-text, and all texts have been collated against the other copy-texts that we have chosen to prioritise. That is, collations for Bradstreet's texts are based on *The Tenth Muse* (1650) and *Several Poems* (1678); those for Philips are based on the Tutin manuscript and *Poems* 1664 and 1667; those for Cavendish on *Poems and Fancies* 1653 and 1664; and those for the first five cantos of Hutchinson's *Order and Disorder* on the Beinecke manuscript and the printed version of 1679. Collation notes for each poem are presented in 'Textual notes' below.

Notes

1 We discuss these contentions further in 'Anthologizing Early Modern Women's Poetry: *Women Poets of the English Civil War*', in Sarah C. E. Ross and Paul Salzman (eds), *Editing Early Modern Women* (Cambridge: Cambridge University Press, 2016), pp. 215–31.
2 See Gillian Wright, 'Textuality, Privacy and Politics: Katherine Philips's Poems in Manuscript and Print', in James Daybell and Peter Hinds (eds), *Material Readings of Early Modern Culture* (Basingstoke: Macmillan, 2010), pp. 163–82.

Textual notes

Anne Bradstreet

The Tenth Muse Lately Sprung up in America, or Several Poems, Compiled with Great Variety of Wit and Learning, Full of Delight (1650; Wing B4167, on *EEBO*) is the copy-text for all poems that occurred in it, collated with their revised versions in *Several Poems, Compiled with Great Variety of Wit and Learning, Full of Delight* (Boston, 1678; Wing B4166, on *EEBO*). *Several Poems* (1678) is the copy-text for poems that occurred only in it. The two versions of 'An Elegy upon that Honourable and Renowned Knight, Sir Philip Sidney' (1650 and 1678) are reproduced in full; these are not collated against each other.

The Prologue

Copy-text: *The Tenth Muse* (1650)
4] And: 1678 = Or
6] verse: 1678 = lines
20] speak afterwards more: 1678 = in future times speak
41] each and all: 1678 = all and each
46] wholesome: 1678 = thyme or
47] ore = 1678 (1650: stuff)

The Four Monarchies

Copy-text: *The Tenth Muse* (1650)
2] did not strive: 1678 = did not proudly strive
6] son = 1678 (1650: sons) Cush: 1678 = Chus

29] Bell: 1678 = Baal

52] 1678 = By force and fraud did under tribute bring

54] Pharmus: 1678 = Thermus

60] drown: 1678 = drowned

67] Philistines' = 1678 (1650: Philistrius')

70] for what: 1678 = for the crime

74] the = 1678 (1650: his)

82] Ninus of her amorous: 1678 = Ninus amorous of her

91] 1678 = That underserved, they blurred her name and fame

92] As: 1678 = By

97] were: 1678 = was

105] Most: 1678 = Some

111] But: 1678 = And

115] beyond: 1678 = above

121] On Shinar ... by the Euphratian: 1678 = In Shinar ... on the Euphratian

124] Staurobates, his country = 1678 (1650: Great King Staurobates, for)

126] man: 1678 = may

129] marvellous: 1678 = wonderful

131] Indus: 1678 = Judas [identified as an error in 1678 errata leaf]

3267–68] omitted in 1678

3272] At Actium slain, his navy: 1678 = At Actium, where his navies

3272] Following this line, 1678 adds: He seeing his honour lost, his kingdom end, / Did by his sword his life soon after send.

3273] Then poisonous asps she sets unto: 1678 = His brave virago asps sets to

3297] that: 1678 = the

3305] But yet: 1678 = Yet shall

3306] that: 1678 = the

3311] a: 1678 = some

3320] *Ne sutor ultra crepidam* = 1678 (1650: *Ne suter ultra crepidum*)

3329] in best: 1678 = in good

3332] into th'world: 1678 = to the world

3338] made: 1678 = kept

3342] walls: 1678 = wall

3351] these: 1678 = those

3360] For: 1678 = Then

3366] Some feigning say to heav'n: 1678 = Some feigning to the gods

3369] is next chosen: 1678 = next chose they

3372] but ope: 1678 = set ope

3375] habit: 1678 = gestures

3377] Goddess: 1678 = The nymph

3380] some: 1678 = a
3384] The: 1678 = This. did = 1678 (1650: do)
3387] conquer, others yield: 1678 = conquer, the other yield
3388] for: 1678 = in
3394] Leaves: 1678 = Left
3402] year th'time: 1678 = years time
3406] 1678 = Who from his country for sedition fled
3414] Much state and glory: 1678 = Some state and splendour
3415] stranger: 1678 = stronger [identified as an error in 1678 errata leaf]
3417] sits upon: 1678 = get into
3435] with speed: 1678 = by force
3440–59] 1678. 'An Apology' is not included in 1650.

A Dialogue between Old England and New

Copy-text: *The Tenth Muse* (1650)
14] weakened fainting: 1678 = fainting weakened
26] wound's: 1678 = wound
29] fraud and force: 1678 = fraud or force
30] And by: 1678 = Or by
46] 1678 = Pray do you fear Spain's bragging armado?
48] do = 1678 (1650: doth)
50] this: 1678 = the
61] and: 1678 = nor
64] Lewis: 1678 = Jews
67–68] omitted in 1678
70] In 1678, two lines are added after line 70: No crafty tyrant now
  usurps the seat / Who nephews slew that so he might be great.
86] thy: 1678 = our
93] And: 1678 = Are
94] trodden = 1678 (1650: is trod)
95] were = 1678 (1650: are)
103] wast: 1678 = wert
104] I: 1678 = was
107] bloods: 1678 = blood
111] which I have: 1678 = by great ones
112] O, Edward's babes: 1678 = Of Edward's youths
115] for thefts, and lies: 1678 = and lies
127–30] omitted in 1678, and replaced with: I then believed not, now I
  feel and see / The plague of stubborn incredulity.
132] 1678 = Some fined, from house and friends to exile went

134] 1678 = Who saw their wrongs, and hath judged righteously
143] yielding: 1678 = yielded
157] hands: 1678 = hearts
161] says: 1678 = said
162] 1678 = 'Tis said, my better part in parliament
163] show: 1678 = showed
166] come: 1678 = came
190] cause: 1678 = strife
193] the worst, the best may overthrow: 1678 = but this may be my overthrow
194–95] omitted in 1678
198] ravished: 1678 = weeping
206–07] 1678: For my relief, do what there lies in thee, /And recompense that good I've done to thee.
210] I once: 1678 = and I
212–13] 1678: Your griefs I pity, but soon hope to see / Out of your troubles, much good fruit to be
214] these: 1678 = those
215] 1678 = Though now beclouded all with tears and blood
222] which do: 1678 = who did
226] them = 1678 (1650: those)
231] prelates: 1678 = popelings
232] out: 1678 = forth
234] such trash: 1678 = such empty trash
238] show whose son thou art: 1678 = with a loyal heart
239] nor country in thy heart: 1678 = nor to the better part
241] By force expel, destroy: 1678 = As duty binds, expel
242–43] omitted in 1678
245] blessèd: 1678 = hopeful
251] will: 1678 = shall
261] for: 1678 = oft
268] thy valour: 1678 = and glory
273] Execute to th'full: 1678 = And on her pour
294] parliament: 1678 = rightest cause

An Elegy upon that Honourable and Renowned Knight, Sir Philip Sidney [1650]

Copy-text: *The Tenth Muse* (1650). See p. 76 for the 1678 version of this poem.
34] Fond = 1678 (1650: Found)

In Honour of Du Bartas, 1641

Copy-text: *The Tenth Muse* (1650)
1] Amongst: 1678 = Among
19] I fitly may compare: 1678 = I may compare
33] And: 1678 = But
55] in him thou didst: 1678 = thou didst in him
56] Pepin, Martel: 1678 = Martel, Pepin
58] in blood, in scars: 1678 = in wars, in blood
64] all men to thee: 1678 = to thee all men
71] are: 1678 = is
72] name = 1678 (1650: names). or: 1678 = and

In Honour of that High and Mighty Princess, Queen Elizabeth, of Most Happy Memory

Copy-text: *The Tenth Muse* (1650)
Title] of Most Happy: 1678 = of Happy
18] greatness: 1678 = praises
24] eleven Olympiads = 1678 (1650: nine Olympiads)
33] had not in force now been: 1678 = in force now had not been
38] once a year = 1678 (1650: twice a year)
43] so: 1678 = more
48] for: 1678 = there
56] Before her picture the proud Tyrone fell = 1678 (1650: And Tyrone bound, before her picture fell)
59] Such soldiers and such captains: 1678 = Such captains and such soldiers
62] her: 1678 = the
63] laden = 1678 (1650 = laded)
65] wit: 1678 = tongue
69] placed: 1678 = built
70] time: 1678 = while
73] at: 1678 = of
81] Proud, profuse: 1678 = Profuse, proud
102] O: 1678 = Yea
109] must: 1678 = shall

David's Lamentation for Saul and Jonathan, 2 Samuel 1:19

Copy-text: *The Tenth Muse* (1650)
13] For there the mighty ones = 1678 (1650: For the mighty ones)
20] Did Saul with bloodless sword: 1678 = With bloodless sword did Saul
22] deaths: 1678 = death
33] wert: 1678 = wast
35] Distressed I am for thee: 1678 = Distressed for thee I am
36] surpassing man = 1678 (1650: passing a man)

An Elegy upon that Honourable and Renowned Knight, Sir Philip Sidney (1678)

Copy-text: *Several Poems* (1678). See p. 59 for the 1650 version of this poem.

The Flesh and the Spirit

Copy-text: *Several Poems* (1678)

The Author to her Book

Copy-text: *Several Poems* (1678)

A Letter to her Husband, Absent upon Public Employment

Copy-text: *Several Poems* (1678)

Another ['As loving hind']

Copy-text: *Several Poems* (1678)

In Memory of my Dear Grandchild Elizabeth Bradstreet, who Deceased August 1605, Being a Year and Half Old

Copy-text: *Several Poems* (1678)

Hester Pulter

Pulter's poems occur only in University of Leeds, Brotherton Collection, MS Lt q 32, which is our copy-text. Some comparisons with Eardley's *Lady Hester Pulter* (2014) are noted.

The Invitation into the Country, to my Dear Daughters

Title: Dear Daughters M.P., P.P.: MS = D: D: M: P: P: P:
Title] Unhappy Hour. Eardley suggests 'Unhappy [Holmby]'.
4] Five: this word has been overwritten in the MS, and is difficult to decipher. Eardley transcribes as 'Fierce'. usurp: MS = usurps
5] planes: Eardley transcribes as 'fanes' (temples).
59] both: In the MS, 'doth' has been crossed out and 'both' inserted above.
67] posies: MS = poses
71–72] The couplet has been inserted into the left-hand margin in Pulter's autograph hand, with its placement after line 70 indicated by an 'x'. In the main text, line 70 leads directly into line 73, without a stanza break, but the inserted couplet implies that there should be one between lines 72 and 73.
95] Mimram: MS = Mimmer
154] Hangs: MS = Hang
155] Napaeae: MS = Napeas
163] violets: MS = vi-letts

The Complaint of Thames, 1647

46] showing: MS = shewing, and Pulter's meaning is not entirely clear. Eardley suggests 'eschewing'.
51] she'd ne'er: MS = she would ne're
55] looked: MS = took
69] Horatius' valour: MS = Horatia's vallure
85] they'd: MS = they would
103] despair: MS = despairs
115] breathe: MS = breaths

On those Two Unparalleled Friends, Sir George Lisle and Sir Charles Lucas

Title] The eighteenth-century annotating hand has added 'who were shot to death at Colchester'.

7] Areopagus: MS = Areopagie

14] two: Eardley transcribes as 'too'

29] t'embrace: MS = to embrace

43] hurrying: MS = hurring. Eardley retains 'hurring' here (which means to snarl or growl).

53] they've: MS = they have

84] In the MS 'triumph' is deleted and 'glory' inserted in its place.

Upon the Death of my Dear and Lovely Daughter, J.P.

28] splendency: MS = splendentie

41] posies: MS = poses

43] The line to close this couplet, 'Like drops of blood upon unsoiled snow', is scored out.

44–52] A pointing finger device and the words 'videre retro 27' (i.e. look back 27') direct the reader to page 27 in the manuscript (fol. 16r), where lines 44–52 of the poem are added into spare space (see Figures 2 and 3).

On the Same ['Tell me no more']

26] Muses': MS = Museses

On the Horrid Murder of that Incomparable Prince, King Charles the First

Title] Murder: MS =Murther

2] unparalled: MS = unparrild

On the Same ['Let none sigh more']

4] sovereign's: MS = sovereign

10] unto: MS = into

15] unparalled: MS = unparrild

'Dear God turn not away thy face'

This poem is untitled in the MS, as are most of Pulter's devotional poems.

The Circle ['Those that the hidden chemic art profess']

1] chemic: MS = Chimick
3] philtres: MS = filterys

On the King's Most Excellent Majesty

The poem seems initially to have been titled 'On the King' (in Pulter's hand, not that of the main scribe), with the alteration and addition made in a different hand.
5] bright Minerva's: These words are written above 'Pallas' sacred' in the MS, but it is unclear which is the preferred reading ('Pallas' sacred' is underlined but not scored out).
11] unparalled: MS = unparrild

To my Dear J.P., M.P., P.P., they Being at London, I at Broadfield

Title] Broadfield: MS = Bradfield
1] lonely: MS = lovly (apparently a scribal error)

'Must I thus ever interdicted be?'

This poem is untitled in the MS, as are most of Pulter's devotional poems.

'Why must I thus forever be confined'

This poem is untitled in the MS, as are most of Pulter's devotional poems.
55] ones': MS = on's
94] I'd: MS = I wo'd

To Sir William Davenant, upon the Unspeakable Loss of the Most Conspicuous and Chief Ornament of his Frontispiece

Title] William Davenant: MS = W^m. D.
9, 33] slight: MS = sleight

The Weeping Wish

Title] The poem is dated January 1665, directly beneath the title.
12] Artemisia's: MS: Artimitius

Emblem 20

8] lay: MS = say
17] Artemesia's: MS = Artimitius
48] In fine: MS = Infine
50] So: MS = To

Emblem 22

19] is pursued: These words are obscured in the MS due to damage.
22] broke: Eardley transcribes as 'breaks'.

Katherine Philips

The autograph 'Tutin' manuscript, National Library of Wales, MS 775B, is our copy-text for poems that occur in it. We have used *Poems by the Incomparable Mrs. K.P.* (1664; Wing P2032, on *EEBO*) for those that are not in Tutin; and we have used *Poems by the Most Deservedly Admired Mrs Katherine Philips, the Matchless Orinda; to which is added Monsieur Corneille's Pompey & Horace, Tragedies; With Several Other Translations Out of French* (1667; Wing P2033, on *EEBO*) for poems that occur in neither of the earlier two copy-texts. Each of these copy-texts is collated against the others. The exceptions to this policy are two poems that occur only in partial copy in the Tutin manuscript,

'To the Right Honourable Alice, Countess of Carbery, on her Enriching Wales with her Presence' and 'Orinda upon Little Hector Philips'. The copy-texts for these poems are the more complete copies in *Poems* (1664) and *Poems* (1667) respectively, and are collated against Tutin.

To my Dearest Antenor, on his Parting

Copy-text: Tutin
13] its own: 1664 = in its

A Retired Friendship, to Ardelia

Copy-text: Tutin
Title] 23rd August 1651: 1664; 1667 [no date]
27] neighbour: 1664; 1667 = neighbouring
27] streams: 1664 = springs
30] Whoever would not: 1664; 1667 = Who would not ever

Friendship's Mysteries, to my Dearest Lucasia

Copy-text: Tutin
Title] Mysteries: 1664; 1667 = Mystery
11] their: 1664; 1667 = the
17] Than Thrones more great and innocent: 1664 = Than greatest thrones more innocent
21] tedious: 1664 = odious

Content, to my Dearest Lucasia

Copy-text: Tutin
9] or: 1664; 1667 = and
28] is: 1667 = he's
37] But: 1664; 1667 = But yet
46] wish: 1664; 1667 = wish for
48] made: 1664; 1667 = born
53] so: 1664 = still

54] Their very griefs imparted lose that name: 1664; 1667 = Their griefs,
   when once imparted, lose their name
61] we who have: 1664 = we have

Friendship in Emblem, or the Seal, to my Dearest Lucasia

Copy-text: Tutin
Stanza 5 ('From smoke ... consumed') is inserted in the manuscript after
the other verses have been transcribed.
28] the other: 1664 = each other; 1667 = this other
44] law: 1664; 1667 = unto
46] and numbers: 1664; 1667 = in number
54] even: 1664; 1667 = ever
58] mine: 1664; 1667 = mind
61] is: 1664; 1667 = are

The World

Copy-text: Tutin
2] too early: 1667; 1664 = untimely
8] mischief: 1664; 1667 = mischiefs
18] And, so far from: 1667 = So far even from
20] an: 1664; 1667 = one
23] are: 1667 = is
45] But: 1664; 1667 = Our
51] Errors: 1664; 1667 = Error
54] we can't: 1667 = cannot
55] men who plod on: 1664; 1667 = men now, who plod
84] or sting: 1664; 1667 = their sting
86] find: overwrites 'seek'. 1664; 1667 = find
93] grope and play and cry: 1664 = grapple, play and cry; 1667 = grovel,
   play and cry

The Soul

Copy-text: Tutin
2] roam: 1664 = come
12] our own: 1664; 1667 = our

33] made body: 1664 = made a body; 1667 = body made
46] her clotty: 1664 = a clotty; 1667 = a sordid
56] immortality: 1664 = mortality
65] shortens: 1664; 1667 = shorten
78] keep: 1664; 1667 = keeps
79] And those who yield to what: 1667 = Who yield to all that does

Invitation to the Country

Copy-text: Tutin
13] laurels pressed their: 1664; 1667 = laurel pressed the
21] fate: 1664 = it
34] sting that: 1664 = thing that
36] wholly: 1664; 1667 = only
42] When: 1664; 1667: Where
49] most: 1664; 1667 = world
50] will: 1664 = can

On the 3rd September 1651

Copy-text: Tutin
5] As if: 1664; 1667 = And as
18] wait upon: 1667; 1664 = else attend
25] Thus captive: 1667; 1664 = And captiv'd
31] thus: 1664; 1667 = so
32] the: 1664; 1667 = a

2 Corinthians 5:19, God was in Christ reconciling the world to himself, 8th April 1653

Copy-text: Tutin
Title] 8th April 1653: 1667 = [no date]
5] Christ: expanded from 'C'' (1664; 1667 = Christ)
9] was in so much misery: 1664; 1667 = in such misery was
10] make: 1664 = made
11] lump: 1664; 1667= load
19–26] omitted in 1667
27] hath made he therefore: 1667 = himself hath made he

28] it's: 1664; 1667 = 'tis
32] 'Tis equal: 1667= Shews more his
34] would: 1664; 1667 = could
47] men: 1664; 1667 = sin

Upon the Double Murder of King Charles I, in Answer to a Libellous Copy of Rhymes Made by Vavasor Powell

Copy-text: 1664
3] dangers: 1667 = danger
5] here's a fair: 1667 = this is a
27–28] omitted in 1667

On the Numerous Access of the English to Wait upon the King in Flanders

Copy-text: 1664
4] 1667 = As Pompey's camp, where'er it moved, was Rome
10] Will itself: 1667 = Itself will
22] so long lost: 1667 = prodigious. did still: 1667 = still did

Arion on a Dolphin, to his Majesty at his Passage into England

Copy-text: 1664
Title] 1667. 1664 = Arion to a Dolphin, on his Majesty's Passage into England
21] Had plots for: 1667 = Plots against
71] Disgusted: 1667 = Discovered

On the Fair Weather Just at Coronation

Copy-text: 1664
Title] 1667 = On the Fair Weather Just at the Coronation, it Having Rained Immediately Before and After
8] a more bright: 1667 = in a bright
12] 1667. The line is missing in 1664, the lacuna indicated by a line of asterisks.

On the Death of the Queen of Bohemia

Copy-text: 1664
3] hath so far: 1667 = so far hath
21] suit begged to have: 1667 = tribute begged t'have
24] bravely: 1667 = greatly
26] the: 1667 = his
39] devotion = 1667 (1664: directions)

To the Right Honourable Alice, Countess of Carbery, on her Enriching Wales with her Presence

Copy-text: 1664 (Tutin contains lines 1–20 only, the leaf containing the
    third stanza having been excised.)
Title] on her Enriching Wales with her Presence: 1667 = at her Coming
    into Wales
In Tutin, the poem begins with an address, on its own line, 'Madam'.
4] so: 1667 = let
5] our = 1667 (Tutin; 1664 = your). deemed: Tutin = doomed
6] in: Tutin = to
12] do't: Tutin = pay't
13] Tutin: It is perfection's misery, that art and wit
23] splendour: 1667 = splendours

To Antenor, on a Paper of Mine which J. Jones Threatens to Publish to Prejudice him

Copy-text: 1664. Hageman believes that the poem was originally in Tutin,
    but has been excised ('Treacherous Accidents', p. 91).
Title] J. Jones: 1667 = J. J.
1] his: 1667 = thy
14] verse: 1664 = Virge; 1667 = verse

A Country Life

Copy-text: 1664
10–12] 1667 = Here taught the multitude; / The brave they here with
    honour fired, / And civilised the rude.
33] Such as: 1667 = Them that

41] roar = 1667 (1664: wear)
59] There: 1667 = Then
61] knew: 1667 = know
85] integrity: 1667 = and humble seat
86] noise: 1667 = strife
87–88] 1667 = I am not forced to make retreat / But choose to spend
  my life.

Upon Mr Abraham Cowley's Retirement. Ode.

Copy-text: 1664
40] thee: 1667 = these
44] will be unconcerned: 1667 = must be unconcerned
48] But of: 1667 = But that of
57] innocence: 1667 = innocent

Epitaph on her Son H.P. at St Sith's Church, where her Body also Lies Interred

Copy-text: 1667

To my Antenor, March 16 1661/2

Copy-text: 1667

Orinda upon Little Hector Philips

Copy-text: 1667 (The first two stanzas of the poem, only, are in the
  Tutin MS.)
Title] Tutin = On the Death of my First and Dearest Child, Hector
  Philips, Born the 23rd of April and Died the 2nd of May 1655. Set
  by Mr Lawes.
1] in = Tutin (1667: of)
6] touch = Tutin (1667: pluck)
8] So = Tutin (1667: For)

Margaret Cavendish

Our first copy-text is *Philosophical Fancies* (1653; Wing N865) for poems that occurred in it. Poems that occurred in *Poems and Fancies* (1653) and *Poems and Fancies* (1664) are taken from *Poems, and Fancies, Written by the Thrice Noble, Illustrious, and Excellent Princess the Lady Marchioness of Newcastle. The Second Impression, Much Altered and Corrected* (1664). British Library shelfmark 1664 G.19054. These poems are collated with *Poems and Fancies* (1653; Wing N869, on *EEBO*, and in the Scolar Press facsimile (Menston, Yorkshire: Scholar Press, 1972)).

Of Sense and Reason Exercised in their Different Shapes

Copy-text: *Philosophical Fancies* (1653)

A Dialogue between the Body and the Mind

Copy-text: *Philosophical Fancies* (1653)

An Elegy

Copy-text: *Philosophical Fancies* (1653)

The Poetress's Hasty Resolution

Copy-text: *Poems and Fancies* (1664)
3] And thinking them so good, thought more to make: 1653 = Thinking them so good, I thought more to write
4] take: 1653 = like
5] thought, lived I many a year: 1653 = I thought, if I lived long
6] thereon to rear: 1653 = to build thereon
9] he: 1653 = she
11] and do: 1653 = said she
13] already hath great store: 1653 = hath already such a weight
14] wherefore do write no more: 1653 = as it is over fraught
15] But: 1653 = Then
16] into th'fire: 1653 = in the fire

18] he: 1653 = she

21] repent with grief: 1653 = with grief repent

A World Made by Atoms

Copy-text: *Poems and Fancies* (1664)

2] For being subtle, every shape they take: 1653 = As being subtle, and of every shape

3] they: 1653 = fit

4] Of forms, that: 1653 = Such forms as

5] or: 1653 = and

9] as they: 1653 = not fit

12] And there remaining close and fast will knit: 1653 = They there remain, lie close, and fast will stick

13] which not fit: 1653 = that unfit

15] Thus by their forms, and motions they will be: 1653 = Thus by their several motions, and their forms

16] Like workmen, which amongst themselves agree: 1653 = As several work-men serve each other's turns

17] so: 1653 = thus

18] predestinate, may work by fate: 1653 = predestinated to work my fate

Of the Subtlety of Motion

Copy-text: *Poems and Fancies* (1664)

3] We should of unknown things dispute no more: 1653 = We should adore God more, and not dispute

4] How they be done, but the great God adore: 1653 = How they are done, but that great God can do't

7] which God in us did raise: 1653 = which nature's God did give

8] To worship him, and in his works to praise: 1653 = Us to adore him, and his wonders with

11] We: 1653 = But

12] But proud: 1653 = Proudly

Of Vacuum

Copy-text: *Poems and Fancies* (1664)

4] should: 1653 = might

5] is like to a: 1653 = like is to the
6] doth go: 1653 = goeth
6] comes: 1653 = takes
7] since: 1653 = though
8] they: 1653 = first
9] filled up: 1653 = first full
10] Room, for succeeding atoms place to take: 1653 = Room for succession, their places for to take
11] Wherefore if: 1653 = But as those
12] They needs must empty places have to go: 1653 = Yet still in empty places must they go

Of Stars

Copy-text: *Poems and Fancies* (1664)
1] that in th': 1653 = in the
2] ne'er did: 1653 = did ne'er
7] who knows but those: 1653 = who doth know, but
10] As our imaginations thither fly: 1653 = As well as can imaginations high
11] we might as little: 1653 = as little may we
12] up do: 1653 = do up

A World in an Earring

Copy-text: *Poems and Fancies* (1664)
1] earring: 1653 = earring round
2] which: 1653 = and
4] learned: 1653 = some wise
8] we call the north and southern-pole: 1653 = which we do call the pole
9] winters: 1653 = winter
11] lightning: 1653 = lightnings
13] Fish there may swim in seas, which ebb and flow: 1653 = There seas may ebb, and flow, where fishes swim
14] wherein do spices grow: 1653 = where spices grow therein
17] Earthquakes may be: 1653 = There earthquakes be
19] Meadows may: 1653 = There meadows
21] fine: 1653 = fresh

23] There may be night and day, and heat and cold: 1653 = There night, and day, and heat, and cold, and so

24] As also life and death, and young and old: 1653 = May life, and death, and young, and old, still grow

25] And: 1653 = Thus

26] infection: 1653 = infections

27] Great cities there may be, and houses built: 1653 = There cities be, and stately houses built

28] Whose: 1653 = Their

29] Churches may they've, wherein priests teach and sing: 1653 = There churches be, and priests to teach therein

30] steeples: 1653 = steeple

31] up run: 1653 = run

33] Markets may be, where things are: 1653 = There markets be, and things both

34] Though th'ear not knows the price their markets hold: 1653 = Know not the price, nor how the markets hold

35] may ... may: 1653 = do ... do

36] And battles may be fought, and many slain: 1653 = And battles fought, where many may be slain

38] Whence they no: 1653 = And yet not

39] this: 1653 = the

43] Rivals may duels: 1653 = There rivals duels

44] And: 1653 = There

48] are into Elysium gone: 1653 = they into Elysium run

The Purchase of Poets, or A Dialogue Betwixt the Poets, and Fame and Homer's Marriage

Copy-text: *Poems and Fancies* (1664)

2] upon which Fame: 1653 = where Fame thereon

4] Of which all those that drink: 1653 = Which those that drink thereof

5] they're all: 1653 = Poets all are

7] might make: 1653 = should get

8] They all agreed they would some counsel take: 1653 = They did agree in council all to sit

9] owner: 1653 = honour

12] That they might: 1653 = And for to

13] a: 1653 = the

14] Some nimbler feet had = 1653 (1664: Some had nimbler feet had)

14] a: 1653 = their

22] did: 1653 = doth

27] Then: 1653 = Straight

28] strove: 1653 = strong

30] For him was Greece and Troy bound; then came in: 1653 = Brought Greece, and Troy for to be bound for him

31] Virgil who brought: 1653 = Virgil brought

32] did come: 1653 = came soon

33] For Juv'nal and Catullus: 1653 = Juvenal, Catullus

35] Tibullus, Venus and her son did bring: 1653 = And for Tibullus, Venus, and her son

36] For him, 'cause wanton verses he did sing: 1653 = Would needs be bound, 'cause wanton verse he sung

38] For Ovid, sealing's bond with several things: 1653 = Ovid, who seals the bond with several things

39] th'senate: 1653 = senate

40] his: 1653 = their

41] Who mustered all i'th'Parthian fields, their hand: 1653 = Mustering them all in the Emathian Fields

42] And seal did freely set to Lucan's band: 1653 = To Fame's bond to set their hands, and seals

44] and would fair Fame: 1653 = fair Fame for to

47] at the: 1653 = all at

48] But: 1653 = Which

50] Who did dispute, which should Fame's husband be: 1653 = Where Fame disputed long, which should her husband be

51] thought it meet: 1653 = first did speak

52] To speak, whose: 1653 = And said, his

53] Ladies, said he, are for varieties: 1653 = Variety, said he, doth ladies please

54] And: 1653 = They

62] whose high praise he in his verse: 1653 = in his verse his praises high

63] Venus: 1653 = fair Venus

64] Let him your husband be, none other take: 1653 = And for your husband no other may you take

65] Then wise Ulysses in a rhet'ric style: 1653 = Wise Ulysses in an orator's style

66] his: 1653 = whose

67] He bowed his head, and thus: 1653 = Bowing his head down low

71] Homer his lofty strain to heav'n flies high: 1653 = Homer's lofty verse doth reach the heavens high

74] He's: 1653 = As

75] Then walks he down to the: 1653 = So walks he down into
77] about: 1653 = above
80] Elysian: 1653 = Elysium
81] Tells you how lovers there: 1653 = There tells you, how lovers
82] how: 1653 = that
83] make by: 1653 = make
84] So do the souls: 1653 = So souls do
86] Th'Olympic: 1653 = At the Olympic
87] how they run, leap, wrestle, swim and ride = 1653: As wrestling, running, leaping, swimming, ride
88] With: 1653 = And
89] ever did before him: 1653 = before him, did ever
90] The gods in heav'n, and devils' names in hell: 1653 = The names of all the gods, and devils in hell
93] elder much than: 1653 = which were before all
96] as: 1653 = else
97] Else: 1653 = It
102] arts brought in: 1653 = brought arts in
103] now made: 1653 = made
104] Which quenched, you'd: 1653 = Quenched out, you
105] heats men's spirits, and: 1653 = It heats the spirits of men
111] you should thieves, that pick the purse: 1653 = thieves, that pick the purse, you should
112] when: 1653 = since
113] servant: 1653 = servants
114] Each from him steals, and so: 1653 = Thieves steal, and with the same
115] 'twill be a heinous fact: 1653 = the world will never care
116] if you from right detract: 1653 = unless you right prefer
119] your: 1653 = thy
120] your: 1653 = thy
121] Then at your word, I'll: 1653 = I, at your word, will
122] prove: 1653 = proves
124] And they were: 1653 = Then were they
128] but: 1653 = were
129] In measure and in time they danced about: 1653 = Then did they dance with measure, and in time
130] the Muses nine took out: 1653 = took out the Muses nine
131] did run their nimble feet: 1653 = their feet did run
132] sung most sweet: 1653 = sung
133] At last the: 1653 = The
134] And there did Homer get: 1653 = There Homer got

A Dialogue betwixt Man and Nature

Copy-text: *Poems and Fancies* (1664)
1] 'Tis most: 1653 = 'Tis
4] Is the greatest: 1653 = Is a great
5] for nought but pains: 1653 = great pains
6] only to be: 1653 = to be
7] reason, and yet not to know: 1653 = sense, and reason too
8] What we are made for, or what we must do: 1653 = Yet know not what we're made to do
9] to heaven: 1653 = heaven up
10] change into new forms: 1653 = into new forms change
11] to the prime matter: 1653 = to matter prime to
12] Thence take new forms, and so always: 1653 = From thence to take new forms, and so
14] which do torment his: 1653 = to torment the
22] they: 1653 = will
23] Which cruelly they: 1653 = Most cruelly do
24] And form it as they please, then build: 1653 = And forms it as he please, then builds
25] to stand, was graced: 1653 = was made to stand
26] by none to be defaced: 1653 = not to be cut by Man
28] no: 1653 = not
29] passions: 1653 = passion
31] before the time, which I: 1653 = I gave, before the time
32] Ordained for them, 's to me an injury: 1653 = I did ordain, the injury is mine
34] And: 1653 = For
36] good: 1653 = either good
37] beasts have sense, feel pain: 1653 = beast hath sense, feels pain
39] Beasts have: 1653 = Beast hath
42] and: 1653 = with
43] Desire doth whip and makes him run amain: 1653 = Desire whips him forward, makes him run
46] though: 1653 = yet
49] and drink, and all be well: 1653 = or drink, or lie stone-still
50] neither for heav'n, nor hell: 1653 = either for heaven, or hell
53] He has this knowledge, that: 1653 = And knowledge hath, that yet
54] And of himself his knowledge is but small: 1653 = And that himself he knoweth least of all
55] think there are: 1653 = thinks there is

58] And striving both they do shut out wise fate: 1653 = By striving both hinders predestinate

60] that contraries: 1653 = Contrariety

61] was: 1653 = were

64] Who: 1653 = Which

A Dialogue between an Oak and a Man Cutting him Down

Copy-text: *Poems and Fancies* (1664)

1] which largely bend: 1653 = both large, and long

2] And from the scorching sun you do defend: 1653 = That keep you from the heat, and scorching sun

3] Which: 1653 = And

4] And kept you free from thund'ring rains and wet: 1653 = From thund'ring rains I keep you free, from wet

5] you'd: 1653 = would

17] And shall thus be requited my: 1653 = And will you thus requite my love

18] That you will take: 1653 = To take away

21] See how: 1653 = And thus

22] And tried: 1653 = Invent

24] Chop off my limbs, and leave me nak'd and thin: 1653 = Hew down my boughs, so chops off every limb

28] this: 1653 = thus

33] you: 1653 = they

37] doth fly: 1653 = flieth

38] and of: 1653 = strong, or

39] do: 1653 = they

41] they: 1653 = do

42] they'll: 1653 = will

43] Grow: 1653 = Grows

46] heav'n has saved: 1653 = heaven saved

47] he dies: 1653 = they die

55] at all times: 1653 = as they ought

56] men's humours, but their crimes: 1653 = their humours but their fault

58] what: 1653 = how

59] Though: 1653 = If

67] you live: 1653 = thou liv'st

68] seek: 1653 = seek'st

69] you down, that knowledge you: 1653 = thee down, 'cause knowledge thou

71] you: 1653 = thou

72] you do: 1653 = thou dost

73] do rise: 1653 = rise high

74] You: 1653 = Thou

75] And bow their lofty heads, their pride to check: 1653 = Their lofty heads shalt bow, and make them stoop

76] Shall set your steady foot upon their neck: 1653 = And on their necks shalt set thy steady foot

77] They; your: 1653 = And; thy

78] your: 1653 = thy

79] you: 1653 = thou

84] run in danger, some: 1653 = dangers run, some new

86] am: 1653 = were

87] shall I: 1653 = I should

88] will: 1653 = would

92] Then: 1653 = So

93] With sails, and ropes men will: 1653 = Besides with sails, and ropes

94] And I: 1653 = Just like

95] such colds shall take: 1653 = shall take such colds

96] through holes, and leak: 1653 = and leak through holes

100] troubles are: 1653 = trouble, is

102] I'll; I'd: 1653 = I; would

106] you: 1653 = thou

107] you: 1653 = thou

109] Your: 1653 = Thy

110] shall you: 1653 = thou shalt

111] i'th': 1653 = in

112] there: 1653 = their

113] and yet: 1653 = yet can

118] With nails and hammers they will often wound: 1653 = And many times with nails, and hammers strong

119] And; round: 1653 = They; on

123] Such vain delights I matter not: 1653 = I care not for these vain delights

128] men: 1653 = man

132] Here you the sun with scorching heat doth burn: 1653 = For here you stand against the scorching sun

133] And all your leaves so green to dryness turn: 1653 = By's fiery beams, your fresh green leaves become

134] Also: 1653 = Withered

135] And: 1653 = Thus

136] I'm happier far, said th'Oak, than you mankind: 1653 = Yet I am happier, said the Oak, than man

137] For I content in my condition find: 1653 = With my condition I contented am

138] Man: 1563 = He

145] them: 1653 = pains

146] you do not know: 1653 = thou understand'st

149] has: 1653 = hath

150] and doth to heav'n: 1653 = doth to the heavens

151] For curiosities he doth: 1653 = A curiosity for to

152] and: 1653 = which

154] afraid: 1653 = as feared

156] as a king, his favourite waxing: 1653 = to a king, his favourite makes so

157] May well suspect, that he his pow'r will get: 1653 = That at the last, he fears his power he'll get

158] a man's: 1653 = man's

159] That: 1653 = A

160–61] For no perfection he at all doth prize / Till he therein the gods doth equalise: 1653 = And never can be satisfied, until / He, like a god, doth in perfection dwell.

A Dialogue between a Bountiful Knight and a Castle Ruined in War

Copy-text: *Poems and Fancies* (1664)

1] how great is thy change: 1653 = how thou now art changed

9] Towers upon: 1653 = And towers on

10] Walls, like a girdle, went about: 1653 = Like to a girdle, walls went round

12] To view; do: 1653 = viewing; did

13] Where like a garden is each field and close: 1653 = Where every field, like gardens, is enclosed

14] grows: 1653 = growed

16] And hear: 1653 = Hearing

17] I'm: 1653 = am

20] held: 1653 = thought

22] has: 1653 = hath

25] those passages you see: 1653 = they passages made out

26] Made, and destroyed the walls that circled me: 1653 = Flung down my walls, that circled me about

27] left: 1653 = let

28] I'm: 1653 = am

33] My windows broke, the winds blow in, and make: 1653 = My windows all are broke, the wind blows in

34] That I with cold like shivering agues shake: 1653 = With cold I shake, with agues shivering

40] I'll: 1653 = will

41] have I: 1653 = I have

42] I'll: 1653 = Will

43] But to restore thy health, and build: 1653 = Thy health recover, and to build

45] then: 1653 = that

46] But all what's: 1653 = For what is

49] This your great: 1653 = For this your

50] and: 1653 = of

The Clasp

Copy-text: *Poems and Fancies* (1664)

1] Give me a free and noble style, that goes: 1653 = Give me the free, and noble style

2] In an uncurbèd strain, though wild it shows: 1653 = Which seems uncurbed, though it be wild

3] For though it runs about: 1653 = Though it runs wild about

8] And not bound up: 1653 = Not to be bound

The Hunting of the Hare

Copy-text: *Poems and Fancies* (1664)

Like several other poems, 'The Hunting of the Hare' is revised heavily between the first edition of 1653 and that of 1664, including the change of the whole poem from present to past tense.

2] Whose body pressed to th'earth, lay close and squat: 1653 = Pressing his body close to earth lay squat

3] did lie: 1653 = close lies

4] With his grey eyes he glared obliquely: 1653 = Glaring obliquely with his great grey eyes

5] set: 1653 = sets

6] His tail when turned, his hair blew: 1653 = If turn his tail his hairs blow

346

7] And made him to get cold; but he being wise: 1653 = Which he too cold will grow, but he is wise

8] Doth keep: 1653 = And keeps

9] rests he all the day, till th': 1653 = resting all the day, till

10] up he riseth his relief: 1653 = riseth up, his relief for

11] And walks: 1653 = Walking

12] Then coming back in's former posture lies: 1653 = Then back returns, down in his form he lies.

14] which came with their dogs: 1653 = with their dogs which came

15] Whom seeing, he got up, and fast did run: 1653 = Seeing, gets up, and fast begins to run

17] had: 1653 = have

18] traced: 1653 = trace

20] echo: 1653 = echoes

22] Seeing each shadow thought the dogs were there: 1653 = Thinks every shadow still the dogs they were

23] their cry: 1653 = the noise

24] did employ: 1653 = new employs

27] been, but straight in's: 1653 = sat, but straight his

29] Then starting up with fear, he leaped, and such: 1653 = Starting with fear, up leaps, then doth he run

30] Swift speed he made, the ground he scarce did touch: 1653 = And with such speed, the ground scarce treads upon

31] straightways he got: 1653 = he straight way gets

32] And; sat: 1653 = Where; sits

33] Where: 1653 = At

34] Brought him such terror, that his heart did ache: 1653 = Did bring such terror, made his heart to ache

39] he sat: 1653 = did sit

43] grey: 1653 = great

47] he was tired: 1653 = weary was

53] The hounds so fast came on, and with such cry: 1653 = Thus they so fast came on, with such loud cries

54] had; could spy: 1653 = hath; espies

56] that: 1653 = the

57] was: 1653 = is

58] was: 1653 = is

59] did: 1653 = doth

60] the grass or track where the scent: 1653 = what grass, or track the scent on

61] *For witty industry is never*: 1653 = *Thus quick industry, that is not*

62] *'Tis like to witchcraft, and brings*: 1653 = *Is like to witchery, brings*

63] But: 1653 = For
65] that: 1653 = it
66] the: 1653 = for th'
69] did: 1653 = they
70] voices round; 1653 = voice around
71] such: 1653 = a
72] That, had they spoken words, 't had been: 1653 = If they but words
   could speak, might sing
73] men did: 1653 = hunters
74] seemed most valiant, poor Wat to: 1653 = valiant seem, poor Wat
   for to
76] Swam; leaped: 1653 = Swim; leap
77] Endangered; they'd ride: 1653 = Endanger; will ride
79] At last: 1653 = For why
80] That their sharp teeth they: 1653 = That they their sharp teeth
81] he fell: 1653 = did fall
82] Gave: 1653 = Gives
83] made: 1653 = make
84] imprisoned had: 1653 = did prisoner take
85] but did: 1653 = do but
87] men do; 1653 = man doth
90] Which doth proceed from others': 1653 = And appetite, that feeds on
92] Kill silly sheep, they say: 1653 = To kill poor sheep, straight say
94] more: 1653 = them
95] God did make: 1653 = that God made
96] And gave: 1653 = To give
98] For to destroy those lives that God did: 1653 = Destroy those lives
   that God saw good to
100] which; 1653 = that
101] gentle and mild: 1653 = gentle, mild
102] of all creatures he's: 1653 = he of creatures is
103] Nay, so proud, that he only thinks to live: 1653 = And is so proud,
   thinks only he shall live
106] Were: 1653 = Was

A Description of an Island

Copy-text: *Poems and Fancies* (1664)
In the 1664 version of this poem, used here, past tense replaces the
present tense of the 1653 version.
Title] A Description of an Island: 1653 = Of an Island

3] not missed: 1653 = don't miss

4] they kissed: 1653 = do kiss

5] Each wave did seem by turn to: 1653 = Where every wave by turn do

6] when as they did flow: 1653 = as they overflow

7] brought: 1653 = bring

8] did glister as: 1653 = do glister like

9] did: 1653 = do

10] Placing them in her havens with great care: 1653 = And in her havens places them with care

11] for no pay they'd: 1653 = They no pay will

12] But as her guard did: 1653 = Yet as her guard they

13] circled: 1653 = circle

14] without: 1653 = still out

15] The winds did serve her, and on clouds did: 1653 = So winds do serve, and on the clouds do

17] Serving as scouts, they searched: 1653 = And serve as scouts, do search

18] galloped in the forests: 1653 = gallop in the forest

19] While she did please the gods, she did live safe: 1653 = And while she please the gods, in safety lives

20] And they all kinds of pleasures to her gave: 1653 = They to delight her, all fine pleasures gives

21] was: 1653 = is

22] were: 1653 = are

23] took; did sing: 1653 = take; do sing

24] did: 1653 = do

25] thrived; for she their roots well fed: 1653 = thrive; this isle their roots do feed

26] And tall with pride, their tops did: 1653 = Grow tall with pride, their tops they

27] Danced; did: 1653 = Dance; do

28] Played; a: 1653 = Play; the

29] did: 1653 = do

30] hopped, and skipped; were: 1653 = hop and skip; are

31] did: 1653 = do

32] And; strived: 1653 = Thus; do strive

33] All; looked: 1653 = And; look

34] were: 1653 = are

35] Th'isle was their mother: 1653 = Their mother the island

37] Who dressed and pruned them often with great care: 1653 = Who takes great care to dress, and prune them oft

38] And washed their leaves with dew to make them fair: 1653 = And with clear dew, he washes their leaves soft

39] Which being done, he wiped: 1653 = When he hath done, he wipes

41] Paint: 1653 = Paints

42] Veiled: 1653 = Veils

42] dressed, their hairy leaves spread out: 1653 = dresses, spreads their hairy leaves

44] Wreathed round their crowns his golden beams about: 1653 = And round their crowns his golden beams he wreaths

45] esteemed: 1653 = esteems

46] he had loved: 1653 = we find he loves

47] Daily he did present her with some gift: 1653 = Presents her daily with some fine new gift

49] came, he put on fair: 1653 = comes, he puts on clean

50] That lovely she and handsome might appear: 1653 = And changes oft, that she may lovely seem

51] from her went: 1653 = goeth from her

52] left; her for: 1653 = leaves; for her

53] Whose name is Cynthia: 1653 = Cynthia she is

55] left his stars to wait on her: 1653 = leaves his stars to wait, for fear

56] Lest she should grieve too much: 1653 = His isle too sad should be

57] clothed: 1653 = clothes

59] brought: 1653 = brings

60] let; lapped: 1653 = lets; laps

61] He mantles rich of equal heat o'erspread: 1653 = With mantles rich of equal heat doth spread

62] covered: 1653 = covers

63] gave: 1653 = gives

65] did: 1653 = doth

66] Like: 1653 = As

67] fringed: 1653 = fringes

68] And; hung; 1653 = Where; hang

69] gave he: 1653 = gives her

71] adorned: 1653 = adorns

72] riv'lets, prospects round: 1653 = prospects, and rills that run

73] Hills over-topped the dales, which level were: 1653 = There hills o'er top the dales, which level be

74] And covered all with cattle, feeding there: 1653 = Covered with cattle feeding eagerly

75] Grass grew: 1653 = Where grass grows

76] lay pleasantly: 1653 = in pleasure lie

79] her love to th'gods willing: 1653 = willing to th'gods her love
81] And temperate seasons gave: 1653 = Gave temperate seasons
82] Warm: 1653 = The

The Ruin of this Island

Copy-text: *Poems and Fancies* (1664)
Title] this: 1653 = the
4] and: 1653 = so
5] and in their stead: 1653 = her own set up
6] Set up her own, and would be worshippèd: 1653 = And she alone would have divine worship
12] That they and mortal men: 1653 = That mortal men, and they
13] thought it did show: 1653 = they thought it showed
14] the gods did not poor men foreknow: 1653 = poor man the gods had not foreknowed
16] did: 1653 = do
17] did man first: 1653 = made, or were
20] Wherefore: 1653 = If so,
24] two: 1653 = to
25] The one pow'r cannot: 1653 = Having no power to
28] Know not: 1653 = Nor know
29] But may't not be the course of God's decree: 1653 = But may not God's decree on this line run
30] wheresoe'er it be: 1653 = whensoe'er it come
31] They from the first a changing power create: 1653 = So from the first variation creates
32] make destiny and fate: 1653 = made destiny and fates
33] It is the mind of man: 1653 = Then 'tis the mind of men
34] The minds of gods are not: 1653 = And not the minds of gods
37] would: 1653 = will
38] Revenge on them, who did: 1653 = Even high revenge, since she
39] like: 1653 = up
40] Bad vapours from the earth, and then did: 1653 = The vapour bad from all the earth, then
41] on: 1653 = in
42] The venom had, got from the world's great ball: 1653 = The venom was, that's got from the world's ball
43] Then: 1653 = Which
44] did like oil their spirit all inflame: 1653 = And like to oil, did all their spirits flame

47] Thinking which way their lusts they might fulfil: 1653 = Studying which way might one another rob

48] Committed thefts, rapes, murders at their will: 1653 = In open sight do ravish, boldly stab

49] Parents and children did unnatural: 1653 = To parents children unnat'rally

50] every friend was turned a: 1653 = former friendship now's turned

51] Nay: 1653 = For

53] they did: 1653 = did they

55] did in tumults rise: 1653 = in a tumult rose

56] And 'gainst the heavens utter blasphemies: 1653 = Blasphemous words against high heaven throws

57] The gods in rage unbound the winds to blow: 1653 = Gods in a rage unbind the winds and blow

58] a strange nation: 1653 = foreign nations

59] themselves did plant, the natives all: 1653 = did plant themselves, no Britons live

60] Were by them killed, for th'gods had sworn their fall: 1653 = For why the gods their lives, and land them give

66] i'th'grave rest quietly: 1653 = in graves shall quiet lie

Wherein Poetry Chiefly Consists

Copy-text: *Poems and Fancies* (1664)
Title] Wherein Poetry Chiefly Consists: 1653 = [without title]
10] but plain, and her skin: 1653 = 'tis plain, and skin is
11] that from her thanks are: 1653 = from her a thanks is
17] the form is, flesh, blood, skin and bone: 1653 = is the form, flesh, blood, bone, skin
18] substance they have none: 1653 = have no substance in
20] of: 1653 = to

A Description of a Shepherd's and Shepherdess's Life

Copy-text: *Poems and Fancies* (1664)
Title] A Description of a Shepherd's and Shepherdess's Life: 1653 = A Description of Shepherds, and Shepherdesses
3] doth: 1653 = do
4] they being: 1653 = being

5] Through the sun's heat their skin doth yellow grow: 1653 = The sun doth scorch the skin, it yellow grows

6] winds that blow: 1653 = wind that blows

7] tops of mountains high: 1653 = mountains top, that's high

8] And: 1653 = Yet

10] moss: 1653 = moist

11] are small, but strong each sinew's string: 1653 = though small, strong are their sinews' string

12] makes: 1653 = make

14] He: 1653 = And

15] as; is: 1653 = to; was

19] He lazy, yawning: 1653 = And yawning, lazy

20] Or on his back, and hath his: 1653 = Or straight upon his back, with

21] his: 1653 = their

22] hobgoblins: 1653 = hobgoblin

23] his: 1653 = their

25] Then takes his knife half broke, but ground again: 1653 = Or takes his knife new ground, that half was broke

26] his sheep-coat up to pin: 1653 = to pin up his sheep-coat

28] amorous tunes, which pleases his love Joan: 1653 = tunes that pleaseth Joan his love at home

30] verse and: 1653 = sonnets

32] follow: 1653 = driving

33] And dance: 1653 = Dancing

35] They would their lovers: 1653 = For they their loves would

38] And: 1653 = With

40] A fair white hand doth hate a: 1653 = A white hand sluttish seems in

The Clasp: Of Fairies in the Brain

Copy-text: *Poems and Fancies* (1664)

Title] The Clasp: Of Fairies in the Brain: 1653 = The Clasp. Of Small Creatures, Such as we Call Fairies

1] that in every: 1653 = in the

2] Those creatures we call fairies: 1653 = Little small Fairies

3] frame: 1653 = make

4] which we fancies name: 1653 = we for fancy take

6] May by their industry be: 1653 = By their industry may

10] they: 1653 = out

11] And thus: 1653 = Thus

12] May fairies: 1653 = Fairies

13] then th'eye's the sea, where by the gale: 1653 = the eye's the sea
they traffic in

14] Of passions, on salt tears their ship doth sail: 1653 = And on salt
wat'ry tears their ship doth swim

15] And when: 1653 = But if

17] There: 1653 = When

18] And fly up to: 1653 = Fly up into

19] great storms: 1653 = storms use

20] Where: 1653 = Which

22] knocking they may: 1653 = knocking hard they

23] a: 1653 = the

25] they, like stone: 1653 = like to stone

Upon the Funeral of my Dear Brother, Killed in these Unhappy Wars

Copy-text: *Poems and Fancies* (1664)

Title] Upon the Funeral of my Dear Brother, Killed in these Unhappy
Wars: 1653 = Of a Funeral

1] my funeral mourner be: 1653 = condole my funeral

2] is allied to me: 1653 = doth my life concern

6] But in my fate, though sad, rejoicèd all: 1653 = But all rejoicèd in
my fate, though sad

8] spleen and: 1653 = and their

9] know: 1653 = have

10] But like fierce beasts in savage wildness go: 1653 = But all in savage
wilderness do delight

11] poor: 1653 = pure

13] my doleful knell ring out: 1653 = ring out my knell

14] hearse about: 1653 = hearse

15] The birds, as mourners on my tomb shall sit: 1653 = And birds as
mourners sit thereon

16] like as a covering grow on it: 1653 = a covering grow upon

17–20] 1653 has additional lines:

> Rough stones, as scutcheons, shall adorn my tomb,
> And glowworm burning tapers stand thereby;
> Night sable covering shall me over-spread,
> Elegies of mandrakes groans shall write me dead.

17] come near me: 1653 = dig me up
18] in peace rest quietly: 1653 = lie quietly in peace
19] He: 1653 = For

Lucy Hutchinson

The copy-text for *De rerum natura* is British Library, Add. MS 19333. The copy-text for 'To Mr Waller upon his Panegyric to the Lord Protector' is British Library, Add. MS 17018. The copy-text for the elegies is Nottinghamshire County Archives, Manuscript DD/Hu2. Although the elegies are not in Hutchinson's hand and therefore we do not know whether she intended them to be presented in a particular order, this edition includes the number of the poems as they appear in the manuscript. The copy-text for *Order and Disorder*, extracts from Cantos 1 and 3, is *Order and Disorder, or, The World Made and Undone being Meditations upon the Creation and the Fall: As it is Recorded in the Beginning of Genesis* (London, 1679; Wing A 3594; on *EEBO*). These extracts are collated against the manuscript version of the poem, Beinecke Rare Book and Manuscript Library, MS Osborn fb 100. The Beinecke manuscript is the copy-text for the extract from Canto 9, which occurs only in it. 'All sorts of men through various labours press' is extant only in Julius Hutchinson's 1808 edition of Hutchinson's *Memoirs of the Life of Colonel Hutchinson*. The manuscript he transcribed from is lost.

De rerum natura

Copy-text: British Library, Add. MS 19333, Lucy Hutchinson, 'De rerum natura'

To Mr Waller upon his Panegyric to the Lord Protector

Copy-text: British Library, Add. MS 17018, fols 213–17
'To Mr Waller upon his Panegyric to the Lord Protector' exists in a single manuscript and is attributed to Lucy Hutchinson in the hand of

Henry Hyde, second Earl of Clarendon ('Mʳˢ Hutchinson's Answer to Mʳ Waller's Panegirique to ~~the~~ Cromwell'). In his article attributing the poem to Hutchinson, David Norbrook also advises caution about the attribution, pointing out some inconsistencies with her political views expressed elsewhere, though argues strongly overall for her authorship ('Lucy Hutchinson versus Edmund Waller').

63] highness's: MS = Highs

Elegy 1. 'Leave off, you pitying friends, leave off'

Copy-text: Nottinghamshire County Archives, Manuscript DD/Hu2
This poem is untitled in the MS.
50] chaste: MS = cheast

Elegy 2. To the Sun Shining into her Chamber

Copy-text: Nottinghamshire County Archives, Manuscript DD/Hu2
1] day: MS = dad

Elegy 2(a). 'Ah! Why doth death its latest stroke delay'

Copy-text: Nottinghamshire County Archives, Manuscript DD/Hu2
This poem is untitled in the MS.

Elegy 3. Another on the Sunshine

Copy-text: Nottinghamshire County Archives, Manuscript DD/Hu2
19] rapine: MS = rampine
21] not: MS = no
37] thrust: MS = thurst

Elegy 7. To the Garden at Owthorpe

Copy-text: Nottinghamshire County Archives, Manuscript DD/Hu2
8] soul: MS = sould
9] just: MS = jus
30] hide: MS = hid

Elegy 10. The Recovery

Copy-text: Nottinghamshire County Archives, Manuscript DD/Hu2
Millman and Wright (eds), *Early Modern Women's Manuscript Poetry*, p.
107: 'the leaves containing this poem are disordered. Lines 45–76 follow
a later poem in the manuscript, "The Consecrated Atoms Sleeping here"'.
See also Norbrook, 'Lucy Hutchinson's "Elegies"', p. 506.
11] centre, all: MS = Centriall
24] enthroned: MS = enthornd
38] cast: MS = cas

Elegy 12. Musings in my Evening Walks at Owthorpe

Copy-text: Nottinghamshire County Archives, Manuscript DD/Hu2
1] groans: MS = groances
7] present: MS = prevent
22] offer: MS = offers
73–74] In the manuscript the final couplet is prefixed by letters that
  remain unexplained:
    A: I: Even then I loathed your flatteries
    B: D: And now your sick souls despise

Elegy 20. 'You sons of England whose unquenched flame'

Copy-text: Nottinghamshire County Archives, Manuscript DD/Hu2
This poem is untitled in the MS.

Order and Disorder: The Preface

Copy-text: *Order and Disorder* (1679)

Order and Disorder: Canto 1, lines 1–150

Copy-text: *Order and Disorder* (1679), collated with Beinecke Rare Book
  and Manuscript Library, MS Osborn fb 100
2] admires: MS = desires
12] Which, though opposing, he must yet fulfil: MS = Which yet he by
  opposing doth fulfil

23] with: MS = in

28] imperfect: MS = unperfect

29] forms: MS = form

39] mortals': MS = mortal

42] bound: MS = bounds

44] *God*: MS = marginal note: *The Creator*

45] *Elohim*: MS = marginal note: *Bara Elohim*

48] Between lines 48 and 49, MS has two extra lines:

> His essence wrapped up in mysterious clouds
> While he himself in dazzling glory shrouds.

55] frail: MS = vain

62] mortal: MS = mortals'

79] Unite: MS = Unity

89] Wherein: MS = In which

92] blessedness: MS = happiness

102] After line 102 the MS has the following instead of lines 103–22:

> And all, in all God's works cooperate
> Although the action we appropriate
> Only unto that person which most clear
> And eminently therein doth appear
> So we the Father the creator name
> Though Son and Spirit joined in the world's frame
> And were that Elohim who first designed

The final line in this section has been corrected (by one of several hands in the MS) as follows:

> Was the great Elohim who first designed

140] magazine: MS = magazines

141] Where power, love, justice, and mercy shine: MS = Where power, love, wisdom, justice, mercy shine

Order and Disorder: Canto 3, lines 91–188

Copy-text: *Order and Disorder* (1679), collated with Beinecke Rare Book and Manuscript Library, MS Osborn fb 100

97] doors: MS = door

99] curtains: MS = curtain

112] thick-set: MS = thickest

113] shows: MS = looks

122] by: MS = in

135] MS: marginal note: 'Paradise'

148] feign: MS = frame

160] tall-growing pines and cedars: MS = tall pines and growing cedars
162] scarcely: MS = not
182] captived Hebrew's: MS = Hebrew captives
184] the: MS = their

Order and Disorder: Canto 9, lines 1–122

Copy-text: Beinecke Rare Book and Manuscript Library, MS Osborn fb 100

'All sorts of men through various labours press'

This poem is extant only in Julius Hutchinson's 1808 edition of Hutchinson's *Memoirs of the Life of Colonel Hutchinson*. The manuscript he transcribed from is lost.

All references to the Bible are from the King James Version of 1611.

Index of first lines